Everyday Spelling

Authors

James Beers • Ronald L. Cramer • W. Dorsey Hammond

Scott Foresman
Addison Wesley

Editorial Offices: Glenview, Illinois • Menlo Park, California
Sales Offices: Reading, Massachusetts • Atlanta, Georgia • Glenview, Illinois
Carrollton, Texas • Menlo Park, California

1-800-552-2259
http://www.sf.aw.com

■ ACKNOWLEDGMENTS

TEXT

p. 133: Untitled haiku by Kikaku from *Word Works* by Cathryn Berger Kaye; illustrated by Martha Weston. Copyright © 1985 by the Yolla Bolly Press. By permission of Little, Brown and Company.

ILLUSTRATIONS

pp. 12-33: Susan Swan; **pp. 12, 38, 64, 81, 90, 116, 129, 132:** Marla Rubin; **pp. 23, 24, 28:** Linda Kinnamon; **pp. 38-59:** Mary Grand Pre; **pp. 40, 44, 47, 48, 51, 52, 55, 56, 59, 60:** John Manders; **pp. 60-62, 86-89, 112-115, 138-141, 164, 165, 167, 184-187, 189, 195, 197, 199, 201, 205-207, 210-213, 215, 219-221, 225-227:** Beth Herman Design Associates; **pp. 60, 63, 88, 210, 211:** Slug Signorino; **pp. 61, 89:** Patti Green; **pp. 62, 113, 166:** Fran Lee; **pp. 63, 86, 87, 89, 115, 139, 165, 204, 207-209, 220, 221:** B.J. Johnson; **pp. 64-85:** Kathy Petrauskas; **pp. 66, 69, 70, 73, 74, 77, 78, 81, 82, 85, 86:** Margaret Spengler; **pp. 87, 114, 140, 141, 202, 203:** Donna Reynolds; **pp. 90-111:** Marianne Wallace; **pp. 113-115, 139, 167, 184, 185, 222, 223:** Linda Kelen; **pp. 115, 138, 166, 192, 193, 214:** Carl Kock; **pp. 116-137:** Darryl Goudreau; **pp. 140, 193, 195, 209, 224, 225, 227:** Tom Herzberg; **pp. 142-163:** Linda Helton; **pp. 148, 152, 156, 164:** Joe Rogers; **pp. 189, 200, 201:** Leon Bishop; **pp. 190, 191:** David Uhl; **pp. 194, 195, 198, 199, 216, 217, 228, 229:** Jacque Auger; **p. 297:** Don Wilson; **p. 304:** Christine Mortensen

PHOTOGRAPHS

pp. 16, 42, 84, 162: Marilyn Meyerhofer; **pp. 77TL, BR, 246B, 261T:** Hans Reinhard/Bruce Coleman, Inc.; **p. 77TR:** Michael & Patricia Fogden; **p. 77BL:** Belinda Wright/DRK Photo; **p. 109L:** Grant Heilman/ Grant Heilman Photography, Inc.; **p. 109R:** Jane Grushow/Grant Heilman Photography, Inc.; **p. 131:** Connie Geocaris/Tony Stone Images; **pp. 153, 271T:** Lawrence Migdale; **pp. 167T, 256B:** Don & Pat Valenti; **p. 167C:** "Life on the Prairie, The Buffalo Hunt" by Currier & Ives, 1862, Library of Congress; **p. 182TR:** Steve McCutcheon; **p. 182TL:** Fred Bruemmer; **p. 182BL:** Francois Gohier/Photo Researchers; **pp. 182BR, 183TL, 183TC, 183TR:** Johnny Johnson/ AlaskaStock; **p. 183BR:** Chris Arend/AlaskaStock; **p. 201:** Dwight R. Kuhn/DRK Photo; **p. 203:** Library of Congress; **p. 210:** Vic Thomasson/Tony Stone Images; **p. 211:** Chris Haigh/Tony Stone Images; **p. 211:** Editions Houvet; **p. 213:** R. Maiman/Sygma; **p. 225L:** Ray Amati/Focus On Sports; **p. 225CL:** Focus on Sports; **p. 225CR:** J. Daniel/ALLSPORT USA; **p. 225R:** Stephen Dunn/ALLSPORT USA; **p. 247:** Dr. Ralph Buchbaum/ Department of Zoology, University of Chicago; **pp. 248T, 274:** Courtesy NASA; **p. 250T:** James L. Ballard/ScottForesman & Co.; **p. 252T:** Robert B. Tolchin/ScottForesman & Co.; **p. 252B:** Michael & Patricia Fogden; **p. 256T:** J. Pickerell/ The Image Works; **p. 260:** Miami Seaquarium; **p. 266B:** Cy Furlan; **p. 268B:** J.C. Stevenson/ Animals, Animals; **p. 270T:** Florida Division of Tourism; **p. 270B:** GemMedia; **p. 273T:** Belinda Wright/DRK Photo; **p. 277:** M. Austerman/ Animals, Animals; **p. 278:** Raymond Schoder; **p. 280B:** Arizona State Museum, University of Arizona, Helga Teiwes, Photographer; **p. 284T:** Jurg Klages; **p. 284B:** Camermann International, Ltd.; **p. 286B:** Lorraine Rorke/The Image Works; **p. 287:** Geo. T. Hillman; **p. 290T:** Daniel L. Feicht; **p. 291:** Carmen Morrison/ScottForesman & Co.; **p. 292:** American Museum of Natural History, New York; **p. 293:** Michael Heron; **p. 299TL:** Robert Frerck/Odyssey/Chicago; **p. 299TR:** Robert Frerck/Odyssey/Chicago; **p. 299B:** Marianne von Meerwall; **p. 300:** Dr. E. R. Degginger; **p. 306:** Jeff Foott; **p. 308:** The Kobal Collection.

All photographs not specifically credited are Scott Foresman Addison Wesley photographs.

UNIT 1

■ CONTENTS

UNIT 3

■ CONTENTS

UNIT 6

Cross-Curricular Lessons

■ CONTENTS

▼ READING

✂ MATHEMATICS

✎ WORK AND PLAY

REFERENCE TOOLS

✳ FREQUENTLY MISSPELLED WORDS!

Lots of words on your spelling lists are marked with green asterisks ✳.
These are the words that are misspelled the most by students your age.*

Pay special attention to these frequently misspelled words as you read,
write, and practice your spelling words.

too	again	everybody	happened	would
a lot	they	off	heard	are
because	Christmas	through	I	enough
there	went	friends	whole	except
their	until	swimming	didn't	friend's
favorite	outside	want	first	probably
that's	said	you're	watch	upon
our	we're	another	people	vacation
when	sometimes	beautiful	always	brought
really	different	I'm	took	house
they're	where	let's	everyone	might
were	caught	then	morning	myself
it's	chocolate	believe	school	basketball
know	friend	cousin	something	hospital
finally	into	especially	with	opened

* **Research in Action** is a research project conducted in 1990–1993. This list of frequently misspelled words is one result of an analysis of 18,599 unedited compositions. Words are listed in the order of their frequency of misspelling.

11

Steps for Spelling Problem Parts

REVIEW THE STEPS FOR SPELLING   Here is the spelling strategy you should use when learning to spell a new word. Read it over step by step.

1. **Look** at the word. **Say** it and listen to the sounds.
2. **Spell** the word aloud.
3. **Think** about the spelling. Do you notice anything special that you need to remember?
4. **Picture** the word with your eyes shut.
5. **Look** at the word and **write** it.
6. **Cover** the word and picture it. **Write** the word again and **check** its spelling.

DISCOVER THE PROBLEM PARTS STRATEGY   If some words are still hard for you to spell, try the problem-parts strategy.

Think | Underline your problem part. | Picture the word. Focus on your problem part.

TRY IT OUT   Practice the problem-parts strategy with words that gave another writer problems. Follow the directions on the next page.

Work with a partner or group. Find the four misspelled words in the description below and write them correctly. Underline the part of each word that gave the writer problems. Use a dictionary if you need help.

I was down on one nee picking up mangoes when the squrrel saw me. It wiggled its nose at me. I bit into a mango and lafed. It turned and ran throgh the trees.

Now practice the problem-parts strategy with your own personal words.

List four words you sometimes misspell. Be sure to spell them right. Underline the part of each word that gives you a problem. Picture the words. Focus on the problem parts.

Have a partner quiz you on your words. Then check the results. How did you do?

LOOK AHEAD   Look at the next five lessons. Write four list words that look hard to spell. Underline the part of each word that you think might give you a problem.

Words with thr, scr, str, squ

SPELLING FOCUS

Some words have consonant blends with three letters pronounced together: **thr**oat, **scr**een, **str**eet, **squ**are.

■ **STUDY** Say each word. Then read the meaning phrase.

WATCH OUT FOR FREQUENTLY MISSPELLED WORDS!

1. *throat* — have a sore **throat**
2. *through* ✳ — strolling **through** the park
3. *screen* — a hole in the window **screen**
4. *scratch* — **scratch** an itchy leg
5. *scream* — a **scream** for help
6. *strange* — a **strange** pig with long tusks
7. *street* — driving down the **street**
8. *strike* — two balls and a **strike**
9. *square* — a **square** box
10. *squeeze* — **squeeze** a lemon to get juice

11. *threat* — the **threat** of war
12. *thrown* — **thrown** from a horse
13. *thrill* — the **thrill** of a roller-coaster ride
14. *scrub* — **scrub** the floor
15. *skyscraper* ✗ — 62-story **skyscraper**
16. *strawberry* — bite a juicy **strawberry**
17. *strength* — the **strength** of a weight lifter
18. *squeal* — the **squeal** of a pig
19. *squirm* — **squirm** in someone's grasp
20. *squirt* — **squirt** water at someone

CHALLENGE!

arthritis
description
instrument
astronaut
squeezable

■ **PRACTICE** Sort the list words by writing
- five words with **thr**
- five words with **scr**
- five words with **str**
- five words with **squ**

■ **WRITE** Choose two phrases to write a riddle.

DRAW YOUR OWN CONCLUSION Write the list word that matches each clue.

1. You might clear this when you begin to speak.
2. A piglet might make this sound if you chase it.
3. Never cross this without looking both ways.
4. A box often has this shape.
5. This is a delicious red fruit.
6. You do this to a match when starting a fire.
7. This is what you might call something odd or unusual.
8. An elevator is necessary if you live or work here.
9. Using soap, do this to get a floor clean.
10. If you have poison ivy, you'll feel the urge to do this.
11. Do this loudly if you are frightened and need help.
12. Sledding down a steep hill may give you this.
13. Little children may do this if they have to sit quietly.
14. An elephant might do this with the water in its trunk.
15. This keeps bugs from flying through an open window.

Take a Hint
This sentence may help you remember the difference between *throne* and *thrown*. The king was thr**own** from the throne he once **own**ed.

WORDS IN CONTEXT Write the list word that is missing from each animal's statement.

16. **Monkey:** I swing ___ the jungle from tree to tree.
17. **Zebra:** I was ___ to the ground by a lion, but I escaped.
18. **Gorilla:** I have the ___ of ten men.
19. **Boa:** I wrap around my prey and ___ very hard.
20. **Mongoose:** I'm so quick, even a cobra is no ___ to me.

Using the Problem Parts Strategy

21.–22. Study the problem parts of words. Write two list words that are hard for you. Underline the part of each word that gives you the problem, and study it extra hard.

15

☰	Make a capital.
/	Make a small letter.
∧	Add something.
ℯ	Take out something.
⊙	Add a period.
¶	New paragraph

PROOFREAD A SIGN Find the misspelled word in the photograph below. Why do you think it is misspelled in this particular way? Write the word correctly.

PROOFREADING TIP

When you create a sign, watch for spelling errors. You don't want people laughing at your message.

CREATE A SIGN Now it's your turn to try to get a message across. Imagine you own The Gyros Stand and want customers to try your exciting new dessert. Use list words to create a sign with a short, sweet message.

Word List

scrub	square	thrill	strike
street	scream	screen	squirm
threat	throat	strength	scratch
skyscraper	strawberry	squeeze	strange
thrown	squeal	through	squirt

Personal Words 1.___ 2.___

Review

PUZZLE IT OUT We are a collection of plans you will use for learning to spell new words. What are we? When you write the boxed words that match the definitions, the answer to the riddle will appear in the box.

1. rub to get rid of an itch
2. odd; unusual
3. a passage from the mouth to the stomach or the lungs
4. having four equal sides and four right angles
5. a road
6. press hard
7. from one side to the other
8. set on fire by rubbing
9. a loud cry for help
10. a glass surface on which information or pictures appear

throat
through
screen
scratch
scream
strange
street
strike
square
squeeze

1. ___ ___ ___ ___ ___ ___
2. ___ ___ ___ ___ ___ ___ ___
3. ___ ___ ___ ___ ___ ___ ___
4. ___ ___ ___ ___ ___ ___
5. ___ ___ ___ ___ ___ ___
6. ___ ___ ___ ___ ___ ___
7. ___ ___ ___ ___ ___ ___
8. ___ ___ ___ ___ ___ ___
9. ___ ___ ___ ___ ___ ___
10. ___ ___ ___ ___ ___ ___

Using a *Dictionary*

GUIDE WORDS At the top of each dictionary page are two guide words in dark type. The first guide word is the first entry word on the page. The second guide word is the last entry word on the page. If the word you are looking for falls alphabetically between these two words, you are on the right page.

When words begin with the same letter, you must look at the second letter, third letter, and so on to alphabetize them. For example, look on page 284 in your Spelling Dictionary. Notice that the word *scree<u>n</u>* follows *scre<u>am</u>* and comes before *scr<u>ub</u>.*

Now, look at each pair of guide words to the right. Which of the boxed words fall between these guide words alphabetically? Write those words.

thought
threat
throat
thrifty
thresh
spray
squirt
squeeze
squeak
squash

1. thrash/thrill

2. square/squirm

Words with kn, gn, wr, mb

SPELLING FOCUS

The underlined consonants stand for only one sound:
kn̲ot, sig̲n, w̲rist, clim̲b.

■ **STUDY** Say each word. Then read the meaning phrase.

1.	*knot*	a **knot** in my shoelace
2.	*unknown*	a painting by an **unknown** artist
3.	*know*	**know** the answer to a question
4.	*sign*	wait at a stop **sign**
5.	*design*	wallpaper with a striped **design**
6.	*writing*	**writing** a novel
7.	*wrist*	a bracelet on one's **wrist**
8.	*wreck*	a rusty old **wreck** of a car
9.	*climb*	**climb** a tree
10.	*thumb*	a baby sucking his **thumb**

11.	*knit*	**knit** a sweater
12.	*knob*	the **knob** on a cabinet door
13.	*kneel*	**kneel** in prayer
14.	*assign*	**assign** a task to someone
15.	*wreath*	a holiday **wreath** on the door
16.	*wrench*	tightening bolts with a **wrench**
17.	*wren*	a chirping **wren** in the tree
18.	*limb*	a tree **limb**
19.	*comb*	**comb** one's hair
20.	*lamb*	a woolly **lamb**

CHALLENGE!

bologna
lasagna
align
cologne
wrestler

■ **PRACTICE** Sort the words by writing
- six words with **kn**
- three words with **gn**
- six words with **wr**
- five words with **mb**

■ **WRITE** Choose three phrases to include in a paragraph.

RHYME TIME   Write the list word that rhymes with each word below.

1. teeth
2. snow
3. biting
4. hum
5. rim
6. bench

7. list
8. clam
9. roam
10. peel
11. when
12. deck

DEFINING WORDS   Write the list word that means the same as the underlined words.

13. The explorers traveled to a land that was <u>not familiar</u> to them.
14. I like to <u>make clothing by looping yarn</u>.
15. We had to <u>use hands and feet to go over</u> the fence to get into our yard.
16. Please <u>tie the ends of</u> this rope tightly.
17. I caught my coat on the <u>handle on a door</u>.

STRATEGIC SPELLING

Seeing Meaning Connections

Write the list word that completes each sentence. The underlined word is a clue.

18. The <u>designer</u> will ___ a dress for her.
19. Please don't ___ another <u>assignment</u>.
20. Write the list word that both of the words you wrote above are related to: ___.

☰	Make a capital.
/	Make a small letter.
∧	Add something.
℮	Take out something.
⊙	Add a period.
¶	New paragraph

PROOFREAD A NOTE   Read the thank-you note that Pat wrote her aunt. Find three misspelled words and three capitalization errors. Write them correctly.

October 10, 1995

Dear aunt Sally,

Thank you for the sweater. I love the desine, especially the lamb on the pocket. did you knitt it yourself? I no I will wear it a lot.

love,

Pat

PROOFREADING TIP

Pat is guilty of three "Capital Crimes"—mistakes with capital letters. Did you find them? If not, check the beginnings of sentences, the names of people, and the opening and closing of her note.

ANSWER THE NOTE   Imagine that you are Pat's aunt. Answer the note above. Use some of your spelling words and personal words in your reply.

Word List

wrist	wreck	wreath	knob
know	limb	assign	wren
thumb	wrench	knot	writing
sign	knit	lamb	climb
unknown	comb	design	kneel

Personal Words 1.___ 2.___

Review

WORD ASSOCIATIONS Write the boxed word that you would associate with each situation described below.

1. a motorist stopping at an intersection
2. bystanders observing the scene of an automobile accident
3. a child making a birthday party list
4. a girl spotting her friend across a crowded room of strangers
5. a team of explorers hiking across a mountain range
6. a boy scout tying two pieces of rope together
7. a mother pulling her young son's hand from his mouth to keep him from sucking
8. astronauts exploring a strange planet
9. a jeweler measuring a customer for a new watch
10. an architect creating a floor plan for a new house

> knot
> unknown
> know
> sign
> design
> writing
> wrist
> wreck
> climb
> thumb

Word *Study*

HINK-PINKS Have you ever played the rhyming game called *Hink-Pink?* Now is your chance. First, you read a question. Then, you answer it with two rhyming words. Here's an example:

> **Q:** What do you call damage done to a pack of playing cards?
> **A:** a deck wreck

Now try to answer the questions below. Hint: One of the words is always a list word.

1. **Q:** What do you call an excellent drawing?

   A: a ___ ___

2. **Q:** What do you call a thin leg?

   A: a ___ ___

3. **Q:** What would you call a fastening made with rope that is lying on a heated stove?

   A: a ___ ___

Consonant Sounds /k/ and /f/

SPELLING FOCUS

Usually the sound /k/ is spelled **c, k,** or **ck: c<u>a</u>re, br<u>a</u>ke, tra<u>ck</u>.** The sound /f/ can be spelled **ff, gh,** or **ph: sti<u>ff</u>, lau<u>gh</u>ed, <u>ph</u>oto.**

■ **STUDY** Say each word. Then read the meaning phrase.

WATCH OUT FOR FREQUENTLY MISSPELLED WORDS!

1.	*care*	**care** about a friend
2.	*because* ✳	**because** she said so
3.	*brake*	using the **brake** to stop
4.	*track*	trains running on a **track**
5.	*pocket*	a hole in my **pocket**
6.	*stiff*	a **stiff,** lacy collar
7.	*enough* ✳	had **enough** to eat
8.	*laughed*	**laughed** at the joke
9.	*photo*	a **photo** of the family
10.	*alphabet*	the **alphabet** from *a* to *z*

11.	*cover*	**cover** a baby with a blanket
12.	*record*	play a phonograph **record**
13.	*Kansas*	the state of **Kansas**
14.	*snack*	ate an after-school **snack**
15.	*attack*	**attack** the weeds in a garden
16.	*muffin*	bit into a blueberry **muffin**
17.	*giraffe*	a long-necked **giraffe**
18.	*rough*	a **rough,** bumpy road
19.	*dolphin*	a sleek, wet **dolphin**
20.	*elephant*	a big, gray **elephant**

CHALLENGE!

cuckoo clock
freckles
sheriff
autograph
headphones

■ **PRACTICE** Sort the words by writing
- four words with **c**
- two words with **k**
- four words with **ck**
- four words with **ph**
- three words with **ff**
- three words with **gh**

■ **WRITE** Choose ten phrases to rewrite as sentences.

POETRY IN MOTION Complete the poem by writing list words.

Sitting by the TV eating a (1).
Watching a train smoking down the (2).
Energetic engineer pulling on the (3).
The gear is (4), so it doesn't take.
I (5) at his antics, sure enough.
Stopping that train was going to be (6).
Cow on the track without a (7).
Train finally stopped without a second to spare.

Take a Hint
Is it *break* or *brake*?
Just remember to
brake at the **lake.**

CLASSIFYING Write the list word that fits in each group.

8. snapshot, picture, ___
9. Iowa, Nebraska, ___
10. pouch, clothes, ___
11. tape, CD, ___
12. letters, *a* to *z*, ___

13. set upon, fight, ___
14. roll, cupcake, ___
15. since, on account of, ___
16. plenty, full, ___

WHO AM I? Write the list word naming each speaker.

17. "I love to swim and dive. I'm a ___."
18. "My sore throats are endless. I'm a ___."
19. "I fill my trunk with water. I'm an ___."

STRATEGIC SPELLING

Seeing Meaning Connections

recover
discover
coverlet

20. Write a list word that is related to the words in the box.

Write words from the box that fit the definitions.

21. to find out
22. to get back a lost item
23. a covering for a bed

☰	Make a capital.
/	Make a small letter.
∧	Add something.
ℰ	Take out something.
⊙	Add a period.
⁋	New paragraph

PROOFREAD A SELF-PORTRAIT

Julio's class is drawing self-portraits and writing short descriptions of them. Find four misspelled words and one incorrect pronoun in Julio's writing. Correct them.

PROOFREADING TIP

Would you ever say "Me go to the zoo"? Well, that's really what Julio did in his sentence. Drop "Mom and ..." to be sure the personal pronoun is correct.

Here I am at the zoo. Mom and me go a lot beacause we like the dofin show. An elefant and a girafe are behind me.

CREATE A SELF-PORTRAIT Draw a picture of yourself doing something you enjoy. Write a description of where you are and what you're doing. Use some of your list words.

Word List

care	Kansas	stiff	enough
snack	brake	dolphin	photo
attack	track	rough	laughed
cover	because	elephant	alphabet
pocket	record	muffin	giraffe

Personal Words 1.___ 2.___

care
because
brake
track
pocket
stiff
enough
laughed
photo
alphabet

DEFINING WORDS   Write the boxed word that means the same as the underlined words.

1. After the accident, my neck was <u>hard to move</u>.
2. At age three, Mira can already recite the <u>letters of the English language arranged in their usual order</u>.
3. Many people <u>are concerned</u> about the future of our planet.
4. Do we have <u>a sufficient amount of</u> food for the party?
5. I went shopping <u>for the reason that</u> I needed new shoes.
6. My best <u>picture made with a camera</u> is the one of my dog.
7. I ran five laps around the race <u>course for running or racing</u>.
8. Della slammed on her <u>device for slowing down the motion of wheels or vehicles</u> pedal to avoid hitting the ducks.
9. Mr. Carter <u>made happy sounds and movements</u> when we explained what had happened on our way to school.
10. I put my lunch money into my <u>pouch sewed into clothing for carrying small items</u>, and now my money is gone.

Multicultural *Connection*

LANGUAGES   Julio saw these signs at the zoo. Each animal is named in English, Swahili, Spanish, and Japanese.

English	giraffe	lion	crocodile	spider
Swahili	twiga	simba dume	mamba	buibui
Spanish	jirafa	león	cocodrilo	araña
Japanese	kirin	raion	wani	kumo

Complete each sentence. Write the missing word in a different language each time.

1. Count the eight legs of the ___.
2. Can you tell the difference between an alligator and a ___?
3. The roaring of the ___ scared the baby.
4. The ___ can reach the treetop.

25

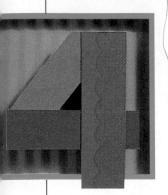

Adding -ed and -ing

SPELLING FOCUS

Here are four things to remember when adding **-ed** and **-ing**:

- Some base words are not changed: **happen, happened, happening.**
- In words that end with **consonant-e,** the **e** is dropped: **dance, danced, dancing.**
- In words that end in **y,** the **y** is changed to **i** when adding **-ed,** but kept when adding **-ing: study, studied, studying.**
- In one-syllable words that end with **consonant-vowel-consonant,** the final consonant is doubled: **stop, stopped, stopping.**

■ **STUDY** Look at each base word. Notice whether the spelling changes when **-ed** and **-ing** are added.

✳
WATCH OUT FOR FREQUENTLY MISSPELLED WORDS!

base word	-ed	-ing
happen	1. *happened* ✳	2. *happening*
open	3. *opened* ✳	4. *opening*
dance	5. *danced*	6. *dancing*
study	7. *studied*	8. *studying*
stop	9. *stopped*	10. *stopping*
chase	11. *chased*	12. *chasing*
worry	13. *worried*	14. *worrying*
dry	15. *dried*	16. *drying*
rob	17. *robbed*	18. *robbing*
slip	19. *slipped*	20. *slipping*

CHALLENGE!

skied
skiing
argued
arguing
occurred
occurring

■ **PRACTICE** Sort the list words by writing
- four words in which the final **e** is dropped
- four words with no spelling changes
- six words in which the final consonant is doubled
- six words in which **y** changes to **i**

■ **WRITE** Choose three words to write a paragraph about a memorable event in your school or community.

CONTEXT CLUES Use list words to finish the sentences.

1. The party-goers were ___ to the music.
2. The thief ___ the man of his wallet.
3. Is she ___ her present now?
4. Dad was very ___ when I was late.
5. The clown ___ on a banana peel.
6. We washed and ___ the dishes.
7. I was ___ for my history test all night.
8. The lion ___ the monkey up a tree.
9. What ___ to the injured ape?
10. We ___ talking to listen to the bird sing.

Did You Know?
The fastest rate ever measured for tap **dancing** is 32 taps per second.

ADD ENDINGS Complete each group with a list word.

11. worry, worried, ___
12. rob, robbed, ___
13. slip, slipped, ___
14. chase, chased, ___
15. open, ___, opening

16. study, ___, studying
17. dry, dried, ___
18. happen, happened, ___
19. stop, stopped, ___
20. dance, ___, dancing

STRATEGIC SPELLING

Building New Words

Use the rules you learned to complete the chart.

Base word	Add -ed	Add -ing
21. scrub	___	___
22. cause	___	___
23. cry	___	___

≡	Make a capital.
/	Make a small letter.
∧	Add something.
ℓ	Take out something.
⊙	Add a period.
⁋	New paragraph

PROOFREAD A BLURB   A **blurb** is a short, favorable description written on the jacket of a book or album. The blurbs below were written about the book *Night of the Twisters.* Find four misspellings and two handwriting errors and write them correctly.

PROOFREADING TIP
Jodie knows how to spell the words, but her handwriting looks as though she doesn't. Not closing letters like **d** and **o** will really frustrate your reader.

"From the moment I opend this book I never stopt reading it!" — Jodie

"Frightening things kept hapeneng. I woried about Dan and Art." — Dana

WRITE A BLURB   Write blurbs about two of the following: a favorite book, an enjoyable movie, or a good record album or tape. Try to use your list words.

Word List

opened	opening	studied	studying
happened	happening	dried	drying
chased	chasing	stopped	stopping
danced	dancing	slipped	slipping
worried	worrying	robbed	robbing

Review

WORDS IN CONTEXT Write the boxed words to complete Terry's story about a strange happening at a carnival.

happened
happening
opened
opening
danced
dancing
studied
studying
stopped
stopping

A strange event <u>(1)</u> on the night the carnival <u>(2)</u>. After Darren and I bought our tickets, we couldn't help <u>(3)</u> to admire the bright lights, rides, exhibits, and games. Teenagers were <u>(4)</u> to rock music pouring from huge speakers. Children were eating the usual carnival treats. Suddenly, the carnival lights dimmed, the music <u>(5)</u>, and the rides slowly came to a halt. "What's <u>(6)</u>?" Darron asked. I <u>(7)</u> his face and could see he was worried. "Look there!" a man shouted as he pointed at the sky. Darren and I peered upward through the <u>(8)</u> between two booths and saw a huge metallic object in the sky. We were <u>(9)</u> its unusual shape and lights that <u>(10)</u> in rhythmic patterns when the object took a sharp turn, shot upward, and disappeared. Then the lights shone brightly again, rides restarted, and everything was just as it had been before, except for one thing—the crowd had just witnessed the most amazing carnival act ever!

Using a *Thesaurus*

ENTRY WORDS Imagine that you are writing about the time you attended a game played by your favorite sports team. Your team won, and the game was the best you had ever seen. You want to express the excitement you felt, but the word *exciting* does not seem quite strong enough to you. You can look up *exciting* in a thesaurus to find synonyms, or other words with similar meanings.

A thesaurus provides a list of **entry words** in alphabetical order. The Writer's Thesaurus on pages 296–309 of your spelling book shows the entry words in color and in large type at the left of the pages.

Find the entry word *worried* in your Writer's Thesaurus. Notice the three synonyms for *worried*. Write the synonyms.

Adding *-er* and *-est*

Here are four things to remember when adding **-er** and **-est:**
- Some base words do not change: **small, smaller, smallest.**
- In words that end with **consonant-e,** the **e** is dropped: **large, larger, largest.**
- In words that end in **y,** the **y** is changed to **i:** **happy, happier, happiest.**
- In one-syllable words that end with **consonant-vowel-consonant,** the final consonant is doubled: **hot, hotter, hottest.**

■ **STUDY** Look at each base word. Notice whether the spelling changes when **-er** and **-est** are added.

small	1. *smaller*	2. *smallest*
large	3. *larger*	4. *largest*
happy	5. *happier*	6. *happiest*
hot	7. *hotter*	8. *hottest*
sad	9. *sadder*	10. *saddest*
deep	11. *deeper*	12. *deepest*
close	13. *closer*	14. *closest*
scary	15. *scarier*	16. *scariest*
funny	17. *funnier*	18. *funniest*
fat	19. *fatter*	20. *fattest*

■ **PRACTICE** Sort the list words by writing
- four words in which the final **e** is dropped
- four words in which the base word does not change
- six words in which the final consonant is doubled
- six words in which **y** changes to **i**

■ **WRITE** Choose ten words to write in sentences.

CHALLENGE!

weirder
weirdest
gentler
gentlest
angrier
angriest

ANTONYM ALERT Write the list word that means the opposite of each word below.

1. larger
2. skinnier
3. smallest
4. colder
5. shallower
6. saddest
7. coldest
8. largest
9. farther
10. happiest
11. skinniest

HAPPY ENDINGS Add an ending to each word in parentheses to form a list word that completes the sentence.

12. (scary) This is the ___ thriller I've read.
13. (funny) Your skit was ___ than mine.
14. (deep) Pike Lake is the___ lake around.
15. (close) Morgan is my very ___ friend.
16. (sad) Was *Sounder* ___ than *Old Yeller?*
17. (large) A gorilla is ___ than a gibbon.
18. (funny) Ribsy is the ___ dog of all time.
19. (happy) Al was ___ with the gift than Di.
20. (scary) I think snakes are ___ than lizards.

> **Did You Know?**
> The **smallest** horse ever recorded, Little Pumpkin, stood only fourteen inches tall and weighed twenty pounds.

STRATEGIC SPELLING
Building New Words

Write the words that complete the chart. Remember what you learned.

Base word	Add -er	Add -est
21. busy	___	___
22. big	___	___
23. strange	___	___

☰	Make a capital.
/	Make a small letter.
∧	Add something.
ℯ	Take out something.
⊙	Add a period.
¶	New paragraph

PROOFREAD AN INVITATION   Lizzy is having a party. Below is the first draft of her invitation. Correct three misspellings and one incorrect comparison.

PROOFREADING TIP

Remember to use **-er** when you compare two things. Use **-est** when comparing more than two.

COME TO A HALLOWEEN PARTY!!!

PLACE: *Lizzy's house —202 Lake St.*

TIME: *October 31 from 3:00 to 6:00 P.M.*

Wear your scaryest costume. We'll carve the fatest pumpkins and drink the hotest cider.

I'll be the sadder ghoul in town unless you come!

WRITE AN INVITATION   What kind of party would you like to give? Write an invitation for it. Use list words.

Word List

deeper	deepest	funnier	funniest
smaller	smallest	happier	happiest
closer	closest	hotter	hottest
larger	largest	fatter	fattest
scarier	scariest	sadder	saddest

Personal Words 1.___ 2.___

Review

ANALOGIES Write the boxed word that completes each analogy.

1. Saddest is to unhappiest as merriest is to ___.
2. Smaller is to littler as bigger is to ___.
3. Loudest is to quietest as biggest is to ___.
4. Tightest is to loosest as happiest is to ___.
5. Nicest is to meanest as coldest is to ___.
6. Quicker is to faster as cheerier is to ___
7. Closer is to nearer as littler is to ___.
8. Thinner is to slimmer as unhappier is to ___.
9. Smallest is to biggest as littlest is to ___.
10. Cooler is to colder as warmer is to ___.

smaller
smallest
larger
largest
happier
happiest
hotter
hottest
sadder
saddest

Word *Study*

EXAGGERATION Liz read a book in which a character "had eyes as large and brown as a coconut." She liked this exaggerated wording and was eager to try it out herself. Exaggeration is often used to emphasize, amuse, or surprise.

Liz practiced using exaggeration in her diary but left a few words out. Choose list words to finish the sentences.

October 31 My party was the (1) I've ever given—spilling over into five states. People came in costumes that were (2) than a barrel of comedians. One tiny kid dressed as a peanut and was (3) than one too! We drank cocoa that was (4) than an oven, and we ate so much that we felt (5) than an overweight elephant. Then we told stories that were (6) than a haunted hotel. It was the (7) time of my life!

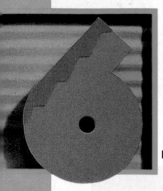

Review

Lesson 1: Words with thr, scr, str, squ
Lesson 2: Words with kn, gn, wr, mb
Lesson 3: Consonant Sounds /k/ and /f/
Lesson 4: Adding -ed and -ing
Lesson 5: Adding -er and -est

REVIEW WORD LIST

1. scratch
2. scream
3. screen
4. scrub
5. skyscraper
6. square
7. squeal
8. squeeze
9. squirt
10. strawberry
11. street
12. thrill
13. through
14. assign
15. climb
16. design
17. kneel
18. knit
19. know
20. sign
21. unknown
22. wreath
23. wreck
24. wren
25. wrench
26. writing
27. alphabet
28. attack
29. because
30. brake
31. care
32. cover
33. dolphin
34. elephant
35. enough
36. Kansas
37. photo
38. pocket
39. rough
40. snack
41. track
42. danced
43. dried
44. opening
45. stopping
46. studying
47. worried
48. worrying
49. scariest
50. smallest

BAKERY SPECIALS

Use the list words to complete the newspaper advertisement.

strawberry
scratch
snack
worrying
alphabet

BELLA'S BAKERY

Every batch is made from (1).

SPECIALS OF THE WEEK:

Monday Fruit pies on sale today! Try (2) or apple.
Tuesday Stop (3) about your next party. Let Bella bake the cake.
Wednesday Children love chewing an initial with our (4) cookies.
Thursday Choose Bella's oatmeal bars for your after-school (5).

get out and have fun

Where do you usually ride your bike? Do you ride all __(1)__ town or just on the __(2)__ you live on? Do you __(3)__ hills or bounce along on __(4)__ trails? Maybe your town has a racing __(5)__. No matter where you ride, you should remember these two tips. ❶ Always wear a helmet. ❷ Keep your bike in good repair, especially the __(6)__ system. Good brakes make __(7)__ safe. Take good __(8)__ of your bike, and it will takc good care of you.

Bret writes articles about outdoor activities for the class news bulletin. Use each list word once to complete this article.

stopping   care   rough   brake   track   through   street   climb

Lindy doesn't like fairy tales, but she had to read one. Use the list words to complete her book review.

Fairy Tales

The Sweetest Princess
A Book Review by Lindy Grach

know
scrub
scariest
danced
wren
scream
kneel
because
knit

This is another one of those stories about a sweet princess and the __(1)__ old queen you could ever imagine. Every day, the princess has to __(2)__ the hard marble floor until it shines. Not a day goes by that the queen doesn't __(3)__ at the princess for some little thing, and the queen demands that the princess curtsey and __(4)__ before her friends. The queen wants the princess to marry a neighboring king __(5)__ he is rich. You probably __(6)__ who the princess wants to marry. Right! A poor young man she __(7)__ with at the fair. The only surprise in the book is that there is no fairy godmother, just a troll who asks the princess to __(8)__ him a sweater from her golden hair. In return, he turns the queen into a __(9)__, and the princess locks her safely in a bird cage. The princess marries the young man, and lives . . . well, you know the rest.

Crafts

Complete the descriptions of the three projects below. Use each list word once.

I. Make an outline picture of a city in winter. Cut squares and rectangles out of newspapers and make a (1) and other such buildings. Glue the buildings along the bottom of a piece of black construction paper. For snow, fill a spray bottle with water and white paint and (2) your paper. Then, (3) your name to your art work.

II. Shape grapevines into a ring to make a festive (4) for your front door. Decorate it with bunches of (5) flowers.

III. Make a picture frame in the shape of a (6). Collect buttons of all sizes and colors. Make sure there are (7) buttons to cover the frame. Arrange them in an interesting (8) and then glue them on the frame.

sign
dried
design
square
squirt
skyscraper
wreath
enough

Pairing Things and Places

Write the list word that relates to each shape.

Kansas   pocket   dolphin   wrench   elephant

 1

2

3

 4

 5

WATER PARK

Complete the announcement below. Use each list word once.

opening
squeal
cover
thrill
assign
worried
photo

Hey Scouts!

Troop #116 is going to the grand (1) of Rocky Valley Water Park on Saturday, August 10. Imagine us as we holler and (2), sliding down the new water slide! Included will be a souvenir (3) of our group for us to take home. So, get ready for the (4) of your life! If you are (5) about how much the trip will cost, here's some good news. The park will (6) the cost for each scout who has earned a service badge. We plan to (7) seats on the bus, so tell Mr. Sato who you'd like to sit with.

Science Fiction

Jason's writing group invented two plots for a science fiction skit. Complete them using each list word once.

The skit might be about alien creatures who come to Earth in a battered (1) of a spaceship plastered with bumper stickers.

The skit could be about time travel. Six students (5) into a small time machine and visit the year 2096.

They have come in the hopes of (2) the human sense of humor.

Their Time-Travel Guide tells them that they will go to a distant place, but the exact location is (6).

In one scene, the very (3) alien, measuring 2 feet, 6 inches, says, "Take me to your ladder!"

In one scene, forces on Planet Circon prepare to (7) Mars with high-impact squirt guns.

He uses it to climb up to the TV (4) so he can watch old Marx Brothers reruns.

When the kids return, they begin (8) a tell-all biography of their amazing adventure.

squeeze
studying
smallest
screen
writing
attack
wreck
unknown

STRATEGY WORKSHOP

Divide and Conquer

DISCOVER THE STRATEGY Do long words give you spelling problems? Help is on the way. It's the divide-and-conquer strategy, and it consists of the following three ways to divide long words:

1. Divide them into syllables.	2. Divide them into prefixes, suffixes, and base words.	3. Divide them into base words if they' re compounds.

choc/o/late	un/known violin/ist	sky/scraper butter/fly

Use the way that works best for you to divide each long word. Then study the word part by part.

TRY IT OUT Now practice the divide-and-conquer strategy yourself. Follow the directions on the next page.

1. Divide into Syllables Use this method with any long word. Remember: A syllable is a word or part of a word that you say as a unit: **(choc/o/late)**.

Write *America, alphabet,* and *elephant.* Listen for the syllables and draw lines between them. Check a dictionary for any words you're not sure of.

2. Divide Prefixes and Suffixes This method will help you see the parts of the word with a prefix or suffix. You will also see if adding a suffix changes the spelling of the base word.

Write *unhappy, beautiful,* and *rewrite.* Draw lines between each base word and any prefixes or suffixes.

Look back at the words you wrote. Underline the base word in which the spelling changed when the suffix was added.

3. Divide Compounds This method will show you that two words have been put together with no letters lost.

Write *everybody, afternoon,* and *something.* Draw a line between the two base words in each compound.

LOOK AHEAD Look ahead at the next five lessons. Write two list words that are long and look hard to spell. Divide each word to make it easier to study.

Words with sh, ch, tch, wh

SPELLING FOCUS

Words can have two or three consonants together that are pronounced as one sound: **punish**, **chapter**, **watch**, **whenever**.

WATCH OUT FOR
FREQUENTLY
MISSPELLED
WORDS!

■ **STUDY** Say each word. Then read the meaning phrase.

1. shown — **shown** how to do something
2. short — a **short** visit
3. punish — **punish** a naughty child
4. March — born in **March**
5. chapter — reading **chapter** two
6. watch ✳ — **watch** an archery contest
7. kitchen — ate in the **kitchen**
8. whatever — **whatever** you do
9. anywhere — can't find it **anywhere**
10. whenever — **whenever** possible

11. shelter — take **shelter** under a tree
12. flashlight — shine a **flashlight** in the dark
13. trash — took out the **trash**
14. chocolate ✳ — ate **chocolate** pudding
15. church — the ringing of the **church** bell
16. pitcher — a **pitcher** on a baseball team
17. catcher — threw the ball to the **catcher**
18. wheat — a piece of **wheat** bread
19. awhile — had to wait **awhile**
20. somewhere — **somewhere** in the city

CHALLENGE!

squash
champion
touchdown
crutches
wherever

■ **PRACTICE** Sort the words by writing
- six words with **sh**
- four words with **tch**
- four words with **ch**
- six words with **wh**

■ **WRITE** Choose four phrases to rewrite as questions and answers.

BURIED WORDS   Each word below is hidden in a list word. Write the list word.

1. eat
2. pitch
3. what
4. pun
5. arch
6. or
7. rash
8. own
9. chap
10. catch

MAKING ASSOCIATIONS   Write the list word that you would associate with each word or phrase below.

11. protection
12. a short time
13. worship
14. clock
15. dark candy
16. cook's place

The Divide and Conquer Strategy

17.- 22. Study long words piece by piece. Write *flashlight, somewhere, anywhere, whenever, chocolate,* and *pitcher.* Draw lines to break each word into smaller parts. Study the parts.

Did You Know?
The word **chocolate** was borrowed from Mexican Spanish. It came from *chocolatl,* a word in Nahuatl, the language of the Aztecs and Toltecs.

☰	Make a capital.
/	Make a small letter.
∧	Add something.
℮	Take out something.
⊙	Add a period.
¶	New paragraph

PROOFREAD A SIGN A spelling error on a large outdoor sign really stands out. Find the mistake in the photograph below, and spell it correctly.

WACH AND
JEWELERY REPAIR

UP TO

PROOFREADING TIP

Watch out! Don't be caught making a big mistake. Keep a dictionary handy when you write signs.

CREATE A SIGN Think of one of your favorite stores. Create a sign for an item that is sold there. Try to use words from your spelling list. Check your sign for careless errors.

Word List

watch	kitchen	somewhere	whenever
anywhere	shown	short	shelter
punish	awhile	catcher	chocolate
church	pitcher	whatever	trash
wheat	flashlight	chapter	March

Personal Words 1.___ 2.___

Review

RHYMES   Write the boxed word that rhymes with the underlined word and makes sense in the sentence.

1. Meet me at the <u>arch</u> on the last day in ___
2. The pilot was ___ where the plane had <u>flown</u>.
3. The <u>men</u> placed the groceries on the table in the ___.
4. The librarian said, "Choose ___ books you like, but <u>never</u> forget to return them."
5. My <u>time</u> visiting the old frontier <u>fort</u> was much too ___.
6. Did you see a <u>bear</u> ___ in Yellowstone National Park?
7. Just ___ me make this <u>blotch</u> disappear from your shirt sleeve.
8. In this ___, I learned that a bird of prey is called a <u>raptor</u>.
9. That <u>clever</u> comedian has his audiences howling with laughter ___ he performs.
10. Carl's parents won't ___ him for breaking the <u>dish</u> accidentally.

shown
short
punish
March
chapter
watch
kitchen
whatever
anywhere
whenever

Using a *Thesaurus*

PARTS OF AN ENTRY   To make your *Writer's Thesaurus* a useful resource, it is important to know all the parts of a thesaurus entry. Study the parts of the entry for the word *show*. Then answer the questions.

1. What part of speech is *show?*
2. Which synonym would you use to tell about a friend who showed you how to make a kite?
3. Which synonym would you use to tell about a boy who showed his kindness by helping an injured child?
4. What cross-references would lead you to other words with related meanings?
5. Write one antonym for *show.*

	Part of speech	Definition

Entry Word → **Show** v. to cause something to be seen. *Patrick wants to show his new shoes to Saburo.*

Synonyms → **Display** to show things in a way that gets attention. *Thalia yawned widely, displaying her braces.*
Exhibit to show something publicly. *Tara exhibited her paintings at the arts and crafts show.*
Demonstrate to show something in a way that helps people understand. *A company demonstrated its new milking machine at the county fair.*
Point out to show where something is or to call attention to something. *Manuel pointed out all the sights of Chicago.*
Cross-References → SEE *guide* and *turn up* for related words.

Words with Double Consonants

Sometimes double consonants stand for one sound. For example, you hear the sound /f/ one time in **different** and the sound /p/ one time in **supper.**

■ **STUDY** Say each word. Then read the meaning phrase.

WATCH OUT FOR FREQUENTLY MISSPELLED WORDS!

1.	*tomorrow*	finish up **tomorrow**
2.	*borrow*	**borrow** someone's pencil
3.	*different* ✳	many **different** animals
4.	*supper*	have **supper** at 5:00
5.	*matter*	does not **matter**
6.	*written*	a **written** party invitation
7.	*bottle*	a **bottle** of juice
8.	*ridden*	has **ridden** a horse
9.	*odd*	an **odd** cat with no hair
10.	*bubble*	blow a big **bubble**
11.	*offer*	**offer** to help
12.	*suffer*	**suffer** from illness
13.	*slippers*	wear **slippers** around the house
14.	*grasshopper*	a **grasshopper** on a leaf
15.	*worry*	**worry** about someone's safety
16.	*current*	study **current** events
17.	*lettuce*	a **lettuce** salad
18.	*paddle*	**paddle** a canoe
19.	*shudder*	**shudder** in the cold
20.	*hobby*	painting as a **hobby**

CHALLENGE!

Mississippi
recess
impossible
antennas
allowance

■ **PRACTICE** First write the words in the list you think are easy to spell. Then write the words you think are difficult. Underline the double consonants in each word.

■ **WRITE** Choose two phrases to write a rhyme.

ANTONYM ARGUMENT   Write the list word that is the opposite of the underlined word in each sentence.

1. Mo and Al are as <u>alike</u> as they can be.
2. At <u>breakfast</u> yesterday they didn't even eat.
3. "Why can't I <u>lend</u> your knit hat?" asked Mo.
4. "Because losing hats is a <u>job</u> with you," said Al.
5. "But I like its <u>ancient</u> style," responded Mo.
6. Mo agreed to a <u>spoken</u> contract before wearing the hat.
7. These <u>ordinary</u> fellows enjoy disagreeing.

WORDS IN CONTEXT   Write the list word that completes each sentence.

8. Both of my parents ___ from allergies.
9. Rabbits eat greens such as ___ and spinach.
10. I forgot to do it today, but I will be sure to do it ___.
11. I am learning how to ___ a canoe.
12. After her bath, she put on a robe and ___.
13. What is the ___ with that howling dog?
14. I bought this gum so I could blow a ___.
15. Do you buy apple juice in a can or a ___?
16. I had never ___ on a Ferris wheel before.
17. The ___ jumped from the leaf to the ground.

FREQUENTLY MISSPELLED WORDS ❋ FREQUENTLY MISSPELLED WORDS ❋

To spell **different** correctly, be sure to pronounce every syllable: **dif fer ent.**

STRATEGIC SPELLING

Building New Words

Write *worry, offer,* and *shudder.* Add **-ed** to complete the chart. Remember: Change the **y** to **i** before adding **-ed.**

	Base word	Add -ed
18.	___	___
19.	___	___
20.	___	___

45

Make a capital.
/ Make a small letter.
∧ Add something.
℮ Take out something.
⊙ Add a period.
¶ New paragraph

PROOFREAD A MESSAGE Lucas read about someone finding an important message in a bottle. He wrote a message of his own. Find four spelling errors and two careless errors and correct them.

PROOFREADING TIP

Lucas is careless with the same word twice. He repeats it in one place, and leaves it out in another. These mistakes are easy to catch if you proofread.

Dare to be diffrent!

If you padel your own canoe today, you you may captain the ship tommorow.

If your buble bursts, can blow another one.

WRITE A MESSAGE Pretend you are writing a message for a bottle. Tell someone what you think is important in life. Use list words and personal words.

Word List

different	grasshopper	written	paddle
offer	tomorrow	matter	shudder
suffer	worry	bottle	odd
slippers	current	lettuce	bubble
supper	borrow	ridden	hobby

Personal Words 1.___ 2.___

Review

CONTEXT CLUES   Use the context in each sentence to help you write the correct boxed word.

1. Whenever I ___ something, I try to return it as soon as possible.
2. Have you ___ on the new roller coaster at the amusement park?
3. A soap ___ floated up from the dishwater and hit me right in the eye.
4. What's the ___ with Tony? He seems upset about something.
5. My friend takes a ___ route to school than I do.
6. I thought it was ___ that the store was closed in the middle of the afternoon.
7. I would have ___ you a note, but I couldn't find a pencil.
8. I tipped over a ___ of juice and it spilled on the floor.
9. I'm busy today, but maybe we can go to a movie ___.
10. In our house, we must be ready to sit down for ___ promptly at 6:00.

tomorrow
borrow
different
supper
matter
written
bottle
ridden
odd
bubble

Word *Study*

ACROSTICS   An **acrostic** is a way of connecting letters to spell different words, often about a particular subject. To make an acrostic, write a noun across or down the page. Then connect words that describe that noun. Try it with *grasshopper.* Use the words shown and add your own, or make up a new acrostic with a noun of your own.

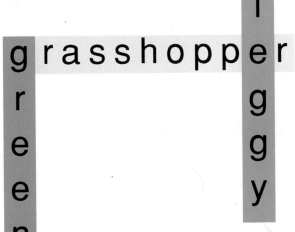

g r a s s h o p p e r

green

leggy

Short e and Long e

Short e is often spelled **e**: w<u>e</u>nt. **Long e** can be spelled **ea** and **ey**: sp<u>ea</u>k, mon<u>ey</u>.

■ **STUDY** Say each word. Then read the meaning phrase.

1.	them	gave it to **them**
2.	went ✳	**went** to see a play
3.	fence	a white picket **fence**
4.	speak	**speak** to a neighbor
5.	reason	a good **reason** for that
6.	beat	**beat** eggs until fluffy
7.	money	**money** to buy food
8.	valley	a river in the **valley**
9.	honey	put **honey** on toast
10.	monkey	a **monkey** in the jungle

11.	credit	buy new furniture on **credit**
12.	engine	a car **engine**
13.	contest	a juggling **contest**
14.	least	the **least** expensive shirt
15.	steal	**steal** someone's property
16.	treat	**treat** a friend to lunch
17.	season	the fall **season**
18.	hockey	play ice **hockey**
19.	alley	trash cans in the **alley**
20.	donkey	a braying **donkey**

✳ **WATCH OUT FOR FREQUENTLY MISSPELLED WORDS!**

CHALLENGE!

escaped
celery
squeaked
bleachers
jersey

■ **PRACTICE** Sort the words by writing
- seven words with **long e** spelled **ea**
- seven words with **long e** spelled **ey**
- six words with **short e** spelled **e**

■ **WRITE** Choose three phrases to include in a paragraph.

WORDS IN CONTEXT   Write the list word that completes each sentence.

1. I can't hear you. Please ___ up.
2. Bees were in the hive making ___.
3. The necklace cost a great deal of ___.
4. Around the yard was a picket ___.
5. She had the most homework and I had the ___.
6. The king gave ___ all silver swords.
7. The child sat upon a long-eared ___.
8. The peasants farmed the fertile ___.
9. The cook ___ the eggs for the omelet.
10. She hid the gold so no one would ___ it.
11. The knight ___ riding off.

Take a Hint
Do you have trouble remembering how to spell **beat** and **beet**? This riddle may help: What do you do when you can't **beat** the **heat**? **Eat** a cool **treat**!

DEFINITIONS   Answer each question with a list word.

12. Which list word is a sport?
13. What can you use to buy things if you have no cash?
14. What animal chatters and often lives in trees?
15. Which word means to think and understand?
16. Which names a narrow driveway behind a building?
17. What piece of machinery gives a car power?
18. Which word describes what winter is?
19. Which names something special that gives pleasure?

STRATEGIC SPELLING

Seeing Meaning Connections

contestant uncontested

20. Write the list word related in spelling and meaning to the boxed words.

Complete the sentences using the words in the box.

Mai was a (21) on a new TV quiz show. All of her answers were correct, so her victory was (22) by her opponent.

☰	Make a capital.
/	Make a small letter.
∧	Add something.
ℰ	Take out something.
⊙	Add a period.
⁋	New paragraph

PROOFREAD A LETTER Find the four misspelled words in this letter to an advice columnist. Write them correctly and add the two missing punctuation marks.

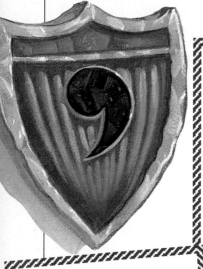

> *May 8, 1997*
>
> *Dear Ms. Understanding*
>
> *Michelle and I have practiced all seson for the dance contist. We whent to the finals last year, but Michelle dropped out at the last second. We didn't speek for weeks! How can I help her?*
>
> *Yours truly*
>
> *Riana*

PROOFREADING TIP

Don't forget what you know about the parts of a letter. What punctuation is needed at the end of the greeting and closing?

ANSWER A LETTER Pretend you are Ms. Understanding. Answer Riana's letter. Use spelling words.

Word List

credit	hockey	reason	steal
speak	went	valley	monkey
alley	contest	money	treat
fence	beat	engine	season
least	honey	them	donkey

Personal Words 1.___ 2.___

Review

CROSSWORD PUZZLE Fill in the crossword puzzle by writing the boxed word that matches each definition.

them
went
fence
speak
reason
beat
money
valley
honey
monkey

Across
3. low land between hills or mountains
5. past tense of go
6. the people being spoken about
9. explanation

Down
1. mix by stirring rapidly with a fork or spoon
2. a wall put around a yard
4. a mammal with a long tail; one of the most intelligent animals
7. a golden liquid that bees make out of nectar
8. coins
10. say with words; talk

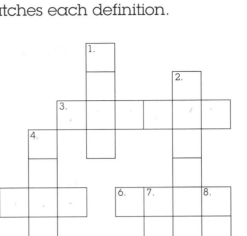

Multicultural Connection

PROVERBS A **proverb** is a short, wise saying. People everywhere use proverbs to pass along common beliefs.

The Chinese proverb **Talk does not cook rice** is much like the English proverb **Actions speak louder than words.**

Write a proverb from the banner that has a similar meaning to these proverbs.

People from Thailand say:
  1. You don't force a buffalo to eat grass.

The Senegalese say:
  2. To catch a monkey requires patience.

The Iranians say:
  3. One finger cannot lift a pebble.

You can lead a horse to water, but you can't make it drink.

In unity there is strength.

Good things come to those who wait.

Short Vowels a, i, o, u

SPELLING FOCUS

> **Short a** is usually spelled **a**: b<u>a</u>nd. **Short i** is usually spelled **i**: <u>i</u>nto. **Short o** is usually spelled **o**: p<u>o</u>nd. **Short u** is usually spelled **u**, but it is also often spelled **ou**: tr<u>ou</u>ble.

■ **STUDY** Say each word. Then read the meaning phrase.

WATCH OUT FOR FREQUENTLY MISSPELLED WORDS!

1. band — joined the school **band**
2. cash — took **cash** to the bank
3. into ✱ — went **into** the castle
4. river — canoe down a **river**
5. with ✱ — going **with** a friend
6. pond — a fishing **pond**
7. block — run around the **block**
8. forgot — **forgot** to return a book
9. trouble — problems that **trouble** me
10. young — too **young** to see the movie

11. January — the month of **January**
12. blanket — warm under the **blanket**
13. backpack — a **backpack** full of books
14. finger — a **finger** pointed at me
15. window — looking out the **window**
16. closet — coats hung in a **closet**
17. chop — **chop** some wood
18. cousin ✱ — my oldest **cousin**
19. couple — just a **couple** of days
20. tough — a **tough**, overcooked roast

CHALLENGE!

package
Pilgrims
ignored
o'clock
southern

■ **PRACTICE** Sort the list words by writing
- five words with **short a** spelled **a**
- five words with **short o** spelled **o**
- five words with **short u** spelled **ou**
- five words with **short i** spelled **i**

■ **WRITE** Choose two phrases to write an advertisement.

DEFINITIONS   Write the list word that fits each definition. Use the Spelling Dictionary if you need to.

1. the first month of the year
2. one of the five slender parts on a hand
3. to the inside of
4. water that flows into a lake or ocean
5. a small room for storing clothes or supplies
6. a group of musicians performing together
7. didn't remember
8. money in the form of coins and bills

> **Did You Know?**
> The word **couple** comes from the Old French word *cople*. *Cople* came from the Latin word *copula*, meaning bond. A married couple is thought to be bonded together.

VOWEL TRADE   Change the vowel in each word to make a list word with the **short o** sound.

9. black   10. chap   11. pend

BASE WORDS   Write the list words that are the base words for the words below.

12. coupled   15. cousins   18. untroubled
13. toughness   16. youngster   19. windowless
14. blanketed   17. backpacking

STRATEGIC SPELLING

Seeing Meaning Connections

| withstand |
| withdraw |
| withhold |

20. Write the list word that is related to the words in the box.

Then write the words from the box that fit the definitions.

21. to draw back or draw away
22. to refuse to give
23. to stand against or resist

■ PROOFREADING AND WRITING

≡	Make a capital.
/	Make a small letter.
∧	Add something.
ℓ	Take out something.
⊙	Add a period.
¶	New paragraph

PROOFREAD A MESSAGE Jane took a message for her cousin, Hiro, from his teacher, Mrs. Cortez. Find four spelling errors and one handwriting error.

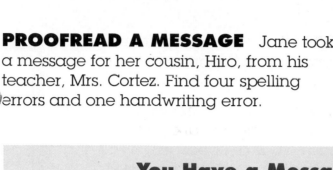

You Have a Message!!!

To: Hiro   **Date:** Janurary 5

Time: 4   A.M. (P.M.)   **From:** Ms. Cortez

Phone #: 555-1219   **Taken by:** Jane

Message

She has the bagpack you left at school. She will drop it off here tomarrow. It's no troble.

PROOFREADING TIP
Did Jane write "7279" or "1219"? When you take a phone message, be sure to write the phone number carefully.

WRITE A MESSAGE Read the following telephone phone message. Write down only the important information.

"Hello, is Jane there? No? Well this is Hiro, her cousin. I'm calling from a pay phone. Tell her I won't be there until 5:00. I'm at school, looking for my backpack."

Word List

cousin	couple	chop	trouble
cash	block	finger	window
into	January	blanket	backpack
closet	river	forgot	tough
with	young	band	pond

Personal Words 1.___ 2.___

54

Review

CONTEXT CLUES   Write the missing boxed words to complete the announcement below.

band
cash
into
river
with
pond
block
forgot
trouble
young

In case you (1)__, Fairview's summer festival will be held on July 2–4 at Merritime Park, just one (2)__ south of Lakeside Road and Briar Street. Here's just a sample of the wonderful entertainment at this year's festival.

- Afternoon and evening performances by the *Romper-Stompers* rock-and-roll (3)__.
- Lovely boat rides on the (4)__ that flows (5)__ our beautiful Lake Opeka.
- A fishing (6)__ with poles and prizes for (7)__ children.
- Food and game booths galore!

Bring your friends (8)__ you.
Admission is $5.00. Bring (9)__ only please.
Avoid (10)__ parking by driving directly to Lot 57.

Using a *Dictionary*

PRONUNCIATION   Dictionaries include a **pronunciation key** on every other page in the book. It helps you pronounce the symbols in the dictionary. It might look like this:

a	hat	i	ice	ʌ	put	´ stands for	
ā	age	o	hot		rule	a	in about
	far, calm	ō	open	ch	child	e	in taken
r	care		saw	ng	long	i	in pencil
e	let		order	sh	she	o	in lemon
"	equal	oi	oil	th	thin	u	in circus
r	term	ou	out	ŧh	then		
i	it	u	cup	zh	measure		

Each word in the dictionary is followed by its **pronunciation** in parentheses. The entry for the word *window* might look like this:

win•dow (win′dō), an opening in an outer wall or roof of a building, or in a vehicle, that lets in air or light. It is usually a wooden or metal frame that surrounds panes of glass or plastic. *n.*

Using the pronunciation key, you see the **i** is pronounced like the **i** in *it,* and the **ow** is pronounced like the **o** in *open.*

The dot between **win** and **dow** tells you that *window* has two syllables. The **accent mark** (′) tells you to say the first syllable in *window* with more force than the second.

Read each pronunciation below. Write the word that each pronunciation stands for. In each two-syllable word, underline the syllable you would say with more force.

1. (tuf)   3. (fər got′)   5. (kuz′n)
2. (kloz′it)   4. (kash)   6. (trub′əl)

Long Vowels a, i, o

SPELLING FOCUS

Long vowels are often spelled with one letter: **station**, **wild**. They can also be spelled **vowel-consonant-e**: **whole**, **hide**.

■ **STUDY** Say each word. Then read the meaning phrase.

WATCH OUT FOR FREQUENTLY MISSPELLED WORDS!

1. *station*   waiting at the train **station**
2. *danger*   staying out of **danger**
3. *April*   **April** showers
4. *wild*   a **wild**, bucking horse
5. *behind*   getting **behind** in one's work
6. *whole* ✳   ate the **whole** apple
7. *broke*   **broke** a glass
8. *drove*   **drove** to the countryside
9. *hide*   run away and **hide**
10. *decide*   **decide** to get a pet

11. *vacation* ✳   a **vacation** by the sea
12. *cable*   a television **cable** into the house
13. *bacon*   cook **bacon** for breakfast
14. *pint*   a **pint** of cream
15. *lion*   the roar of a **lion**
16. *smoke*   **smoke** from a campfire
17. *remote*   a **remote** cabin in the woods
18. *stole*   **stole** into their hideaway
19. *invite*   **invite** the queen to dinner
20. *arrive*   will **arrive** at noon

CHALLENGE!

operation
behavior
private
Rhode Island
apologize

■ **PRACTICE** Sort the list words by writing
- six words with **long a**
- eight words with **long i**
- six words with **long o**

■ **WRITE** Choose ten phrases to rewrite as sentences.

COMPARE Write a list word that has the same first letter, last letter, <u>and number of syllables</u> as each word below.

1. lotion
2. beacon
3. stallion
4. Abdul

5. ramble
6. veteran
7. drier
8. divide

9. pant
10. wood
11. beyond
12. inside

VOWEL TRADE Change the vowel in each word to make a list word with the **long o** sound.

13. whale
14. brake

15. drive
16. stale

STRATEGIC SPELLING

Using the Rhyming Helper Strategy

A rhyming helper rhymes with a word and is spelled the same at the end. Write *hide, cable, arrive,* and *smoke.* Write a rhyming helper alongside each word. Underline the matching letters. Be sure your helper is spelled right.

	List Word	Rhyming Helper
17.	___	___
18.	___	___
19.	___	___
20.	___	___

FREQUENTLY MISSPELLED WORDS Can't remember when to use **whole** or **hole?** Remember this: A complete **whole** has a wide **w,** while **hole** has just an empty middle.

≡	Make a capital.
/	Make a small letter.
∧	Add something.
ℯ	Take out something.
⊙	Add a period.
⁋	New paragraph

PROOFREAD A SUMMARY

Shanieka's class enjoyed a documentary film about Africa. Shanieka wrote a summary of what she saw. Correct four spelling errors and one run-on sentence.

PROOFREADING TIP

Shanieka forgot this simple rule: To avoid a run-on sentence, use a comma and and.

> Africa has deserts, jungles, and large cities. It is a place where willd animals roam and buildings touch the sky. A line roars loudly smock floats from a house. It would be a wonderful place to vacashun.

WRITE A SUMMARY
Think of an interesting film you saw lately. Write a summary of the film. Try to use some of your list words and personal words.

Word List

smoke	behind	broke	drove
cable	remote	station	hide
whole	lion	stole	bacon
invite	vacation	arrive	wild
April	pint	danger	decide

Personal Words 1.___ 2.___

Review

ANALOGIES Write the boxed word that completes each analogy.

1. Rider is to rode as driver is to ___.
2. Some is to all as part is to ___.
3. Pardon is to blame as show is to ___.
4. Ship is to port as bus is to ___.
5. Study is to examine as determine is to ___.
6. Wednesday is to Thursday as March is to ___.
7. Here is to there as front is to ___.
8. Kind is to cruel as calm is to ___.
9. Swim is to swam as break is to ___.
10. Rough is to bumpy as hazard is to ___.

> station
> danger
> April
> wild
> behind
> whole
> broke
> drove
> hide
> decide

Word *Study*

IDIOMS An **idiom** is a word picture that means something more than the words in it would suggest. One idiom has an interesting history.

Long ago in France, the people of Paris did not want Henry IV as their king. Henry decided to make war on them to "teach them a lesson." A wise counselor said to Henry, "If you destroy Paris, you will be king of a dead city. Would you chop off your nose to teach your face a lesson?" Henry spared Paris, became a popular king, and helped coin the idiom **cut off one's nose to spite one's face.**

Use the phrases in the box to help you write the meaning of each idiom below.

1. bring home the bacon ___

2. blow one's own horn ___

3. lose one's head ___

4. lead by the nose ___

> **praise oneself; boast**
>
> **earn a living**
>
> **have control over**
>
> **get excited**

Review

Lesson 7: Words with sh, ch, tch, wh
Lesson 8: Words with Double Consonants
Lesson 9: Short e and Long e
Lesson 10: Short Vowels a, i, o, u
Lesson 11: Long Vowels a, i, o

REVIEW WORD LIST

1. anywhere
2. catcher
3. chocolate
4. church
5. flashlight
6. kitchen
7. pitcher
8. shelter
9. somewhere
10. trash
11. watch
12. whatever
13. bottle
14. lettuce
15. odd
16. offer
17. slippers
18. supper
19. tomorrow
20. alley
21. beat
22. contest
23. fence
24. season
25. speak
26. them
27. treat
28. backpack
29. blanket
30. chop
31. couple
32. forgot
33. into
34. river
35. tough
36. trouble
37. window
38. with
39. young
40. April
41. bacon
42. decide
43. drove
44. invite
45. remote
46. smoke
47. station
48. stole
49. vacation
50. whole

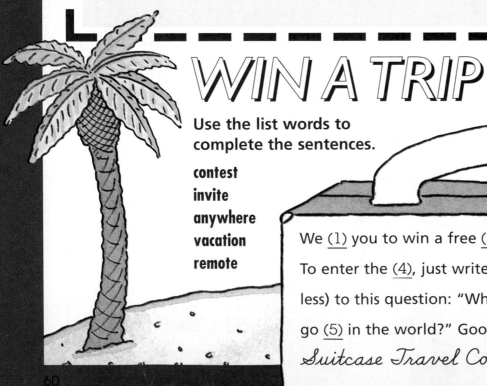

WIN A TRIP

Use the list words to complete the sentences.

contest
invite
anywhere
vacation
remote

We (1) you to win a free (2) to a (3) island in the Pacific. To enter the (4), just write the answer (in 50 words or less) to this question: "Where would you go if you could go (5) in the world?" Good Luck!

Suitcase Travel Company

Nat's Story

Nat is telling the story of *Aladdin* to his classmates, but he has forgotten a few of the details. Use the list words to complete his story.

ALADDIN AND THE MAGIC LAMP

Aladdin is a (1) man who finds a magic lamp. He rubs the lamp and an (2) fellow, called a genie, floats out in a puff of (3). The genie gives Aladdin (4) he asks for. Aladdin falls in love with the Emperor's daughter and must (5) how to win her. The genie helps (6), and the happy (7) are finally married.

couple
them
whatever
smoke
young
decide
odd

While in Los Angeles, Aponi sent her friend Ray this postcard. Use the list words to complete her message.

church
April
window
river
speak
season
station

POSTCARD FROM L.A.

Dear Ray,   April 3, 1995

We arrived in Los Angeles on the first of (1). Our train pulled into the (2) at midnight. It's supposed to be the rainy (3), but each day is sunny. It's fun to (4) Spanish with my friend Carlota. Today we visited Watts Towers. They look like steeples on a (5). I can see them from my bedroom (6). Tomorrow we will find a (7) and do some fishing. Have fun.

Aponi

Household Chores

Complete the list of weekly chores using each list word once.

forgot   with
offer   trash
fence   slippers
bottle   alley

SUNDAY: Feed the fish. —You (1) to do this last week—

MONDAY: Clean the hamster s water (2).

TUESDAY: Mend torn bedroom (3).

WEDNESDAY: Help Mom Remember to (4) to wash dishes.

THURSDAY: Clean the tub (5) scouring powder.

FRIDAY: Take old newspapers and other (6) out to the (7).

SATURDAY: Paint the picket (8).

pitcher
stole
watch
catcher
beat
drove
into
tough
trouble

The Big Game

Kelly couldn't wait to write in her journal after the championship baseball game. Complete the sentences. Use each list word once.

We played the big game against Evanston yesterday and we (1) them by one run!!! Dad said it was an incredibly exciting game to (2). It sure was a (3) game to play! We had a lot of (4) getting on base the first five innings, but then Chris got to first and (5) two bases. I (6) home the winning run! Our (7) struck out five of their batters, and our (8) tagged two runners sliding (9) home. The final score was 2-1.

A Family Meal

The local high school is offering a family cooking class. Complete the description using each of the list words once.

Cooking Together 101

If you want to (1) your family to a great time, this course is for you. Come into the (2) and learn how to prepare an entire (3). You will learn how to make a delicious omelet, using eggs, (4) milk, and crisp (5). Children will enjoy making Caesar salad, using fresh garden (6). They will also learn how to (7) and arrange vegetables for a dip. Dessert will be a (8) cake you prepare without flour! Only five families per class.

supper	kitchen	chocolate
treat	lettuce	chop
bacon	whole	

Camping Out

Use the list words to complete the conversation.

Place: Middle of the woods
Time: Twilight

tomorrow
somewhere
shelter
blanket
flashlight
backpack

Lewis: I'm glad we set up camp here. The trees will give us (1).

Lewis: Gosh, it's cold. I hope you packed an extra (3).

Lewis: It's here (5), but I can't find it. It's too dark.

Clark: Can you help me take off this heavy (2)?

Clark: It may be in here, but I can't see anything. It's so dark. I need the (4).

Clark: Let's just roll out our sleeping bags. We'll find everything (6), when it's light.

Meaning Helpers

DISCOVER THE STRATEGY Even a short word like every can be hard to spell—until you discover where it comes from.

You don't hear the second **e** when you say every, but you <u>do</u> hear it when you say ever. Ever is a meaning helper for every because a sound clue in ever helps you spell every.

TRY IT OUT Now try the meaning-helper strategy yourself. Follow the directions on the next page.

Work with a partner to figure out what sound clue in the top word helps you spell the bottom word. The first two pairs are done for you.

major
majority

The **long a** in **major** reminds me that **majority** is spelled with an **a** too. The sound of **a** is different in the two words, but the spelling of that sound is the same.

act
action

The sound of **t** in **act** reminds me that **action** is spelled with a **t** too.

1. press
   pressure

2. fast
   fasten

Write a meaning helper of your own for each word below. Mark the letter or letters that give the sound clue.

3. national   4. election   5. confession

LOOK AHEAD   Look ahead at the next five lessons. Write two list words and the helpers that would help you use this strategy. Underline the letters that give the sound clues.

Related Words

Related words often have parts that are spelled the same but pronounced differently: **able**, **ability**; **sign**, **signal**.

■ **STUDY** Say each word. Then read the meaning phrase.

1. *able* **able** to do a back flip
2. *ability* the **ability** to juggle
3. *sign* a stop **sign**
4. *signal* **signal** a left turn
5. *mean* didn't **mean** to hurt you
6. *meant* **meant** what I said
7. *deal* **deal** the number cards
8. *dealt* **dealt** six math fact cards
9. *soft* a **soft,** dreamy song
10. *soften* **soften** my dry skin

11. *relate* **relate** well to one's sister
12. *relative* a distant **relative**
13. *heal* medicine to **heal** a burn
14. *health* grateful for good **health**
15. *meter* about 39 inches in a **meter**
16. *metric* a **metric** measurement
17. *compose* **compose** a symphony
18. *composition* a new piano **composition**
19. *crumb* ate every **crumb** of the cake
20. *crumble* **crumble** to the ground

CHALLENGE!

direct
direction
personal
personality
invade
invasion

■ **PRACTICE** Write the related word pairs. For each pair, first write the word that is easier for you to spell. The easier word should help you spell the related word.

■ **WRITE** Choose two phrases to write an advertisement, slogan, or saying.

CONTRASTS   Write list words to complete the sentences.

1. A small bit of water is a drop.
   A small bit of bread is a ___.
2. Lack of rest and a virus may cause sickness.
   Rest and medicine may bring about ___.
3. If you fail at something, you are unable to do it.
   If you finally succeed, you are ___ to do it.
4. A person who helps you is kind.
   A person who harms you is ___.
5. You use your voice in spoken language.
   You use your hands in ___ language.
6. Apples should be sweet and hard.
   Raisins should be sweet and ___.

Take a Hint
Watch out for the **mean ant** in **meant.**

SYNONYMS   Write the list word that means the same as the underlined word or words. Use the Spelling Dictionary.

7. I wrote a <u>short essay</u> about my dog.
8. Please shuffle and <u>pass out</u> the division facts cards.
9. The <u>arrangement of beats</u> in a polka is very quick.
10. Mozart was able to <u>put together</u> twenty-two operas.
11. She was able to <u>tell</u> the exact details of the event.
12. Is that what you <u>intended</u> to say?
13. The cut will <u>become well</u> in a few days.
14. Dogs have the <u>power</u> to hear high-pitched sounds.
15. A red light is a <u>sign giving notice</u> to stop.
16. The old wall was beginning to <u>decay</u>.
17. Asia uses the <u>measurement-that-counts-by-tens</u> system.

STRATEGIC SPELLING

Using the Meaning Helper Strategy

18.–20. Meaning helpers can help you spell words. Write the list words related to *soft, relate,* and *deal.* Mark the letters that match the underlined letters in the helpers.

☰	Make a capital.
/	Make a small letter.
∧	Add something.
ℯ	Take out something.
⊙	Add a period.
¶	New paragraph

PROOFREAD A PERSUASIVE PARAGRAPH
Min and her friends are trying to convince their principal to allow music during lunch. They are writing their reasons on index cards to be delivered on a cafeteria tray. Correct the five spelling errors Min has made.

PROOFREADING TIP

Min wrote *brother* when she meant to write something else. Always proofread your writing for words that are spelled correctly but have the wrong meaning.

It is meen not to let us listen to music at lunch. Good music is good for our helth. It helps us relax and be abel to face the next class. We will only play sof music. It won't brother anyone.

Min Yi

WRITE A PERSUASIVE PARAGRAPH
Think of something you would like to persuade someone to do or to allow you to do. Write about it. Try to use list words and a personal word.

Word List

crumb	soften	meter	ability
crumble	mean	metric	relate
sign	meant	deal	relative
signal	heal	dealt	compose
soft	health	able	composition

Personal Words   1. ___ 2. ___

Review

CONTEXT CLUES Mr. Chambers asked his students to list their talents and good qualities. One of his students made the list below. Write the boxed word that completes each sentence in the list.

| able |
| ability |
| sign |
| signal |
| mean |
| meant |
| deal |
| dealt |
| soft |
| soften |

My Talents and Good Qualities

I have the (1) to make friends easily.
I am never (2) or spiteful towards anyone.
I have (3), shiny hair.
When I am misunderstood, I always take the time to explain what I (4).
I am (5) to do a cartwheel and a handstand.
I have helped my mother the times she has (6) out food at the homeless shelter. I spend a good (7) of my free time doing volunteer work like that.
I obey every street (8) and traffic (9) when riding my bike.
I know how to (10) the hurt feelings of others with kind words.

Word *Study*

TRIPLETS Here's a challenging vocabulary game called **Triplets.** It's a game in which you supply the one word that is often associated with three others. For example, what list word would you associate with the three words below?

post   language   up

The answer is **sign,** as in **signpost, sign language,** and **sign up.** Here are more for you to try. Remember, the missing word always goes in front. Use the boxed words for help.

| soft | night | whole | music | dry |

1. drink   boiled   soap
2. cleaner   run   ice
3. gown   crawler   mare
4. video   hall   box
5. milk   note   wheat

Consonant Sounds /j/, /ks/, /kw/

The sound /j/ can be spelled **ge** and **dge**: cha**nge**, e**dge**. The sounds /ks/ and /kw/ can be spelled **xc**, **x**, and **qu**: e**xc**ept, e**x**plain, **qu**ick.

■ **STUDY** Say each word. Then read the meaning phrase.

WATCH OUT FOR FREQUENTLY MISSPELLED WORDS!

1. change — **change** my wet clothes
2. village — a charming country **village**
3. edge — the **edge** of a cliff
4. except ✳ — everyone **except** me
5. excited — **excited** about a trip
6. explain — **explain** how to do something
7. expect — **expect** a package in the mail
8. Texas — a ranch in **Texas**
9. quick — a **quick** dance step
10. equal — all **equal** under the law

11. charge — **charge** a purchase
12. bridge — a **bridge** across a river
13. fudge — delicious chocolate **fudge**
14. excellent — an **excellent** orchestra
15. relax — **relax** and listen to music
16. extra — **extra** credit for doing more work
17. queen — the **queen** of a Pacific island
18. quart — a **quart** of milk
19. liquid — medicine in **liquid** form
20. quilt — a **quilt** made of colorful scraps

■ **PRACTICE** Sort the list words by writing
- eight words with the sound /ks/ spelled **x** or **xc**
- six words with the sound /j/ spelled **ge** or **dge**
- six words with the sound /kw/ spelled **qu**

■ **WRITE** Choose three phrases to include in a paragraph.

CHALLENGE!

advantage
pledge
excess
explosion
question

TONGUE TWISTERS   Write the list word that would best complete each tongue twister.

1. Fran fasts Fridays, frequently forgetting flavorful ____.
2. The ____ quickly quashed the quarrelsome quibbler.
3. Tula took trips to ____ a total of ten times.
4. Beside the bay ____, Binita built a bungalow.
5. Running relentlessly, Russ will rarely ____ or rest.
6. Chang's chum can ____ cheese into cheesecake.
7. This Vermont ____ is veiled in the vast verdant valley.
8. Lassie lapped at the ____ in the ladle.
9. Ed is edgy at the ____ of the edifice.

WORD SEARCH   Find the ten list words in the puzzle below. They may be printed down or across. Write them.

```
c  e  x  c  e  l  l  e  n  t  e  e
h  x  e  q  u  a  r  t  e  a  x  x
a  p  e  x  t  r  a  q  u  i  c  k
r  e  x  p  l  a  i  n  q  u  e  e
g  c  e  x  c  i  t  e  d  e  p  p
e  t  q  u  i  l  q  u  i  l  t  x
```

STRATEGIC SPELLING

Seeing Meaning Connections

| equator |
| equally |
| equation |

20. Write a list word that is related in spelling and meaning to the words in the box.

Finish the sentences with words from the box.

21. Divide this ____ among you.
22. (2 x 2) + 3 = 7 is a math ____.
23. The ____ circles the earth.

≡	Make a capital.
/	Make a small letter.
∧	Add something.
ℓ	Take out something.
⊙	Add a period.
¶	New paragraph

PROOFREAD A RECIPE Read the following recipe. Correct four misspellings and one place where *good* is used incorrectly.

PROOFREADING TIP

Good food, good kids, good home are good ways to use the word good. Good describes a person, place, or thing. Use *well* to describe how you do something: cook well.

Here's a recipe for very good fuge.

In a pan over low heat mix together good:

2 tablespoons butter

2 cups marshmallows

2 cups exellent chocolate

2 cups sugar

Pour liqid into pan. Allow to cool.

Cut into bars. For a good snack, freeze exdra pieces.

WRITE A RECIPE Think of something you enjoy eating. Find out how to make it and write the recipe. You might want to make the dish and share it with your classmates.

Word List

bridge	quart	expect	equal
queen	edge	quick	excellent
except	extra	explain	quilt
change	village	Texas	excited
relax	liquid	charge	fudge

Personal Words   1. ___ 2. ___

Review

CONTEXT CLUES Isabella was in a hurry when she wrote this letter to her friend. Write the missing boxed words to complete her letter.

| change |
| village |
| edge |
| except |
| excited |
| explain |
| expect |
| Texas |
| quick |
| equal |

Dear Nina,

I'm having a great time on my trip in the southwest. The weather here has been a nice (1) from the cold weather we left in Minnesota. Temperatures have been in the nineties every day (2) one day when it was over one hundred. Standing on the (3) of the Grand Canyon was awesome! Nothing is (4) to its beauty. I saw a Pueblo Indian (5) where the people live in houses called adobes. When I see you I'll (6) how they are made. Tomorrow we make a (7) stop in Santa Fe where we catch a flight to Dallas, (8). We (9) to see a rodeo there. I'm (10) about that! I'll write again soon.

Love,
Isabella

Using a *Dictionary*

FINDING THE RIGHT MEANING If someone said, "I can't eat without my bridge," would you understand the person? *Bridge* has many meanings. If you look it up in a dictionary, you might find these definitions. ——→

The second definition is followed by a **sentence.** This sentence helps you to see how the word is used.

At the end of the entry, each definition is identified by its **part of speech** (whether noun, verb, adjective, etc.). These are called part-of-speech labels.

Look at the entry for *bridge* again. Write the number of the definition that answers each question below.

1. Which definition of *bridge* fits the meaning, "I can't eat without my bridge"? ___
2. Which definition of *bridge* is part of a stringed instrument? ___
3. Which definition is a verb? ___

bridge (brij), **1** something built over a river, road, or railroad, so that people can get across. **2** to build a bridge over: *The engineers bridged the river.* **3** the false tooth or teeth in a mounting fastened to natural teeth. **4** a thin, arched piece over which the strings of a violin and other stringed instruments are stretched. 1, 3–4 *n.,* 2 *v.,* **bridged, bridg•ing.**

Adding -s and -es

SPELLING FOCUS

Add **-s** to words ending in a **vowel** and **y** and to most words: **monkeys, flowers.** Change **y** to **i** and add **-es** to words ending in a **consonant** and **y: supplies.** Add **-es** to words ending in **sh, ch, s, ss, x: beaches.**

■ **STUDY** See whether **-s** or **-es** is added to each list word.

monkey	1.	*monkeys*
flower	2.	*flowers*
friend	3.	*friends*
supply	4.	*supplies*
enemy	5.	*enemies*
eyelash	6.	*eyelashes*
beach	7.	*beaches*
circus	8.	*circuses*
class	9.	*classes*
tax	10.	*taxes*

tiger	11.	*tigers*
holiday	12.	*holidays*
delay	13.	*delays*
hobby	14.	*hobbies*
memory	15.	*memories*
mystery	16.	*mysteries*
ash	17.	*ashes*
bunch	18.	*bunches*
glass	19.	*glasses*
suffix	20.	*suffixes*

WATCH OUT FOR FREQUENTLY MISSPELLED WORDS!

CHALLENGE!

accidents
skis
injuries
libraries
couches

■ **PRACTICE** Sort the words by writing
- five words in which **y** has been changed to **i**
- nine other words in which **-es** is added
- six words in which **-s** is added

■ **WRITE** Choose ten words to write in sentences.

MAKING COMPARISONS Complete each comparison using a list word.

1. The children chattered like ____ in a tree.
2. Her sweet perfume smelled like fresh ____.
3. The long threads were as thin and dark as ____.
4. Their faces were as dry and gray as ____.
5. The play had more problems than one of my math ____.
6. Tho two round puddles shined like a pair of ____.
7. The floor was as sandy as ten ____.
8. Deep-sea photography is like having two ____ in one.
9. They ate the roast like ferocious, snarling ____.

WORD ASSOCIATIONS Write the list word that you would associate with the words or phrases below. Use the Spelling Dictionary for help.

10. stops along the way
11. grapes in groups
12. July 4, Thanksgiving
13. groups at war
14. clowns and acrobats
15. money citizens pay

16. sleeping bags, canteens,
17. good pals
18. puzzling secrets
19. -ment, -ly, -ous
20. things remembered

STRATEGIC SPELLING
Building New Words

Write the plural form of each word. Remember what you learned.

21. scratch ____. 22. guess ____. 23. play ____.

Take a Hint
Here's another way to remember when to add -es: Say the plural form aloud. If the ending you hear adds a syllable, the ending you add is -es: watch•es tax•es

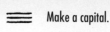

☰	Make a capital.
/	Make a small letter.
∧	Add something.
ℰ	Take out something.
⊙	Add a period.
¶	New paragraph

PROOFREAD A DESCRIPTION

Byron wrote this description of reggae, his favorite music. Read what he wrote, and then correct three misspellings and one pronoun error.

PROOFREADING TIP

My friends and I means the same thing as we. Byron should use one or the other, never both.

> In Jamaica, my homeland, my freinds and I we listen to reggae music. Reggae has a strong beat, like rock music. It is not as hard as rock, though, because it was born on island beachs. It is like the blues, but brighter. It has the sound of sunshine and floweres.

WRITE A DESCRIPTION

Write a description of your favorite music. Use list words and personal words.

Word List

friends	monkeys	circuses	hobbies
tigers	ashes	glasses	enemies
flowers	eyelashes	classes	memories
holidays	beaches	taxes	mysteries
delays	bunches	suffixes	supplies

Personal Words   1. ___   2. ___

Review

WORD ASSOCIATIONS Write the boxed word that belongs in each group.

1. leopards, zebras, ___
2. chin, nose, ___
3. students, learning, ___
4. foes, rivals, ___
5. allowances, wages, ___
6. carnivals, fairs, ___
7. buddies, pals, ___
8. sunbathers, lifeguards, ___

> monkeys
> flowers
> friends
> supplies
> enemies
> eyelashes
> beaches
> circuses
> classes
> taxes

CATEGORIZING Write the boxed word that is a name you would give to each group.

9. pens, paper, ruler
10. roses, daisies, petunias

Multicultural *Connection*

ENVIRONMENT People of all nations use flowers to express feelings and to symbolize love. The flowers pictured below are national flowers. Write the boxed word that matches each description. Use your Spelling Dictionary to look up the flowers you don't know.

> **lotus**
>
> **almond blossom**
>
> **cattleya orchid**
>
> **edelweiss**

1. a small flower that grows in Austria, made famous in a song

2. a bright, showy flower that grows in the tropics of Costa Rica

3. a kind of water lily found in India

4. the flower of the almond tree, often seen in Israel

Using Just Enough Letters

Pronouncing a word correctly and picturing how it looks can help you avoid writing too many letters.

■ **STUDY** Say each word. Then read the meaning phrase.

WATCH OUT FOR FREQUENTLY MISSPELLED WORDS!

1.	*coming*	**coming** to your house
2.	*always* ❋	**always** buckle seat belts
3.	*almost*	**almost** finished her homework
4.	*didn't* ❋	**didn't** want to go
5.	*upon* ❋	sat **upon** a bench
6.	*wasn't*	**wasn't** ready to begin
7.	*until* ❋	wait **until** later
8.	*during*	quiet **during** the concert
9.	*want* ❋	**want** a glass of milk
10.	*father*	a **father** with six children
11.	*hamster*	a furry little **hamster**
12.	*a lot* ❋	like to dance **a lot**
13.	*ugly*	an **ugly** duckling
14.	*washed*	**washed** the dinner dishes
15.	*hotel*	a **hotel** in the city
16.	*missed*	**missed** my bus
17.	*eleven*	**eleven** different flavors
18.	*crazy*	performed a **crazy** stunt
19.	*lazy*	felt **lazy** all day
20.	*feelings*	hurt someone's **feelings**

CHALLENGE!

delivery
magnet
replied
drowned
mustard

■ **PRACTICE** Sort the list words by writing
- the only two-word form
- one word that has three syllables
- three words that have one syllable
- fifteen words that have two syllables

■ **WRITE** Choose two phrases to write a riddle.

CLASSIFYING   Write the list word that fits in each group.

1. sister, mother, ____
2. ten, ____, twelve
3. inn, resort, ____
4. wish, desire, ____
5. in the course of, at the time, ____

6. foolish, nutty, ____
7. emotions, thoughts, ____
8. careless, not working, ____
9. guinea pig, gerbil, ____

WORDS IN CONTEXT   Write the missing list words to complete the paragraph below.

Once (10) a time there was a little boy who thought of himself as an (11) duckling, although his grandmother always told him, "You're truly a handsome fellow." She (12) kidding, but the boy (13) believe her. He would frown at himself in a mirror (14) his face would begin to hurt. Other children would ask him to play quite (15), but he would (16) find an excuse to smile and say, "Not today, thanks." One day a little girl invited him to a party. He (17) didn't go, but his grandmother convinced him that the girl would feel hurt if he stayed home. When he finally arrived at the party, his friend rushed to him, saying, "I was worried you weren't (18)! We would have (19) your friendly face!"

STRATEGIC SPELLING
Using the Meaning Helper Strategy

20. Write a list word that is related to the words in the box.

| wishy-washy |
| washable |
| washcloth |

Now write words from the box that fit the clues.

21. Use it when you take a bath. ____

22. If asked an opinion, don't be this. ____

23. Your play clothes should definitely be this. ____

≡	Make a capital.
/	Make a small letter.
∧	Add something.
ℯ	Take out something.
⊙	Add a period.
¶	New paragraph

PROOFREAD A WARNING One morning the sign below appeared beside the cage of Scratch the Hamster. Correct four misspellings and one place where the punctuation is wrong.

PROOFREADING TIP

Remember that *it's* has an apostrophe because it's short for *it is*. Say *it is* aloud when you write *it's* or *its*. If *it is* doesn't fit, take out the apostrophe.

WARNING

This hamster is on strick untill it's cage is cleaned. Hamsters have feellings too. Please, allways be aware of its needs!

WRITE A WARNING Think of a warning sign you would like to write. Try to use your list words and your personal words.

Word List

hamster	always	eleven	wasn't
a lot	father	didn't	almost
ugly	missed	upon	want
washed	until	crazy	feelings
hotel	coming	lazy	during

Personal Words   1. ___   2. ___

Review

ANTONYMS Complete each phrase by writing the boxed word that means the opposite of the underlined word.

1. not a <u>mother</u>, but a ___   2. not <u>going</u>, but ___

DRAW YOUR OWN CONCLUSIONS Write the boxed word that matches each clue.

3. before, ___, after
4. This word is used in the following phrase that starts many fairy tales: *Once ___ a time.*
5. This word means the same as *nearly.*
6. was + not = ___
7. ___, sometimes, never
8. This word means the same as *desire.*
9. did + not = ___
10. This word means "up to the time when."

| coming |
| always |
| almost |
| didn't |
| upon |
| wasn't |
| until |
| during |
| want |
| father |

Word *Study*

WORD PLAY Janna thinks that the word *ugly* looks just like what it means. "It's an ugly word," she says. "Just look at that open, gaping **u** and the hanging **g** and **y.** It just says 'ugly' to me!" Janna drew the word *ugly* to illustrate her point.

Lee had other ideas. "That's a neat drawing, Janna," he said, "but I don't see it that way. I think there's some beauty to be found in the word *ugly.*" Lee drew the word his way.

Now it's your turn. Find a way to make a word look like what it means. You might want to take Lee's approach and do the opposite.

Contractions

SPELLING FOCUS

In contractions, an apostrophe replaces omitted letters. **We will** becomes **we'll**; **I am** becomes **I'm**.

■ **STUDY** A **contraction** is a shortened form of two words. Say each pair of words and then say its contraction.

WATCH OUT FOR FREQUENTLY MISSPELLED WORDS!

we + will	=	1. we'll
I + am	=	2. I'm ✳
I + would	=	3. I'd
you + would	=	4. you'd
I + will	=	5. I'll
we + have	=	6. we've
it + is	=	7. it's ✳
that + is	=	8. that's ✳
what + is	=	9. what's
does + not	=	10. doesn't

he + will	=	11. he'll
she + will	=	12. she'll
they + will	=	13. they'll
they + would	=	14. they'd
he + would	=	15. he'd
would + have	=	16. would've
could + have	=	17. could've
would + not	=	18. wouldn't
should + not	=	19. shouldn't
let + us	=	20. let's ✳

■ **PRACTICE** Sort the list words by writing
- five words ending in **-'ll**
- four words ending in either **-'ve** or **-'m**
- four words ending in **-'d**
- seven words ending either in **-'t** or **-'s**

■ **WRITE** Choose ten words to write in sentences.

CHALLENGE!

it'll
who'll
might've
mustn't
we'd

HOMOPHONES   Write the contraction that sounds just like each word below.

1. heed
2. weave
3. aisle
4. eyed
5. heel
6. lets

CREATING CONTRACTIONS   Write the contractions for the words below.

7. they will
8. we will
9. what is
10. they would
11. that is
12. could have
13. would have
14. she will

DON'T QUOTE ME   Write list words to help the famous people below complete sentences they might have said.

15. Nathan Hale: "____ sorry I have but one life to give."
16. Rosa Parks: "I ____ give up my seat on the bus."
17. Mohandas Gandhi: "One should resist oppression, but one ____ use violence to do so."
18. Pablo Picasso: "Painting isn't beautiful, ____ magical."
19. Confucius: "Do to others what ____ want done to you."
20. Amelia Earhart: "Peace comes with courage. It ____ come easily."

> **Did You Know?**
> *I* is a capital because in old handwritten manuscripts, a small *i* would often be lost or attached to a neighboring word. A capital *I* helped separate it.

STRATEGIC SPELLING
Building New Words

Add the contraction for *will* to the base words. Remember what you learned.

Base word	Contraction with -'ll
21. you	——
22. who	——

☰	Make a capital.
/	Make a small letter.
∧	Add something.
ℓ	Take out something.
⊙	Add a period.
¶	New paragraph

PROOFREAD A SIGN The photograph below contains a misspelled word. Since a question is being asked, the punctuation is also incorrect. Write the word correctly as well as the punctuation mark.

PROOFREADING TIP

When making a sign, it's easy to make a mistake in a word with an apostrophe. Be sure you carefully proofread your sign before others see it.

WRITE A SIGN Isn't there a question you'd like to ask in a big way? Use a few list words to create your message.

Word List

I'm	I'll	it's	shouldn't
I'd	he'll	that's	doesn't
you'd	she'll	what's	we've
they'd	we'll	let's	would've
he'd	they'll	wouldn't	could've

Personal Words 1. ___ 2. ___

Review

CONTEXT CLUES   Write the missing boxed words to complete the paragraph below.

we'll
I'm
I'd
you'd
I'll
we've
it's
that's
what's
doesn't

(1) convinced that my dog Rusty is the world's naughtiest dog! That (2) mean I don't love him. After all, (3) been great pals ever since he was a pup, and (4) always be the best of friends. But (5) rather he didn't get into so much mischief! (6) never forget the time he saw the kid across the street with a big ice cream cone. There isn't any treat that Rusty loves more than ice cream, ('/) tor sure! Well, he ran lickety-split toward that kid, jumped all over him and started licking his cone. Then there was the time that Rusty jumped into the bathtub when Dad was giving my younger brother Joel a bath. I bet (8) have laughed like I did though if you saw how Dad couldn't get a hold of Rusty. What a mess! You never know (9) going to happen next with Rusty around, but you can bet (10) going to be BIG TROUBLE!

Word *Study*

PYRAMID SENTENCES   **Pyramid sentences** start with one word, the subject, and get longer and longer. Each word that is added must begin with the same letter. Arranged one atop the other, the sentences look like a pyramid. Here's an example:

Subject word: *she'll*

She'll sing.

She'll sing songs.

She'll sing six songs.

Shelly says she'll sing six silly songs.

Now you try writing your own pyramid sentences. Begin with one of these words: *They'll, I'm, It's, He'd,* or *We'll.*

Review

Lesson 13: Related Words
Lesson 14: Consonant Sounds /j/, /ks/, /kw/

Lesson 15: Adding -s and -es
Lesson 16: Using Just Enough Letters
Lesson 17: Contractions

REVIEW WORD LIST

1. ability
2. able
3. compose
4. composition
5. crumb
6. heal
7. health
8. meter
9. relative
10. signal
11. soft
12. change
13. charge

14. edge
15. excellent
16. excited
17. explain
18. extra
19. fudge
20. liquid
21. quart
22. quick
23. quilt
24. relax
25. Texas
26. village

27. beaches
28. bunches
29. classes
30. flowers
31. friends
32. glasses
33. holidays
34. memories
35. a lot
36. always
37. eleven
38. father

39. feelings
40. lazy
41. missed
42. want
43. washed
44. didn't
45. doesn't
46. I'm
47. it's
48. let's
49. shouldn't
50. we'll

℞ for Good Health

The students in health class put together the rules below. Supply the missing words and see how the rules apply to you.

Take (1) of your own life. Eat sensibly! Exercise!

To maintain good (2), always get plenty of rest.

Don't be (3)! Get out and do things!

Exercise is an (4) way to reduce stress.

If a sore doesn't (5), see your doctor.

If we follow these simple rules, (6) all stay healthy.

excellent
lazy
we'll
heal
charge
health

Daily Record — Mon, May 7

N'Jabi decided to keep a record of his daily routine. Complete the entry for Monday, May 7.

5:30 (1) __ up and dressed.

5:40 Breakfast: two (2) __ of orange juice. 7-grain cereal, and ½ (3) __ of 2% milk

6:30 30 sit-ups

7:00 My (4) __ comes in and says, "Son, (5) __ talk."

7:05 I tell him I'm not (6) __ to take the time.

7:30 I run 5 miles, worrying about hurting Dad's (7) __.

8:30 Home to change clothes for school.

9:00 Take a shortcut that (8) __ go anywhere.

10:00 I'm so late for school, I've missed two (9) __! Tomorrow will be better.

quart
glasses
father
able
feelings
classes
I'm
doesn't
let's

GOOD SPORTS

Use the words below to complete each person's statement.

signal
missed
beaches
always

I MADE TEN BASKETS AND ONLY (1) __ ONCE.

I RIDE THE WAVES RIGHT ONTO THE SANDY (2) __.

GIVE ME THE (3) __, AND I'LL TACKLE ANYTHING IN SIGHT.

I (4) __ TRY TO SERVE AND VOLLEY.

Off the Shelf

a lot   extra   change
quick   shouldn't   want

The items below are missing words.
Complete each item with a list word.

SLICK SHOES

If you want to be (1), wear
Slick. They'll (2) the way
you run... for the better!"

WHEAT CRUNCHIES
Breakfast of Eaters

with (5) helping
of honey clusters

MY FLIGHTY LIFE
by Carl Canary

"You (6) miss this one!"

the ROACHES
SING
the BEETLES

"I liked it (3)."
— Paula McCartney

"You'll (4) to hear more!"
— Ringlet Starr

Interview

Karli loves music and wondered what it would be like
to discuss it with a famous composer. She wrote this
imaginary interview with J. S. Bach.

KARLI: Mr. Bach, can you (1) why you became a composer?

J. S.: Yes. I (2) want to do anything in my life but (3) music.

KARLI: Did you have musical (4) at a young age?

J. S.: I believe so. I wrote my first (5) as a young man.

didn't
meter
ability
compose
excited
it's
explain
soft
composition

KARLI: What was it about music that (6) you?

J. S.: Everything! The notes, the (7), the harmonies!

KARLI: You write music that is loud and triumphant

or (8) and romantic. Which do you prefer?

J. S.: I think (9) all a challenge. Music is my life.

88

Visiting the Lone Star State

Rafael gave a talk to his class about a place that is very important to him. Use the list words to complete his sentences.

- EL PASO
- PECOS
- SOCORRO

holidays   friends   relative   Texas
eleven   memories village

I love the state of (1) .

I have wonderful (2) of El Paso. I spend all my school (3) there.

My good (4) Juana and Paul live in Pecos. I have (5) cousins who live in the small (6) of Socorro.

I am the only (7) who doesn't live in this state.

School Fund-Raiser

Martin Luther King, Jr. School is having its annual fund-raiser. Use the list words to finish the posters.

fudge
quilt
washed
crumb
edge
relax
flowers
bunches
liquid

Raffle Tickets
Take a chance on this beautiful handmade (1) . Notice the scallop along each (2) .

Fresh garden (5)
Daisies, Roses, Snapdragons, and more!! Buy two (6) in a big bouquet, get one free! Hurry while the supply lasts!!

Quench Your Thirst
25¢ each
Sodas, apple juice, and other (9) refreshments. Straw-free.

Homemade Chocolate (3) for sale here. You'll gobble up every (4) ! Fifty cents apiece

CAR WASH $2.50
We'll have it (7) in 5 minutes. You just sit back and (8) .

Strategy Worksho[p]

Memory Tricks

DISCOVER THE STRATEGY   Some words seem so tricky to spell that we need to outsmart them with tricks of our own. Follow these steps.

1. Mark the letters that give you a problem.	2. Find words you know with those same letters.	3. Use your problem wo[rd] [a]nd the word you know [in a] phrase or sentence.

Your memory trick might be more than one word. It might rhyme. Just be sure you can spell the helping word and that the problem letters match. Here are more memory tricks.

wheat—Heat the wheat.
liquid—quick liquid
young—You are young.
bubbles— big beautiful bubbles.

TRY IT OUT   Now practice the memory-tricks strategy yourself. Follow the directions on the next page.

Complete each memory trick using a word from the box to the right.

1. Ride ____ the lion.
2. A couple is ____.
3. Flick the kitchen ____.
4. Give ____ the lettuce.

switch

on

Bruce

plenty

With a partner, write your own memory tricks for each pair of words below. It's all right if they sound silly. The point is to find ways to remember how to spell tricky words. Underline the matching letters.

5. hotel—Elvis
6. blanket—thank
7. window—down

Make a memory trick for one of the words in the box to the right. Follow steps 2 and 3 on page 90. Mark the matching letters.

8. ____

cable

closet

season

tomorrow

LOOK AHEAD Look ahead at the next five lessons. Find one list word that looks hard to spell and write a memory trick for it. Share your trick with the class.

Getting Letters in Correct Order

SPELLING FOCUS

Watch for letter combinations that are hard to keep in order, and pay special attention to those parts: **friend, said.**

■ **STUDY** Say each word. Then read the meaning phrase.

WATCH OUT FOR FREQUENTLY MISSPELLED WORDS!

1. *piece*   a **piece** of cake
2. *friend* ✳   help a **friend**
3. *field*   a **field** full of corn
4. *said* ✳   couldn't hear what she **said**
5. *again* ✳   doing it over **again**
6. *asked*   **asked** for my help
7. *only*   **only** on Tuesdays
8. *brought* ✳   **brought** a friend along
9. *heard* ✳   **heard** the good news
10. *build*   **build** a new tree house

11. *believe* ✳   **believe** someone's story
12. *heart*   a kind **heart**
13. *weird*   **weird** shadows on the wall
14. *height*   a **height** of six feet six inches
15. *weight*   a **weight** of two hundred pounds
16. *neighbor*   my next-door **neighbor**
17. *rattle*   a **rattle** for the baby
18. *pickle*   a sour **pickle**
19. *toes*   wiggling their **toes**
20. *hospital* ✳   in the **hospital** with a broken leg

CHALLENGE!

interview
poetry
sword
tongue
unusual

■ **PRACTICE** Decide which of the list words you use most in your writing. Then write them in order, from the ones you use most to the ones you use least. Underline any letter combinations that are hard for you to keep in order.

■ **WRITE** Choose three phrases to include in a paragraph.

EQUATIONS   Write each list word using the math clues.

1. a + gain =
2. on + lye -e =
3. we + bird -b =
4. ask + led -l =
5. rat + tile -i =
6. fried -d + nd =

7. is -i + aid =
8. pick + led -d =
9. outfield -out =
10. built -t + d =
11. be + lie -e + eve=
12. neigh + born -n =

HOMOPHONES   Write the list word that sounds like each word below.

13. herd
14. peace

15. wait
16. tows

17. hart

Strategic Spelling

Using the Memory Tricks Strategy

Use memory tricks to help you spell. Write a list word to complete each trick. Underline the matching letters.

18. <u>eight</u> feet in ____

19. <u>p</u>at<u>i</u>en<u>t</u>s <u>i</u>n <u>t</u>raction in a ____

20. I ____ <u>g</u>rapes, <u>h</u>oney, and <u>t</u>ea to the party.

> **Take a Hint**
> Is it **peace** or **piece?**
> Just remember:
> Slice a **pie**ce of **pie.**

≡	Make a capital.
/	Make a small letter.
∧	Add something.
ℓ	Take out something.
⊙	Add a period.
¶	New paragraph

PROOFREAD A DESCRIPTION

While blindfolded, Bria felt an object and then wrote a description of it. First correct three misspellings and two careless errors in her description below. Then write the name of the object. Hint: It's a list word.

PROOFREADING TIP

Bria tried so hard to get the description right that small words were left out. Such mistakes are easy to catch if you proofread.

It is a long peice of plastic with a round part on top.

Its weight is about two ounces.

Its hight about five inches.

It makes wierd sound when you shake it.

What is it? _____

WRITE A DESCRIPTION
Play this guessing game with your classmates. While blindfolded, each player feels a different object and writes a description of that object. After everyone has written descriptions, read them aloud one by one and guess the names of the objects.

Word List

believe	height	heard	asked
friend	weight	heart	toes
piece	neighbor	rattle	build
field	said	pickle	only
weird	again	brought	hospital

Personal Words 1.___ 2.___

piece
friend
field
said
again
asked
only
brought
heard
build

Review

WORDS IN CONTEXT Write the missing boxed words to complete the dialogue below.

"Have you (1)?" (2) Louie. "There's a new pizza place called Pepe's Premium Pizza Palace across from the baseball (3) on Fifth Street. You can get a (4) of pizza there for (5) seventy-five cents."

"Oh, I bet that's the place that Ramon was telling me about," Ricky replied. "He (6) the pizza is great and he can hardly wait to get back there (7). I heard that the owners are planning to (8) a video arcade right next door too."

"Let's go over there for lunch," said Louie. "I (9) some money with me. It'll be my treat."

"Thanks! You're a great (10)!" Ricky said, just as his stomach let out an approving growl. "My stomach thanks you too."

Word *Study*

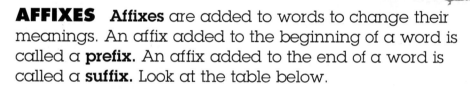

AFFIXES **Affixes** are added to words to change their meanings. An affix added to the beginning of a word is called a **prefix.** An affix added to the end of a word is called a **suffix.** Look at the table below.

	PREFIXES			SUFFIXES	
	Meaning	Example		Meaning	Example
un-	not	(unhappy = not happy)	**-less**	without	(hopeless = without hope)
re-	again	(replay = play again)	**-ly**	in a ___ way	(slowly = in a slow way)
mis-	badly	(misbehave = behave badly)	**-ness**	being ___	(happiness = being happy)

Use the list words below and the affixes in the chart to make new words that will finish the sentences. One sentence will need a word with two affixes.

build   friend   heard   weight

1. The cat's noisy meowing was ___ by its sleeping owner.
2. The astronauts floated around in a ___ state.
3. The beavers were able to ___ their home after it was destroyed by a flood.
4. I backed away from the growling, ___ dog.

Vowels with r

The vowel sound in **fourth** and **storm** is the same, but it is spelled differently: **our, or.** The same is true of **serve** and **dirty: er, ir.**

■ **STUDY** Say each word. Then read the meaning phrase.

WATCH OUT FOR FREQUENTLY MISSPELLED WORDS!

1.	*fourth*	entering **fourth** grade
2.	*course*	take a **course** in woodworking
3.	*storm*	trees bending in a **storm**
4.	*morning* ✳	woke up early in the **morning**
5.	*forest*	a deep, green **forest**
6.	*serve*	**serve** a salad with dinner
7.	*herself*	finished the job **herself**
8.	*certain*	be **certain** a problem is solved
9.	*dirty*	**dirty** after a week of camping
10.	*first* ✳	be the **first** in line

11.	*pour*	**pour** a glass of milk
12.	*fourteen*	**fourteen** apartments in a building
13.	*court*	met on the tennis **court**
14.	*Florida*	eat an orange from **Florida**
15.	*form*	filled out an application **form**
16.	*nerve*	have the **nerve** to sing a solo
17.	*perfect*	**perfect** weather for a picnic
18.	*girlfriend*	trust the advice of a **girlfriend**
19.	*thirsty*	**thirsty** after a hard game of soccer
20.	*skirt*	wore a **skirt** and blouse

CHALLENGE!

resources
unfortunately
commercial
determine
whirl

■ **PRACTICE** Sort the list words by writing
- five words with **er**   - five words with **or**
- five words with **ir**   - five words with **our**

■ **WRITE** Choose four phrases to write as questions and answers.

MAKING CONNECTIONS   Write the list word that answers each question.

1. What follows second and third?
2. In what kind of place could you see many trees?
3. What type of clothing is often worn with a blouse?
4. What do you call that special female pal?
5. What does a waiter do with the meal you order?
6. When you play basketball, what do you play it on?
7. What comes next: myself, yourself, himself,____?
8. If something is absolutely wonderful, what is it?

POETRY   Write the list words that complete the poem.

Early one (9) in their Michigan dorm,
The students could hear the raging (10).
They hadn't the (11) to go out the door,
Because rain continued to pour and (12).
Then the temperature dropped to a cold (13).
Snow mounds began to (14) all over the green.
Said one, "I'm (15) now of nature's force.
Mother Nature always takes her own (16)."
Well, they did the same—on the (17) bus they could reach.
They arrived in sunny (18) and headed for the beach.

> **Take a Hint**
> If you think it may r**ain,**
> But you're not quite cert**ain,**
> Spare yourself some p**ain.**
> Open up the curt**ain.**

Strategic Spelling

Using the Memory Tricks Strategy

19.–20. Write *dirty* and *thirsty*. Write the forms of these words that complete the chart. **Remember:** In words that end in **y,** you change the **y** to **i** before adding **-er** or **-est.**

Spelling Word	Add -er	Add -est
19. ——	——	——
20. ——	——	——

≡	Make a capital.
/	Make a small letter.
∧	Add something.
✃	Take out something.
⊙	Add a period.
¶	New paragraph

PROOFREAD AN ADVERTISEMENT

The ad below was written for a small travel magazine. Correct four misspelled words and two incorrect verbs.

PROOFREADING TIP
The writer used the verbs swam and saw incorrectly. It's swim, swam, (have) swum. Check a dictionary for how to handle see.

Have you ever swam in the ocean?

Have you ever eaten fresh lobster?

Have you ever saw grate blue herons flying?

No? Then you must visit **Flordia!**

It is the perfect vacation for anyone

thursty for sun and fun!

Call us today. **Travel Masters**

WRITE AN ADVERTISEMENT

Write an advertisement for a place you think others might like to visit. Use a few list words and personal words.

Word List

pour	fourth	nerve	certain
morning	forest	dirty	thirsty
course	fourteen	first	perfect
Florida	form	serve	skirt
storm	court	girlfriend	herself

Personal Words 1.___ 2.___

98

Review

fourth
course
storm
morning
forest
serve
herself
certain
dirty
first

WORDS IN CONTEXT   Write the boxed word that completes each person's statement.

1. **TV Weatherman:** "A severe ___ warning is in effect for Greenfield County until 10:00 P.M."
2. **Teacher:** "The ___ and ___ grades will be performing together at this year's fall concert."
3. **Waitress:** "I'm happy to ___ you this evening. May I take your order?"
4. **Softball Coach:** "If Marilyn wants to be on the softball team, she must train ___ to be on time for practice."
5. **News Reporter:** "At the top of the news this ___ is the president's visit to Chicago."
6. **Park Ranger:** "I am ___ that you will enjoy the many hiking trails, plants, and wildlife in the ___."
7. **Student:** "I plan to take a ___ in history at college."
8. **Laundromat Worker:** "Our brand new washing machines will do a good job cleaning those ___ clothes."

Word *Study*

ONOMATOPOEIA   This big word is pronounced
on′ ə mat′ ə pē′ ə. It's what we call words like *buzz, hum,*
and *splash.* When you use **onomatopoeia,** the words sound
like the sounds they describe. Read the poem aloud.
Emphasize the words that are examples of onomatopoeia.

Whack! The tennis ball is served.
It whizzes 'cross the net.
Bing! It bounces on the court.
Wham! It's hard to get.
Then...thud!
Oh...
No!
It's collapsed into the net.

Now use onomatopoeia to write words
you might use to describe the sounds of

1. walking on leaves in wet tennis shoes
2. bees building a honeycomb
3. dropping pebbles in a puddle
4. eating soup and salad

Vowel Sounds in *put* and *out*

The vowel sound in **put** is spelled **oo** in **took** and **u** in **bush**. The vowel sound in **out** is spelled **ow** in **power** and **ou** in **loud.**

WATCH OUT FOR FREQUENTLY MISSPELLED WORDS!

■ **STUDY** Say each word. Then read the meaning phrase.

1. stood — **stood** at the door
2. took ✳ — **took** an afternoon nap
3. wood — **wood** for the fireplace
4. bush — birds sitting in a **bush**
5. July — vacation in **July**
6. power — a senator with great **power**
7. however — **however** you prefer
8. loud — heard a **loud** bang
9. house ✳ — build a brick **house**
10. outside ✳ — went to play **outside**

11. cushion — a soft sofa **cushion**
12. butcher — meat from the **butcher**
13. pudding — ate chocolate **pudding**
14. football — throw a **football**
15. brook — a little bubbling **brook**
16. shower — took a hot **shower**
17. crowd — a large **crowd** of moviegoers
18. mountain — high atop the **mountain**
19. cloud — a billowy white **cloud**
20. proud — **proud** of your success

CHALLENGE!

barefoot
jury
coward
thousand
announced

■ **PRACTICE** Sort the list words by writing
- six words with **ou**
- four words with **ow**
- five words with **u**
- five words with **oo**

■ **WRITE** Choose ten phrases to rewrite as sentences.

SYLLABLE SCRAMBLE   Each group of letters is one syllable of a two-syllable word. Match one from each column to make list words.

1. moun		ball
2. butch		ly
3. foot		er
4. cush		ding
5. Ju		tain
6. pud		ion

RHYME TIME   Write the list words that rhyme with the underlined words and make sense in the sentences. Circle the list word that ends differently than its rhyming word.

The tiny <u>mouse</u> crept through the (7).
With one swift <u>push</u> I fell into the (8).
Lee <u>Loud</u> looked up at a fluffy white (9)
The actors <u>bowed</u> before the cheering (10).
"Milk a <u>cow</u>? Never!" "You may have to, (11)."
I (12) a <u>book</u> and read beside the (13).
Tired Ms. <u>Good</u> (14) beside the cut (15).
<u>Gower</u> lacked the (16) to turn off the dripping (17).
Mr. <u>Doud</u> shouted out (18) because he was so (19).

Strategic Spelling

Seeing Meaning Connections

Words with *out*
outlook
outside
outcast

Write the words from the box that fit the definitions.

20. a person who is driven away from home and friends ____

21. not inside; outdoors ____

22. a way of looking at things; point of

view ____

Take a Hint
If you have trouble with **wood** and **would,** remember the two round knotholes in **wood.**

≡	Make a capital.
/	Make a small letter.
∧	Add something.
ℯ	Take out something.
⊙	Add a period.
⌐	New paragraph

PROOFREAD A LIST Lamont has written a list of the things he must do Saturday morning. Correct four misspelled words and two words that should be capitalized.

PROOFREADING TIP
Lamont has developed a "lazy-lower-case" habit. He forgets to capitalize people's names and the days of the week. Don't let this happen to you.

saturday chores

1. Take a shouwer.

2. Help auntie clean the hous.

3. Make puding for party.

4. Practice foot ball.

WRITE A LIST Write a list of the things you plan to do this weekend. Use some of your list words and a few personal words.

Word List

took	butcher	shower	however
cushion	stood	mountain	cloud
football	pudding,	power	crowd
July	bush	proud	loud
brook	wood	house	outside

Personal Words 1.____ 2.____

Review

CROSSWORD PUZZLE Complete the crossword puzzle by writing the boxed word that matches each definition.

stood
took
wood
bush
July
power
however
loud
house
outside

Across
1. past tense form of the verb *take*
5. a woody plant
7. past tense form of the verb *stand*
8. in whatever way
10. strength

Down
2. outdoors
3. the opposite of quiet
4. the seventh month of the year
6. a building in which people live
9. parts of trees used for building houses and making furniture

Multicultural *Connection*

SPORTS All over the world, sports are played in which players try to move a ball from one place to another. Use the pictures and the labels at the right to help you name each sport described. Your Spelling Dictionary may also help.

1. North American Indians invented this game. It is played with a small rubber ball and sticks, or "crosses." It is called ___.

2. South Americans play a very fast game using a small, hard ball called a "pelota." Curved baskets are worn on the hands. The game is called ___.

3. This is the most popular game in the world. It is played without using the hands. Most Africans and Europeans call it "football," but you may know it as ___.

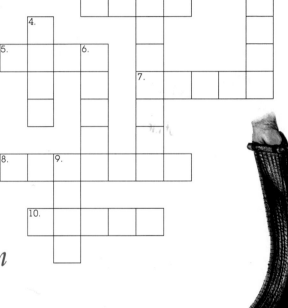

lacrosse

jai alai   soccer

Vowel Sounds in *few* and *moon*

The vowel sound in **few** can be spelled **u-consonant-e**, **ew**, or **u**: exc<u>u</u>se, f<u>ew</u>, p<u>u</u>pil. The vowel sound in **moon** can be spelled **oo** or **ui**: c<u>oo</u>l, j<u>ui</u>ce.

■ **STUDY** Say each word. Then read the meaning phrase.

WATCH OUT FOR FREQUENTLY MISSPELLED WORDS!

1.	*huge*	a **huge** office building
2.	*excuse*	no **excuse** for rudeness
3.	*few*	waited a **few** minutes
4.	*usual*	took the **usual** route home
5.	*pupil*	a **pupil** in the third grade
6.	*cool*	**cool** weather for July
7.	*mood*	in a bad **mood**
8.	*fruit*	ate three pieces of **fruit**
9.	*suit*	a blue business **suit**
10.	*juice*	drank a glass of **juice**

11.	*confuse*	**confuse** her with her sister
12.	*nephew*	a **nephew** in college
13.	*curfew*	in before 9:00 **curfew**
14.	*fuel*	**fuel** a car with gasoline
15.	*menu*	order food from a **menu**
16.	*shoot*	**shoot** a few baskets
17.	*school* ✳	ride the bus to **school**
18.	*shampoo*	**shampoo** my hair
19.	*bruise*	a purple **bruise** on her leg
20.	*cruise*	a Caribbean **cruise**

CHALLENGE!

commute
universe
reunion
fireproof
pursuit

■ **PRACTICE** Sort the list words by writing
- five words with **oo**
- six words with **u-consonant-e** or **ew**
- five words with **ui**
- four words with **u**

■ **WRITE** Choose two phrases to write an advertisement, slogan, or saying.

ANALOGIES Write the list word that completes each phrase.

1. hot and warm, cold and ____.
2. most and many, least and ____.
3. aunt and uncle, niece and ____.
4. small and tiny, large and ____.
5. carrot and banana, vegetable and ____.
6. apple and sauce, orange and ____.
7. teeth and toothpaste, hair and ____.
8. train and schedule, restaurant and ____.
9. doctor and patient, teacher and ____.

> **Did You Know?**
> The word *curfew* comes from the French words *covrir*, to cover, and *feu*, fire. When the curfew bell rang, people covered, or put out, their fires each night.

TONGUE TWISTERS Write the list word that would best complete each tongue twister.

10. Being bucked by a bronco brought about Brian's ____.
11. The sensational singer sported a silky silver ____.
12. Should Shelly snap the shutter and ____ the shy sheep?
13. Curt's camp counselor calls "Come in!" at ____.
14. Maybe Maya managed to maintain a merry ____.
15. Chemistry quiz questions ____ and confound Cornelius.
16. Chris chartered a craft to ____ the Caribbean.
17. The extravagant explorers had an ____ for the expensive expedition.

Strategic Spelling

Seeing Meaning Connections

Write the list word that completes each sentence. The underlined word is a clue. Circle the letters in each list word that are the same as in the underlined word.

18. The <u>schoolwork</u> at our ____ is very challenging.
19. I am <u>usually</u> on time if I take the ____ route.
20. We had to stop and <u>refuel</u> when we ran out of ____.

☰	Make a capital.
/	Make a small letter.
∧	Add something.
ℓ	Take out something.
⊙	Add a period.
¶	New paragraph

PROOFREAD DIRECTIONS The owner of Cozy's Café left these directions for her after-school assistant. Correct four misspelled words and add three missing end marks.

PROOFREADING TIP

Cozy forgot to use an exclamation mark in her final sentence. What other mark did she forget (twice)?

> P. J.,
>
> How was shcool Please squeeze oranges and cut up apples. Type up a new menu to include frut salad and fresh orange joos. Are you in the mude to make one of your special soups They are terrific
>
> Cozy

WRITE DIRECTIONS Isn't there something you'd like to ask someone to do in writing? Use spelling words and personal words to write your directions.

Word List

bruise	mood	pupil	huge
cool	suit	few	curfew
juice	shoot	fuel	confuse
school	cruise	excuse	usual
fruit	shampoo	nephew	menu

Personal Words 1. ___ 2. ___

huge
excuse
few
usual
pupil
cool
mood
fruit
suit
juice

Review

WORDS IN CONTEXT Maybe you have seen advertisements for vacation spots much like the one below. Write the boxed words to complete the advertisement.

Is the hot weather putting you in a bad (1)? Do you need to get away for a (2) days? Imagine this:

- Taking a dip in the ocean to (3) off
- Having fresh (4), including slices of watermelon, honeydew, and bananas, with your breakfast every morning
- Sipping a cool fruit (5) as you relax under a palm tree
- Being a (6) in one of Peter Orca's famous scuba diving classes

The Sand and Surf Hotel in southern Florida has a special limited offer. Instead of the (7) tiny rooms you find at other vacation spots, you can stay in a (8) room at a very low cost. So don't make the (9) that you can't afford a vacation. Call a travel agent NOW and make your reservation. See you at the Sand and Surf soon, and don't forget your bathing (10)!

Word *Study*

COLLECTIVE NOUNS You know the phrase, "a herd of elephants," but did you know a group of geese is called a "gaggle"? Words like *herd* and *gaggle* are called **collective nouns.** Sometimes they reflect a quality possessed by the subject. This is why we speak of a *pride* of lions—because they seem proud to us.

Find the collective noun at the right that names each group below. Your Spelling Dictionary will help you.

swarm
school
skulk

1. Just one is called a goldfish.
   Two are goldfish or goldfishes.
   As a group, they are called a ___.
2. One alone is a bee.
   More than one are bees.
   As a group, they are called a ___.
3. One is called a fox.
   Two or more are called foxes.
   As a group, they are called a ___.

Homophones

A homophone is a word that sounds exactly like another word but has a different spelling and meaning: **wood, would.**

■ **STUDY** Say each word. Then read the meaning phrase.

WATCH OUT FOR FREQUENTLY MISSPELLED WORDS!

1.	wood	chopped a pile of **wood**
2.	would ✳	asked if I **would** help
3.	too ✳	**too** tired to stay up
4.	to	went **to** work
5.	two	**two** sisters and a brother
6.	there ✳	have never been **there** before
7.	their ✳	finished **their** work
8.	they're ✳	if **they're** not too busy
9.	your	borrowed **your** book
10.	you're ✳	asked when **you're** going
11.	beat	**beat** a drum
12.	beet	ate a pickled **beet**
13.	break	**break** a glass
14.	brake	**brake** at a stop sign
15.	clothes	bought some new **clothes**
16.	close	told me to **close** the door
17.	piece	ate a **piece** of cheese
18.	peace	hoped for world **peace**
19.	thrown	has **thrown** her old toys away
20.	throne	a queen on her **throne**

CHALLENGE!

guessed
guest
aisle
isle
waist
waste

■ **PRACTICE** First write the homophone groups that may be difficult for you to keep straight. Then write the rest of the homophones.

■ **WRITE** Choose two phrases to write a dialogue, or conversation, between two or more people.

HOMOPHONE PHOTOS   Write the list word that labels each photograph. Below that word, write another list word that sounds just like it.

1.____   3.____   5. ____

2.____   4.____   6. ____

HOMOPHONE QUOTES   Complete the statements of the people below by writing list words that sound alike.

King: "I was so unpopular, I was (7) from my (8)."
Teacher: "If they stay (9), I know (10) going to miss (11) bus."
Twins: "The (12) of us would like (13) ride the bus (14)."
Driver: "If I (15) suddenly, the dishes in the back will (16)."
Dentist: "Tino, (17) going to have to brush (18) teeth more."

Strategic Spelling

Using the Memory Tricks Strategy

Use memory tricks to help you spell. Write a list word to complete each trick. Underline the matching letters.

19. a ____ of pie

20. ____ for people all over

FREQUENTLY MISSPELLED WORDS * *FREQUENTLY MISSPELLED WORDS*

The word **too** is often misspelled by students. Think of **too** as meaning "extra," then be sure to include the "extra" **o** in such phrases as "**too** tired."

☰	Make a capital.
/	Make a small letter.
∧	Add something.
℮	Take out something.
⊙	Add a period.
¶	New paragraph

PROOFREAD AN OUTLINE Sara is giving a speech tomorrow. Read her outline. Correct four misspelled words and two errors in capitalization.

> How to Build a Birdhouse
> I. Gather your materials
>   A. Seven squares of wod
>   (sides, bottom, roof)
>   B. Hammer and nails
> II. assemble you' re materials
>   A. Cut hole in one peace
>   B. Nail four sides together
>   (opening in front)
>   C. nail bottom to sides
>   D. Nail the last to pieces on top for roof
> III. Paint your birdhouse

PROOFREADING TIP

Sara knows that the first word in each main topic and subtopic of her outline must be capitalized. Proofreading would have helped her do just that.

WRITE AN OUTLINE Write an outline of a speech you would like to give. Use list words.

Word List

beat	would	your	too
beet	clothes	you're	two
break	close	thrown	there
brake	piece	throne	their
wood	peace	to	they're

Personal Words 1. ___ 2. ___

Review

POETRY   Write the boxed words that complete the poem.

Hair, oh hair,
It's just not fair!
Give me (1) hair, (2) hair,
Any hair but MY hair!

I'd say (3) lucky, (4) lucky (5),
To have such a fine-looking, stylish hairdo.
Mine is neither here nor (6),
Usually it's ho-hum hair.

Wait! Look in that window. STOP!
See that head made of (7) with a wig on top?
It's curly! I do declare,
I simply MUST have that hair!

Could you, (8) you spare a dollar or (9),
And help me (10) get a brand new exciting hairdo?

wood
would
too
to
two
there
their
they're
your
you're

Using a *Dictionary*

HOMOGRAPHS   If you looked up *brake* in
a dictionary, here is what you would find: ——▶

There is more than one entry for *brake. Brake*
is a **homograph.** Homographs are spelled
exactly alike, but they have different word
histories and different meanings. The raised
number alerts you to this.

Study the entries for *brake.* Write *brake¹* or
brake² to answer each question below.

1. Which entry can be more than one part of speech?
2. Which entry has an example sentence?
3. Which entry would you find in a forest?

brake¹ (brāk), **1** anything used
to slow or stop the motion of
a wheel or vehicle by
pressing or scraping or by
rubbing against. **2** show or
stop by moving a brake:
*The driver braked the
speeding car and it slid to a
stop.* **1** *n.,* **2** *v.,* **braked,
brak•ing.**

brake² (brāk), **1** a thick growth
of bushes; thicket. *n.*

111

Review

Lesson 19: Getting Letters in Correct Order
Lesson 20: Vowels with r
Lesson 21: Vowel Sounds in put and out

Lesson 22: Vowel Sounds in few and moon
Lesson 23: Homophones

REVIEW WORD LIST

1. again	14. dirty	27. cushion	39. nephew
2. believe	15. Florida	28. football	40. school
3. friend	16. forest	29. July	41. shampoo
4. heard	17. fourteen	30. mountain	42. suit
5. heart	18. fourth	31. pudding	43. usual
6. height	19. morning	32. shower	44. clothes
7. hospital	20. nerve	33. few	45. there
8. neighbor	21. perfect	34. fruit	46. they're
9. pickle	22. skirt	35. fuel	47. too
10. piece	23. storm	36. huge	48. two
11. rattle	24. butcher	37. juice	49. wood
12. toes	25. cloud	38. menu	50. your
13. weight	26. crowd		

CLARINETISTS' COMPLAINT

Band members are filing an official complaint with their leader.
Write the words they left out.

usual
suit
clothes
believe
crowd

Dear Mr. Seifworth,

    We, the Woodwind Section, (1) it is unfair that we must wear (2) pants to play in school concerts. The (3) comes to hear us play, not to admire our (4). Please consider letting us wear our (5) school clothes at future concerts.

        Thank you,
        The Woodwinds

Labels

Tess received a small label maker and went around her house labeling items. Match the name of each item to the number next to it.

football
heart
forest
skirt
cushion
shower
fourteen

Descriptions

Guess what each person is describing below. Write your answers.

cloud
hospital
wood
storm
nephew

It may look fluffy and white, but a (2) is simply water vapor. I predict there will be a major (3) moving in from the east.

There's nothing like the smell of freshly cut pine (4).

She's my dad's sister, and I'm her (1).

I spend long hours operating in the (5).

Wally

– a cartoon by Sam

Help Sam finish his comic strip about a big baby named Wally.

Wally is bigger than most babies. Actually, he is (1).

He can wiggle his gigantic (2). He makes music by shaking his (3).

Wally loves mud puddles!

I'm all (4)!

But he hates (5)!

You have some (6) messing with my hair!!!

He is a (7) to all animals.

dirty
rattle
shampoo
friend
nerve
huge
toes

Pen Pals

Read Marissa's card to her pen pal in Moscow, Russia. Supply the missing words.

fourth school height your too they're July weight again

Chicago

May 2, 1997

Dear Svetlana,

I enjoyed reading (1) letter. Here are some facts about me: My birthday is (2) 22. My (3) is 4 feet 2 inches. My (4) is 62 pounds. I am in the (5) grade. I go to (6) on a bus. I like to wear sweat shirts because (7) so comfortable. Please write once (8). I want to hear more about you (9)!

Sincerely,

Marissa

114

piece
fuel
neighbor
heard
morning
mountain
there
menu

PETITE POEMS

Read each short poem below and supply the missing rhyming word.

$hopping List

Denzel left this list for Jacqui.
Write the missing items.

few
butcher
fruit
Florida
juice
two
pickle
perfect
pudding

- fresh orange juice from (1)
- a large dill (2)
- oranges, apples, bananas, and other (3)
- one gallon of sweet apple (4) —not cider
- six red roses—must be (5) !
- one stick of butter and (6) loaves of bread
- just a (7) sprigs of parsley
- ready-made thick chocolate (8)
- Have the (9) cut up a three-pound chicken.

Here's a handy driving rule:
Don't go on the highway
when you're low on (1).

When you've lost something,
you look everywhere.
The last place you look, it's sure
to be (2).

Did I hear the squawks of the
early bird? For an hour and a half
it was all I (3)!

Do yourself a great big favor.
Get to know your next-door (4).

It's easy to order a fine meal when you,
Take a good look at the restaurant's (5).

If this arguing doesn't cease,
The cake will vanish; no one gets a (6).

The storm came up without a warning,
And rocked the city early one (7).

Here's one thing you can always count on:
A hill is never as large as a (8)!

MOSCOW

115

STRATEGY WORKSHOP

Pronouncing for Spelling

DISCOVER THE STRATEGY 1   To avoid making the mistake Josh made in the cartoon below, use this strategy:

1. Pronounce the word carefully and correctly. Listen to the sound of each letter.
2. Pronounce the word again as you write it.

TRY IT OUT   Now practice this strategy yourself.

Pronounce each word in dark type slowly and correctly. Pay special attention to the sounds of the underlined letters. Pronounce each word again as you write it.

1. Say **sur**prise (NOT su-prise)

2. Say **pic**ture (NOT pi-ture)

3. Say **streng**th (NOT strenth)

4. Say **diff**erent (NOT diff-rent)

5. Say **chas**ing (NOT chas-in)

DISCOVER THE STRATEGY 2   Pronouncing the word correctly won't work for a word like *thumb*. How can you remember to include the silent **b?** Use the "secret pronunciation" strategy below.

1. Pronounce any silent letters to yourself. Don't worry if the word sounds funny. Say the **b** in *thumb* and the **k** in *knit.* Say "thum-**b**" and "**k**-nit."

2. Exaggerate or change a sound in the word. You might pronounce *million* by exaggerating the smaller word *lion* inside it. Say "mil-**li-on**" to yourself.

TRY IT OUT   Now practice this strategy.

With a partner, make up secret pronunciations for the words below. Pay special attention to the underlined letters. Write each word correctly. Say its secret pronunciation to yourself.

1. lamb
2. knit
3. wrist
4. guess
5. everyone

6. talk
7. once
8. hour
9. clothes
10. movie

LOOK AHEAD   Look ahead at the next five lessons. Write four list words you could use these strategies with. Mark the part of each word that you'll pay special attention to when you pronounce it.

1.___
2.___

3.___
4.___

117

Including All the Letters

SPELLING FOCUS

Some words have more letters than you might expect. To spell these words, pronounce each syllable carefully.

■ **STUDY** Say each word. Then read the meaning phrase.

WATCH OUT FOR FREQUENTLY MISSPELLED WORDS!

1. often   **often** read comic books
2. might *   **might** go to a movie
3. they *   if **they** want to
4. remember   **remember** an important event
5. finally *   **finally** heard from my pen pal
6. really *   see things as they **really** are
7. several   **several** close friends
8. everyone *   asked **everyone** for an opinion
9. interesting   an **interesting** science experiment
10. everybody *   saw **everybody** at the party

11. known   **known** as a fine student
12. caught *   **caught** the ball
13. surprised   **surprised** to see you
14. island   an **island** in the Pacific Ocean
15. swimming *   **swimming** in the lake
16. camera   took a picture with her **camera**
17. December   cold weather in **December**
18. evening   an **evening** of entertainment
19. beginning   **beginning** to learn sign language
20. February   a valentine in **February**

CHALLENGE!

broccoli
kindergarten
cabinet
serious
temperature

■ **PRACTICE** Sort the list words by writing
- four words with one syllable
- five words with two syllables
- eight words with three syllables
- three words with four syllables

■ **WRITE** Choose ten phrases to rewrite as sentences.

PUZZLE IT OUT   What do you shoot people with that makes them smile? When you write the list words that match the clues, the answer to this riddle will appear in the box.

1. the twelfth month
2. truly; actually
3. call back to mind
4. early part of night
5. astonished; shocked
6. grabbed; took and held
7. The answer to the riddle is a ___.

1. _ _ _ _ _ _
2. _ _ _ _ _
3. _ _ _ _ _ _ _
4. _ _ _ _ _ _ _
5. _ _ _ _ _ _ _
6. _ _ _ _ _

SYLLABLE ALERT   Write the list word that starts and ends with the same letter and has the same number of syllables as each word below.

8. ballooning
9. keen
10. eventfully
11. tray
12. sweeping

13. exercise
14. inward
15. open
16. moat

STRATEGIC SPELLING

Pronouncing for Spelling

We sometimes misspell words because we say them wrong. Write *February, finally, interesting,* and *several.* Now say each word carefully. Be sure to pronounce the underlined syllable.

17. ___

18. ___

19. ___

20. ___

F·E·B·R·U·A·R·Y

S	M	T	W	T	F	S

Take a Hint:
Do you say *brr* in the February cold?
That's how to remember to write the
br in February!

≡	Make a capital.
/	Make a small letter.
∧	Add something.
ℯ	Take out something.
⊙	Add a period.
¶	New paragraph

PROOFREAD A MATH PROBLEM

Ms. Yasutaki's class is keeping a math journal. Read the journal entry below and correct four misspelled words and add the missing quotation marks.

PROOFREADING TIP

A speaker's exact words are called a **quotation.** Quotations begin with a capital letter and have quotation marks at the beginning (") and end (") of the speaker's words.

I multiplied 22 X 15 in 3 seconds! Everyone was suprised by my speed. They asked, How do you do it? I finely told them this secret: "You know 22 X 10 is 220. Half of 220 is 110. So just add them up to get 330.

Math is intresting if you now the shortcuts!

WRITE A MATH PROBLEM

You probably have a math shortcut or interesting problem you'd like to share. Use list words as well as personal words.

Word List

camera	everyone	surprised	evening
finally	they	might	swimming
really	remember	often	several
known	February	island	beginning
everybody	December	caught	interesting

Personal Words   1. ___   2. ___

Review

SYNONYMS Write the two boxed words that have similar meanings.

DEFINING WORDS Write the boxed word that means the same as the underlined word or words in each sentence.

| often |
| might |
| they |
| remember |
| finally |
| really |
| several |
| everyone |
| interesting |
| everybody |

3. Our team <u>at last</u> has won a game against the mighty Falcons.
4. Eddie was absent from school for <u>more than two or three</u> days when he had the flu.
5. The program about the grizzly bears in Yellowstone National Park was <u>holding my attention</u>.
6. I <u>frequently</u> stop to talk with Mrs. Griffin when I see her out in her yard.
7. Do you <u>truly</u> think that I bake good cookies?
8. I <u>will possibly</u> want to go bike riding with my friends on Saturday.
9. Do you <u>call back to mind</u> what time the train is due to arrive this evening?
10. The kittens are hungry and <u>the animals spoken about</u> need a good home.

Using a *Dictionary*

WORDS THAT AREN'T ENTRIES You won't find **inflected forms,** words like *surprised* and *dirtiest,* as entry words in most dictionaries. If a dictionary included words like these as entries, it would be too large and heavy to use! To find inflected forms, look for the base words. You will find *dirtiest* at the end of *dirty* and *surprised* at the end of *surprise.*

Write the entry word you would look for in order to find the definition of each word below.

1. smuggled
2. funnier
3. speeches
4. largest

dirt•y (dėr′tē), **1** soiled by dirt; not clean: *I got dirty emptying the garbage.* **2** not fair or decent: *Fooling me was a dirty trick. adj.,* **dirt•i•er, dirt•i•est.**

sur•prise (sər prīz′), **1** a feeling caused by something that happens suddenly. **2** to cause to feel surprise; astonish: *The news surprised us.* **3** something unexpected: *I have a surprise for you. 1 n., 2,3 v.,* **sur•prised, sur•pris•ing.**

Compound Words

SPELLING FOCUS

A compound word is made of two or more words.
Keep all the letters when spelling compounds:
base + ball = baseball.

■ **STUDY** Say each word. Then read the meaning phrase.

**WATCH OUT FOR
FREQUENTLY
MISSPELLED
WORDS!**

1. *baseball*   play **baseball** after school
2. *basketball* ✳   a tall **basketball** player
3. *upstairs*   in an **upstairs** closet
4. *myself* ✳   gave **myself** a haircut
5. *highway*   lots of traffic on the **highway**
6. *classroom*   a **classroom** full of students
7. *anyway*   did what I shouldn't **anyway**
8. *newspaper*   read a **newspaper** article
9. *something* ✳   have **something** on your mind
10. *sometimes* ✳   **sometimes** read action stories

11. *chalkboard*   wrote the answer on the **chalkboard**
12. *earrings*   beautiful golden **earrings**
13. *nighttime*   raccoons hunting in the **nighttime**
14. *motorcycle*   rode a red **motorcycle**
15. *downstairs*   went **downstairs** to watch TV
16. *softball*   play **softball** all summer
17. *weekend*   spent the **weekend** at Grandma's
18. *classmate*   asked my **classmate** for a pencil
19. *doorbell*   rang the **doorbell** twice
20. *driveway*   cars pulling into a **driveway**

CHALLENGE!

courtroom
ourselves
heartbroken
teammate
skateboard

■ **PRACTICE** Write the words in alphabetical order.

■ **WRITE** Choose three phrases to include in a
paragraph.

CLASSIFICATIONS   Add the list words that belong in each group. The words already listed are clues.

Sports	School	Time
football	*homeroom*	*weeknight*
1. _____	4. _____	6. _____
2. _____	5. _____	7. _____
3. _____	*schoolmate*	*sometime*

JOINING WORDS   Find two words in each sentence that can be joined to make a list word. Write the word.

8. Because I was so worried, I was not my old self.
9. Were there any sights along the way?
10. The dog ran to the door when the bell rang.
11. The good news is that I got an A on my paper.
12. Here are some crackers for that thing in the cage.
13. I got up and walked to the stairs near the porch.
14. When the sirens blast, my ear always rings.
15. There are some of us who enjoy good times.
16. The chalk was ordered by a member of the board.
17. He fell and went rolling down the stairs.
18. The washer's motor failed, so the cycle didn't finish.

STRATEGIC SPELLING

Seeing Meaning Connections

Words with *way*
driveway
runway
highway

Write the word from the box that answers each question.

19. Where does an airplane take off? ___
20. Where do cars go whizzing along? ___
21. Where might a car be parked? ___

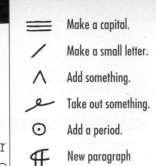

■ PROOFREADING AND WRITING

≡	Make a capital.
/	Make a small letter.
∧	Add something.
ℯ	Take out something.
⊙	Add a period.
¶	New paragraph

PROOFREAD AN ESSAY Nan wrote this essay about an important event in her life. Correct four misspelled words and one incorrectly used adjective.

PROOFREADING TIP
Nan forgot this rule about using the adjectives *more* and *most*: Don't use *more* or *most* with words that end in -er or -est.

My Proud Moment

I play basket ball in the Adapted Athletics Program. At first it was hard dribbling from my wheelchair, but I soon got more better at it. Once, I faked out my classmat, Pete. I drove my self around him and swished the ball trough the net. I felt like Supergirl!

WRITE AN ESSAY Write about one of your proud moments. Use your spelling words and a personal word.

Word List

basketball	chalkboard	upstairs	classroom
something	earrings	downstairs	classmate
sometimes	nighttime	newspaper	doorbell
baseball	myself	softball	driveway
anyway	motorcycle	weekend	highway

Personal Words 1. ___ 2. ___

Review

WORDS IN CONTEXT   Write the missing boxed words to complete the following letter.

Dear Jessica,

It's supposed to rain on Saturday, but I'm glad you're coming for a visit (1). Here are directions to my house.

Go to the intersection of Davis Street and Grant Avenue. Get on the (2) that takes you north to Cedar City. You will be on this road for about thirty miles.
Get off at the Dillard Street exit and turn left at the first stoplight. You will see a park with a (3) court on the corner. That's where I (4) shoot baskets either with a few other kids on my block or all by (5).
My house is the white one across from the (6) field. The Little League will probably be in the middle of a game.

I'll be looking for you from the (7) window of my room. When you get here, we'll check the movie section in the (8) to see what's playing. If you'd rather do (9) else, that's all right. Oh, I almost forgot. My school will be open on Saturday, so I'll show you all the neat stuff in my new (10).

Your friend,
Marguerita

baseball
basketball
upstairs
myself
highway
classroom
anyway
newspaper
something
sometimes

Multicultural *Connection*

ARTS   Throughout history, people have worn jewelry. Read about the handcrafted jewelry pictured at the right. Then complete each description below by writing the name of one of the items pictured.

1. The ancient Egyptians used blue and red gemstones in jewelry, such as this beautiful pin, or ___.
2. The Greeks valued fine metalwork and often used lacelike *filigree,* or ornamental gold or silver wire, as seen in the center of this ___.
3. Carved jade and metal ornaments like this white jade hanging ornament, or ___, were popular in China .
4. The Inca of South America worked with gold and silver. This ___ shows their craftsmanship in making strings of ornaments for wearing around the neck.

pendant

earring

brooch

necklace

Suffixes -ful, -ly, -ion

SPELLING FOCUS

When adding **-ful**, **-ly**, or **-ion** to most base words, the base stays the same: **slowly**. To words ending in **y**, change the **y** to **i**: **beautiful**. To words ending in **e**, drop the **e**: **location**.

■ **STUDY** What happens when each suffix is added?

WATCH OUT FOR FREQUENTLY MISSPELLED WORDS!

power + ful =	1.	*powerful*
peace + ful =	2.	*peaceful*
beauty + ful =	3.	*beautiful* ✳
slow + ly =	4.	*slowly*
safe + ly =	5.	*safely*
day + ly =	6.	*daily*
sudden + ly =	7.	*suddenly*
careful + ly =	8.	*carefully*
act + ion =	9.	*action*
locate + ion =	10.	*location*

cheer + ful =	11.	*cheerful*
pain + ful =	12.	*painful*
thought + ful =	13.	*thoughtful*
week + ly =	14.	*weekly*
late + ly =	15.	*lately*
truthful + ly =	16.	*truthfully*
hopeful + ly =	17.	*hopefully*
invent + ion =	18.	*invention*
correct + ion =	19.	*correction*
pollute + ion =	20.	*pollution*

CHALLENGE!

grateful
suspenseful
completely
exactly
separation

■ **PRACTICE** Sort the list words by writing
- nine words with the suffix **-ly**
- six words with the suffix **-ful**
- five words with the suffix **-ion**

■ **WRITE** Use three words to write about a friend.

SUFFIX ADDITION   Write the list word that has each meaning and ending shown below.

1. gladness and joy + ful
2. seven days + ly
3. feeling hope + ly
4. not early + ly
5. quiet and still + ful
6. without warning + ly
7. good looks + ful
8. not fast + ly
9. feeling hurt + ful
10. free from harm + ly
11. strength and might + ful
12. twenty-four hours + ly

WORD FORMS   Add **-ion, -ly,** or **-ful** to the base words below to make list words. Write the list words. Circle the word in which the spelling changed when the suffix was added.

13. act ___

14. thought ___

15. pollute ___

16. invent ___

17. truthful ___

18. careful ___

Did You Know?
The word *pollution* comes from a Latin word meaning "soiled," "dirty."

STRATEGIC SPELLING

Using the Meaning Helper Strategy

Use meaning helpers to help spell hard words. Write the list word that goes with each meaning helper. Mark the letter that matches the underlined sound clue.

19. correct ___   20. locate ___

	Make a capital.
/	Make a small letter.
∧	Add something.
ℯ	Take out something.
⊙	Add a period.
¶	New paragraph

PROOFREAD CAPTIONS Hassan and his friend Bill have written captions for the photos they took on their camping trip. Correct four misspellings and one sentence that contains more than one negative word.

PROOFREADING TIP
No and *not* are **negative words.** Contractions formed with the adverb *not* are also negative words. Use ONLY ONE negative word per sentence.

Here we are in beatiful Mesa Verde.

We carfully climb the ladder to the house.

Our campsite is in a peacefull locashun.

This deer didn't have no fear of humans.

WRITE A CAPTION Think about a photo that shows you and a friend doing something. Draw a picture of it. Then write a caption for the picture. Use a spelling word and a personal word.

Word List

peaceful	beautiful	lately	invention
thoughtful	safely	daily	correction
powerful	slowly	truthfully	action
cheerful	weekly	carefully	pollution
painful	suddenly	hopefully	location

Personal Words 1. ___ 2. ___

Review

ANALOGIES   Write the boxed word that completes each analogy.

1. Eagerly is to anxiously as thoroughly is to ___.
2. Narrow is to wide as ugly is to ___.
3. Edge is to rim as place is to ___.
4. Politely is to courteously as unexpectedly is to ___.
5. Week is to weekly as day is to ___.
6. Lazy is to hardworking as hostile is to ___.
7. Gently is to roughly as swiftly is to ___.
8. Stillness is to calmness as movement is to ___.
9. Generously is to selfishly as dangerously is to ___.
10. Tricky is to clever as mighty is to ___.

powerful
peaceful
beautiful
slowly
safely
daily
suddenly
carefully
action
location

Word *Study*

CODES   Many different kinds of codes can be used to disguise what we write. Can you read the message below?

When you understand how the **tick-tack-toe code** works, the message is easy to read.

A	B	C
D	E	F
G	H	I

J	K	L
M	N	O
P	Q	R

S	T	U
V	W	X
Y	Z	

All the letters of the alphabet are on three tick-tack-toe grids. To spell a word in code, look at where the letter is on the grid. Then draw the lines that appear around it. If there are dots, draw those too. So, B =⌊⌋ M = .⌉ F =⌊ Now read the words above and write them.

129

Suffixes -less, -ment, -ness

■ **SPELLING FOCUS**

When **-less, -ment**, or **-ness** is added to most base words, the base stays the same: **goodness**. If the base word ends in a **consonant** and a **y**, the **y** is changed to **i** before adding the suffix: **business**.

■ **STUDY** What happens when each suffix is added?

help + less	=	1. *helpless*
care + less	=	2. *careless*
hope + less	=	3. *hopeless*
pay + ment	=	4. *payment*
state + ment	=	5. *statement*
move + ment	=	6. *movement*
good + ness	=	7. *goodness*
soft + ness	=	8. *softness*
bright + ness	=	9. *brightness*
busy + ness	=	10. *business*

spot + less	=	11. *spotless*
breath + less	=	12. *breathless*
worth + less	=	13. *worthless*
use + less	=	14. *useless*
pave + ment	=	15. *pavement*
treat + ment	=	16. *treatment*
punish + ment	=	17. *punishment*
great + ness	=	18. *greatness*
fair + ness	=	19. *fairness*
dark + ness	=	20. *darkness*

CHALLENGE!

assignment
appointment
announcement
homelessness
consciousness

■ **PRACTICE** Sort the list words by writing
- seven words ending in **-ness**
- six words ending in **-ment**
- seven words ending in **-less**

■ **WRITE** Choose ten words to write in sentences.

ADDING ENDINGS Complete each sentence by adding **-less**, **-ment**, or **-ness** to the word in parentheses.

1. (busy)   She was out of town on ___.
2. (pay)   He just made his last car ___.
3. (help)   The trapped fox was ___.
4. (use)   This old map is ___.
5. (move)   I watched the dancer's graceful ___.
6. (great)   The child was destined for ___.
7. (state)   The lawyer began her closing ___.
8. (hope)   Our unfortunate situation looked ___.
9. (good)   He helped us out of the ___ of his heart.
10. (worth)   Throw away that ___ old inner tube.
11. (breath) I ran so fast I was soon ___.
12. (pave)   We rode our bikes on the concrete ___.
13. (fair)   In all ___, I don't want to take sides.
14. (soft)   The child loved the ___ of the blanket.

Take a Hint
It's easy to leave out the **i** in **business** because you don't say it. Just remember this phrase: Take the **bus in** when you have **busin**ess in town.

MATCH UP Match each word with one of the suffixes below to form a list word. Write each word.

ness	less	ment

15. care   17. bright   19. dark
16. treat   18. spot   20. punish

STRATEGIC SPELLING

Building New Words

Add the suffix to each base word to make a new word.

Base word	Suffix	New word
21. home	-less	___
22. enjoy	-ment	___
23. cold	-ness	___

≡	Make a capital.
/	Make a small letter.
∧	Add something.
ℒ	Take out something.
⊙	Add a period.
⌗	New paragraph

PROOFREAD A COMIC STRIP

LaDonna and Jake created a superhero named WizKid, who fights crime by using brain power. Read WizKid's words and correct four misspellings and two careless errors.

PROOFREADING TIP

LaDonna and Jake made a great superhero, but they also made two super errors. Words such as *to* and *for* may be small, but they should never be left out.

> What is this I see on the pavment? It's a hepless bird with clipped wings!

> This is the work of my flightless foe, the Ostrich! Little bird, can you lead me that worthes evildoer?

> Release those nestlings, Ostrich! You've clipped your last wing! Get ready your punisment!

WRITE A COMIC STRIP
Practice writing your own comic strip dialogue. Use list words.

Word List

pavement	punishment	darkness	spotless
statement	greatness	brightness	helpless
movement	fairness	business	useless
payment	goodness	breathless	hopeless
treatment	softness	careless	worthless

Personal Words   1. ___ 2. ___

PUZZLE IT OUT What is a name for action figures that are brave, strong, and good? Write the boxed words that match the clues. Then use the numbered letters to solve the riddle.

helpless	movement
careless	goodness
hopeless	softness
payment	brightness
statement	business

1. shininess
2. amount of money paid
3. motion
4. the opposite of badness
5. fluffiness
6. unable to take care of oneself
7. the opposite of confident
8. work; occupation
9. done without enough thought or effort
10. remark; declaration

1. _ _₈ _ _ _ _ _ _ _₁
2. _ _ _ _ _₇ _ _
3. _ _ _₁₀ _ _ _ _
4. _ _ _ _ _₄ _ _
5. _ _₉ _ _ _ _
6. _ _ _₃ _ _ _
7. _₆ _ _ _ _ _
8. _ _₂ _ _ _ _
9. _ _ _₅ _ _ _
10. _₁₁ _ _ _ _ . _ , _ _

_1 _2 _3 _4 _5 _6 _7 _8 _9 _10 _11

Word *Study*

HAIKU Long ago in Japan, a contest was held in which competitors added lines to existing poems. Those who created the best lines won. The name **haiku** (hī′kü) comes from this contest. Read the two haiku below.

*The falling flower
I saw drift back to the branch
was a butterfly.*

Poor crying cricket,
perhaps your little husband
was caught by our cat.

A haiku is usually three lines long and often describes a scene in nature. The first line has five syllables, the second line has seven syllables, and the third line has five syllables.

Write your own haiku. Start with the line at the right. Use a dictionary if you need help counting syllables.

Raindrops on a leaf.

133

Prefixes dis-, in-, mis-, re-

SPELLING FOCUS

When prefixes **dis-**, **in-**, **mis-**, and **re-** are added to words, make no change in the spelling of the base word: **dis + like = dislike.**

■ **STUDY** Notice that each base word below does not change when a suffix is added.

dis + like	=	1. *dislike*
dis + appear	=	2. *disappear*
in + complete	=	3. *incomplete*
in + dependent	=	4. *independent*
in + correct	=	5. *incorrect*
mis + place	=	6. *misplace*
mis + spell	=	7. *misspell*
mis + led	=	8. *misled*
re + build	=	9. *rebuild*
re + use	=	10. *reuse*

dis + trust	=	11. *distrust*
dis + honest	=	12. *dishonest*
dis + agree	=	13. *disagree*
in + visible	=	14. *invisible*
in + active	=	15. *inactive*
mis + treat	=	16. *mistreat*
mis + behave	=	17. *misbehave*
re + act	=	18. *react*
re + place	=	19. *replace*
re + call	=	20. *recall*

CHALLENGE!

disobedience
incredible
inconvenient
misfortune
recycling

■ **PRACTICE** Sort the list words by writing
- five words with **dis-**
- five words with **in-**
- five words with **re-**
- five words with **mis-**

■ **WRITE** Choose ten words to write in sentences.

SUPER ANTONYMS   Complete each statement with a list word that means the opposite of the underlined word.

1. Superguy said, "I <u>like</u> good guys, but I ___ criminals."
2. Spygirl stated, "I <u>trust</u> that you won't ___ me."
3. X-ray Man boasted, "What is <u>visible</u> to me is ___ to you."
4. Wiseguy said, "<u>Treat</u> others <u>well</u> and they won't ___ you."
5. Plastic Woman asked, "Do you <u>agree</u> or ___ with me?"
6. Supergirl warned, "The <u>honest</u> are rewarded, but the ___ are never happy."

PREFIX ADDITION   Write the list word that has each beginning and meaning indicated below.

7. re + do something
8. dis + come into sight
9. in + without mistakes
10. mis + put down
11. re + put into service
12. in + finished
13. mis + went in front of
14. in + ready to do things
15. re + put down
16. mis + act politely
17. in + needing help
18. re + speak or shout
19. mis + write words
20. re + put pieces together

STRATEGIC SPELLING

Building New Words

Add the prefix **dis-** or **re-** to each word to make a new word. Remember what you learned.

21. able ___
22. design ___
23. charge ___
24. band ___

Take a Hint
Miss Pell will never misspell the word misspell!

≡	Make a capital.
/	Make a small letter.
∧	Add something.
℮	Take out something.
⊙	Add a period.
¶	New paragraph

PROOFREAD A LETTER Editors at a textbook publisher received the letter below. Correct four misspellings and four handwriting errors.

PROOFREADING TIP

People appreciate hearing your opinion, but they have to be able to read what you write. Make it easy for them—always cross your *t*'s and loop your *l*'s.

April 8, 1995

Dear Editors,

Your spelling book is fun and some times challenging, but we all have sertain lessons we dislik. We enjoy finding words other writers mispell.

Sincerely,

Lill School Fourth Graders

WRITE A LETTER Let the editors of one of your textbooks know what you think of their product. Use list words.

Word List

disappear	invisible	misplace	react
distrust	incorrect	misspell	replace
dishonest	incomplete	mistreat	recall
disagree	inactive	misled	rebuild
dislike	independent	misbehave	reuse
Personal Words	1. ___	2. ___	

136

Review

WORD ASSOCIATIONS Write the boxed word that you would associate with each situation described below.

1. a town repairing buildings that were damaged by a tornado
2. a child choosing activities he likes instead of just doing what everyone else wants to do
3. a student accidentally adding an extra letter as she is writing a word
4. a man saving a piece of paper to write on again
5. a student handing in a written assignment with missing answers
6. a customer discovering that a salesperson directed him to the wrong department
7. a student giving the wrong answer on a math test
8. a child not eating broccoli
9. a child forgetting where she left her library book
10. a boat sinking into a lake

dislike
disappear
incomplete
independent
incorrect
misplace
misspell
misled
rebuild
reuse

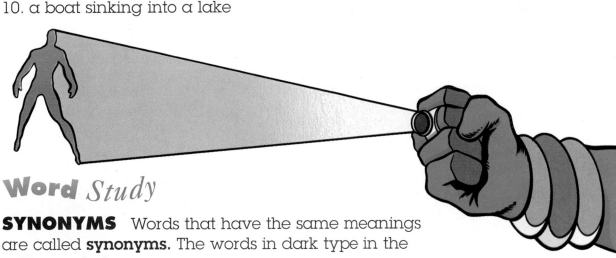

Word *Study*

SYNONYMS Words that have the same meanings are called **synonyms**. The words in dark type in the sentences below are synonyms.

When I rub my powerful ring, my assistant will **disappear.**

When I rub my powerful ring, my assistant will **vanish.**

Write the list word that is a synonym for each underlined word or words below.

1. I'm sorry that the number I gave you was <u>wrong</u>.
2. Doctors often <u>differ</u> about the way to treat patients.
3. You've made a good start, but your work is <u>unfinished</u>.
4. I cannot <u>remember</u> the words to that song.

Review

Lesson 25: Including All the Letters
Lesson 26: Compound Words
Lesson 27: Suffixes -ful, -ly, -ion
Lesson 28: Suffixes -less, -ment, -ness
Lesson 29: Prefixes dis-, in-, mis-, re-

REVIEW WORD LIST

1. camera
2. caught
3. December
4. evening
5. everybody
6. everyone
7. finally
8. interesting
9. island
10. often
11. remember
12. several
13. surprised
14. swimming
15. baseball
16. classmate
17. classroom
18. downstairs
19. myself
20. newspaper
21. nighttime
22. something
23. beautiful
24. carefully
25. daily
26. invention
27. painful
28. peaceful
29. powerful
30. suddenly
31. thoughtful
32. brightness
33. business
34. fairness
35. greatness
36. hopeless
37. pavement
38. spotless
39. statement
40. treatment
41. worthless
42. disagree
43. disappear
44. dislike
45. incomplete
46. independent
47. invisible
48. rebuild
49. recall
50. reuse

Adopt-a-Pet

These animals are looking for good homes. Read their stories and supply the words that are missing.

brightness
newspaper
independent
daily
dislike
rebuild

Rico

Rico is a quiet cat. He's a bit of a loner and very (1). The (2) of his wide, green eyes will delight you. Rico likes kids but would (3) living with another cat.

Mim

When Mim first arrived, she distrusted everyone. Help her (4) her trust by giving her a loving home. Mim must have (5) exercise. She loves to fetch the (6)!

Tricks of the Trade

Read the chapter subtitles from the book *Magic to Annoy Those Around You.* Write the words that have been left out.

1. Writing on your Grandpa's best shirt with ___ ink

2. New ways to ___ old paper towels

3. Ten foolproof ways to grab cookies without getting ___

4. Making your little sister ___ without a trace

5. Throwing your voice all the way ___ when you are upstairs

6. Convincing ___ at home that you're asleep when you're not

7. Creating ___ snowstorms in July with the spurting whipped-cream trick

reuse
downstairs
everybody
invisible
December
caught
disappear

classmate
powerful
baseball
island
several
camera
swimming

Necessities of Life

Use list words to complete the list below.

I would want these things along if I were stranded on a desert (1) :

my (2) cap—for cool dips in the sea

my (3) Alex—for good company

a (4) — to capture the sights

a (5) to toss around with Alex

(6) books—about wilderness camping

a (7) speedboat—for escape— HA HA!

Story Book Secrets

Jack and the Beanstalk and the Three Little Pigs had their sides of the story told, but what do the giant and the wolf have to say? You supply the missing words.

Giant Tells All

Bigtown, Austria—The giant of the beanstalk legend has (1) agreed to share his story. He feels that the (2) the press has given him lacks (3). "I strongly (4) with what's been written about me," he said. "Jack stole my (5) harp and golden eggs! He brought disorder to my once quiet, (6) household. He gets to be the hero, and I'm the (7) one! Well, I'm here to defend (8)!"

disagree
peaceful
myself
beautiful
treatment
worthless
fairness
finally

painful
recall
pavement
evening
statement
often

From the Trial of B. B. Wolf

Bailiff: Do you swear that the (1) you are about to give is the whole truth and nothing but the truth?

Wolf: I do.

Bailiff: Be seated.

Defense Lawyer: Tell us, Mr. Wolf, do you (2) the night of August 6?

Wolf: Yes, I think about it (3). It is the night I huffed and puffed and blew....

Defense Lawyer: To be sure, but how were you feeling that particular (4)?

Wolf: I had a terrible cold. My sinuses were blocked and very (5). Whenever I sneezed, a house fell to the (6)!

Defense Lawyer: So it wasn't your intention to destroy the homes of these squealing piglets?

Wolf: Certainly not! I am a peaceful wolf who minds his own business.

The Leszczynsky family is celebrating the birthday of their dog, Spot. Supply the words that are missing from the card they wrote.

surprised   spotless
everyone   nighttime
remember

to One Fine Canine

You know (1) said that we were thoughtless,
For naming you Spot, although you are (2)!

Will you be (3) to find steak in your bowl,
And to have us take you for a (4) stroll?

Just (5), dear old Spot,
We all love you quite a lot!

Hugs and kisses,
Your family

Benjamin Banneker– American Genius

By Yael Rubin

Learning about Benjamin Banneker was very (1). He became famous for the (2) of his mathematical abilities.

He was (3) taught to read and write by his grandmother. He was further educated in the (4) of a Quaker school. George Ellicott, who owned a large flour mill (5), also encouraged Benjamin's (6) pursuit of knowledge.

Write the words that are missing from Yael's report on a famous American.

business
carefully
interesting
thoughtful
classroom
greatness

At the age of 24, Benjamin built a clock that struck the hour. This clock is thought to be the first such (7) made in the United States.

Later, Benjamin was appointed by George Washington to help plan Washington, D.C. The chief architect (8) left the project, so the work was (9). The architect had taken the plans with him, and re-creating them seemed (10). Benjamin came to the rescue, drawing all the plans from memory. The building of the capital city is (11) people can thank Benjamin Banneker for.

invention   **hopeless**
suddenly   **incomplete**
something

Choosing the Best Strategy

DISCOVER THE STRATEGY You've learned that it is important to use the Steps for Spelling when studying spelling words. Don't forget to also use the strategies you've learned when a spelling word gives you a problem. Read about the strategies in the chart below.

Steps for Spelling	**Divide and Conquer**	**Memory Tricks**
Use the step-by-step strategy for studying most spelling words. 1. Look and say. 2. Spell. 3. Think. 4. Picture. 5. Look. 6. Cover and write.	Divide long words into shorter pieces. choc/o/late un/known	Link the tricky word with a helper you know how to spell. <u>You</u> are <u>you</u>ng. <u>qui</u>ck li<u>qui</u>d
Problem Parts	**Pronouncing for Spelling**	**Meaning Helpers**
Identify the problem and study it extra hard. <u>w</u>rong lau<u>gh</u>ed	Pronounce the word correctly, say a silent letter, or exaggerate a sound. Say "thum**b**." Say "mil-**li-on**."	Find a related word that gives you a sound clue. ev<u>e</u>r—ev<u>e</u>ry a<u>c</u>t—a<u>c</u>tion

TRY IT OUT Now it's time to practice choosing the best strategies. Read the exercises below and on the next page. Write the name of each strategy. Use the chart.

1. Which tricky strategy helps you remember the two **r**'s in *arrives?*

2. Which strategy helps you conquer a long word like *caterpillar?*

3. Which strategy helps you remember to pronounce the **o** in *favorite?*

4. Name the meaningful strategy that is helpful when trying to remember that *operation* is spelled with a **t.**

5. Which strategy would you use if a certain part of the word were giving you a spelling problem?

Compare your results with others in the class. It's fine to have different choices as long as you can explain them.

LOOK AHEAD Look ahead at the next five lessons. Find three words that look hard to spell. Write the word and strategy you would use to help spell each word.

Vowels with No Sound Clues

SPELLING FOCUS

In many words, the vowel sound gives no clue to its spelling: m**a**chine, mom**e**nt, an**i**mals, ir**o**n, s**u**pport.

■ **STUDY** Say each word. Then read the meaning phrase.

WATCH OUT FOR FREQUENTLY MISSPELLED WORDS!

1. machine   fix the sewing **machine**
2. especially ✳   like sports, **especially** soccer
3. usually   **usually** asleep by now
4. probably ✳   **probably** on her way
5. giant   saw a **giant** panda
6. moment   stopped for a **moment**
7. animals   saw the **animals** in the zoo
8. iron   need to **iron** a shirt
9. support   offer a friend **support**
10. suppose   **suppose** it would be all right

11. buffalo   **buffalo** roaming the plains
12. Canada   a vacation in **Canada**
13. canoe   **canoe** down a stream
14. relatives   **relatives** in Bombay
15. stomach   a growling **stomach**
16. cement   pour **cement** for a sidewalk
17. yesterday   finished it **yesterday**
18. favorite ✳   my **favorite** teacher
19. welcome   **welcome** visitors
20. August   go swimming in **August**

CHALLENGE!

dictionary
separate
multiplication
salmon
recognize

■ **PRACTICE** Sort the words by writing those you know how to spell. Then write the ones you think are difficult. You can use a memory trick like this for learning hard words: The **stomach** is an eating **machine**. Tell which strategy you will use for learning the hard words.

■ **WRITE** Choose ten phrases to rewrite as sentences.

144

DRAWING CONCLUSIONS Write a list word that fits the clues below.

1. A bricklayer uses this material to keep things in place.
2. If you want to paddle down a river, do it in this.
3. These people may be your aunts, uncles, and cousins.
4. When friends come to visit, greet them with a big one.
5. This is what you call the one you like more than others.
6. Use this to straighten out a wrinkled shirt.
7. A fairy tale might include one of these large fellows.
8. This is the month before September.
9. To sew a dress quickly, learn to operate one of these.
10. Sit-ups firm up the muscles in this part of your body.
11. This country is the United States neighbor to the north.

SYNONYMS Write the list word that means the same as each word below. Use the Spelling Dictionary for help.

12. particularly; chiefly
13. assume; believe
14. help; comfort
15. instant; short time
16. normally; customarily

STRATEGIC SPELLING
Choosing the Best Strategy

17.–20. Write *yesterday, probably, buffalo,* and *animals.* Which strategy could help you spell all four words? Name the strategy and tell why you chose it. Compare choices with a partner. For a list of strategies, see page 142.

Name of strategy: ____
Why I chose it: ____

FREQUENTLY MISSPELLED WORDS

To be an **especial**ly good speller, include the word **special** inside e**special**ly whenever you write it.

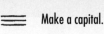

■ PROOFREADING AND WRITING

☰	Make a capital.
/	Make a small letter.
∧	Add something.
ℓ	Take out something.
⊙	Add a period.
¶	New paragraph

PROOFREAD A LETTER Anya wrote this letter home after her first day at camp. Correct five misspelled words, one of which is an incorrectly formed plural.

PROOFREADING TIP
Remember, to make words that end in a consonant and **y** plural, you must change the **y** to **i** and add **-es.**

July 8, 1997

Dear Mom and Aunt Carol,

I arrived yesturday. Flies are everywhere. My canoe tipped over. The food is relly bad. I supose one day I'll have fond memorys of camp, but so far this is not my favrite place.

Love,

Tenderfoot

WRITE A LETTER Pretend you are at camp. Write a letter home telling all about your first day. Use list words.

Word List

animals	August	canoe	cement
buffalo	suppose	machine	yesterday
especially	usually	moment	probably
favorite	iron	relatives	support
giant	Canada	stomach	welcome

Personal Words 1. ___ 2. ___

146

 **Review**

CROSSWORD PUZZLE Complete the crossword puzzle by writing the word that matches each definition.

Across
3. help
5. living things that are not plants
8. likely
9. huge
10. a very short space of time

Down
1. more than others
2. press
4. commonly; ordinarily
6. consider as possible
7. an object for doing work

machine
especially
usually
probably
giant
moment
animals
iron
support
suppose

Using a Dictionary

FINDING A WORD WHEN YOU CAN'T SPELL IT
Many sounds in the English language can be spelled lots of different ways. Take the sound /s/, for example. It can be spelled **s**upport, **c**ement, **sc**ent, li**s**ten, wal**tz,** and about six other ways. So if you wanted to look up *sword* and only knew it began with the sound /s/, what would you do?

You'd check the Spellings of English Sounds chart in your dictionary (and in this book on page 245). It shows you all the ways any given sound in English can be spelled.

Look at each pronunciation below. Write the word you would look up in the dictionary to find its spelling. If you are unsure, check the Spellings of English Sounds chart. Then check your Spelling Dictionary for the correct spelling.

1. (hwēt)   2. (brij)   3. (fō′tō)

147

Vowels in Final Syllables

■ **STUDY** Say each word. Then read the meaning phrase.

**WATCH OUT FOR
FREQUENTLY
MISSPELLED
WORDS!**

1.	other	no **other** news
2.	number	wore the **number** ten
3.	color	the **color** green
4.	doctor	saw the **doctor** for an injury
5.	people ✳	many **people** at the beach
6.	simple	give **simple** directions
7.	model	a role **model** to a young cousin
8.	broken	a **broken** flowerpot
9.	sudden	caught in a **sudden** rainstorm
10.	common	a **common** summer vegetable

11.	October	a cool **October** evening
12.	another ✳	**another** day of fun
13.	motor	the **motor** in a car
14.	angle	a right **angle** of 90 degrees
15.	title	the **title** of a book
16.	barrel	rainwater in a **barrel**
17.	angel	an **angel** with silvery wings
18.	oven	a roast in the **oven**
19.	gallon	a **gallon** of milk
20.	button	**button** a child's jacket

CHALLENGE!

receiver
counselor
article
citizen
cinnamon

■ **PRACTICE** Sort the list words by writing
- seven words that end with **or** and **er**
- seven words that end with **el** and **le**
- six words that end with **en** and **on**

■ **WRITE** Choose three phrases to include in a paragraph.

CONTEXT CLUES Write the list word that ends like the underlined word and completes the sentence.

1. An ___ with wings was carved into each door panel.
2. Tex was my ___ when I learned how to yodel.
3. The little squirrel jumped into the wooden ___.
4. To cure a pimple, try this ___ solution.
5. No one ___ than Mother will be waiting.
6. The inventor built a new automobile ___.
7. My cotton shirt is missing a ___.
8. I would not bother to look for ___ pen.
9. Drinking tea with lemon is ___ in many countries.
10. A ___ rainstorm will sadden picnickers.
11. The poor little chicken had a ___ wing.

ABBREVIATIONS Write the list word that corresponds to each abbreviation below. Use the Spelling Dictionary if you need help.

12. Dr.
13. Oct.
14. gal.
15. no.

Did You Know?
The word *angel* comes from a Greek word meaning "messenger."

CATEGORIZING Write the list word that names the category to which you would assign each group below.

16. men, women, children
17. turquoise, mauve, orange
18. your highness, her majesty
19. gas, electric

Seeing Meaning Connections

rectangle
triangle

20. Write a list word that is related to the words in the box.

Write the words from the box that fit the definitions.

21. a three-sided shape

22. a four-sided shape

149

≡	Make a capital.
/	Make a small letter.
∧	Add something.
ℰ	Take out something.
⊙	Add a period.
¶	New paragraph

PROOFREAD A CARD Indira received this card from a friend at school. Correct five misspelled words and two careless errors.

PROOFREADING TIP
You may leave out words when you're writing a card you're in a hurry to mail. Take a minute to proofread. Your reader will thank you.

GET WELL SOON!

I sorry about your brokin leg. Does it hurt? Is your docter nice? All the peopel at shcool miss you a lot. Hurry back. I want sighn your cast.

Michael

WRITE A CARD Pretend you are Indira. Write a response to your friend's card. Use a few list words and some personal words.

Word List

people	angle	sudden	doctor
gallon	number	another	oven
color	barrel	button	title
broken	motor	other	angel
October	model	simple	common

Personal Words 1. ___ 2. ___

VOCABULARY BUILDING

Review

WORDS IN CONTEXT Write the missing boxed words to complete the following news story.

other
number
color
doctor
people
simple
model
broken
sudden
common

Jimmy Thundercloud got quite a surprise during his demonstration of a (1) of the new XK-2000 vacuum cleaner at Mulberry's Department Store. "Most vacuum cleaners have a hard time picking up pet hair, but that task is (2) for the XK-2000," Mr. Thundercloud announced to the large (3) of (4) who were admiring the bright red (5) of the machine. Just as Mr. Thundercloud turned on the machine, the loud roar of the motor could be heard in all the (6) departments. All of a (7), the powerful suction turned the hose into a wild monster. It thrashed about wildly and hit Mr. Thundercloud in the arm with a loud *smack.*

"The arm is (8) and will be in a cast for about six weeks," says Mr. Thundercloud's (9).

A (10) reaction might be anger, but in an interview, Mr. Thundercloud chuckled and said, "I guess that machine just doesn't like me!"

Word *Study*

WORD WEBS Suppose you wanted to write a report about spiders. The first thing you'd want to do is ask yourself what you know about them. "What do they look like? What do they do? What makes them special?" Your next step would be to create a **word web** like the one below.

eight-legged   *small*

spider

builds webs   *eats insects*

Now suppose you were a spider, spinning a word web about people. Write the words you would use in your web.

(1)   (2)

people

(3)   (4)

151

Capitalization and Abbreviation

SPELLING FOCUS

Holidays, days and months of the year, titles, and words that are part of an address are always capitalized: **Christmas, May.** Abbreviations should be capitalized and followed by a period: **Dr., Rd., Sun.**

■ **STUDY** Notice that these words are capitalized. Some have periods.

WATCH OUT FOR FREQUENTLY MISSPELLED WORDS!

1. Memorial Day
2. Christmas *
3. Sun.
4. May
5. June
6. September
7. Dec.
8. Dr.
9. Mrs.
10. Rd.
11. Hanukkah
12. Kwanzaa
13. Chinese New Year
14. Valentine's Day
15. November
16. Feb.
17. Wed.
18. Ms.
19. Mr.
20. Ave.

■ **PRACTICE** Sort the list words by writing
- six words that name holidays
- two words that name days
- six words that name months
- four words that name people
- two words that name types of streets

■ **WRITE** Choose three words to write an invitation to a holiday party.

CHALLENGE!

Fourth of July
St. Patrick's Day
English
Blvd.
etc.

ABBREVIATIONS Write the abbreviation on your spelling list that stands for each word below.

1. doctor
2. avenue
3. December
4. Wednesday

5. February
6. mister
7. Sunday
8. road

IDENTIFICATION Write the list word that matches each clue below.

9. This is the ninth month of the year.
10. On this day we remember those who have died.
11. This is the fifth month of the year.
12. This is the eleventh month of the year.
13. This is a title put in front of a married woman's name.
14. This is the sixth month of the year.
15. On this day we may send a card to a sweetheart.
16. This is a title put in front of a woman's name, married or unmarried.

STRATEGIC SPELLING
The Divide and Conquer Strategy

17.–20. Sometimes it helps to study long words piece by piece. Write *Kwanzaa, Hanukkah, Christmas,* and *Chinese New Year.* Draw lines between the syllables. Study each word syllable by syllable. Use the Spelling Dictionary for help.

Did You Know?
Both **Hanukkah** and **Kwanzaa** can be spelled in different ways. You may also see **Hanukkah** spelled **Chanukah. Kwanzaa** may also be spelled **Kwanza.**

Make a capital.

/ Make a small letter.

∧ Add something.

 Take out something.

⊙ Add a period.

  New paragraph

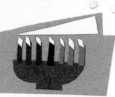

PROOFREAD AN ANNOUNCEMENT

The announcement below was posted on a school bulletin board. Find five misspelled words and four handwriting errors. Write them correctly.

PROOFREADING TIP

Did you stop and try to figure out what an aulhor and an audilorium were? Uncrossed **t**'s can cause confusion. You can catch these errors if you proofread.

Ms Jan Dure to Speak on Novenber 5

Here the aulhor of <u>Hannah's Hannuka</u>, <u>Cal's Cristmas</u>, *and* <u>Kestra's Kwanzaa</u> *speak aboul her wriling.*

Time: Wed. 6:00 PM

Place: School Audilorium

WRITE AN ANNOUNCEMENT

Now it's your turn to write an announcement about a visiting author. Use list words and personal words.

Word List

Ms.	Rd.	Hanukkah	Memorial Day
Mr.	Sun.	Christmas	May
Mrs.	Wed.	Kwanzaa	June
Dr.	Feb.	Chinese New Year	September
Ave.	Dec.	Valentine's Day	November

Personal Words   1. ___ 2. ___

Memorial Day
Christmas
Sun.
May
June
September
Dec.
Dr.
Mrs.
Rd.

Review

MAKING INFERENCES Complete each group by writing the missing boxed word.

1. April, ___, June
2. Oct., Nov., ___
3. August, ___, October
4. Sat., ___, Mon.
5. May, ___, July

MAKING ASSOCIATIONS Write the boxed word that you would associate with each group of words below.

6. December, tree, celebration
7. woman, married, title
8. person, professional, medicine
9. street, address, abbreviation
10. holiday, May, remembering

Multicultural Connection

HOLIDAYS People everywhere celebrate important occasions. Read the descriptions of the holidays below. Then answer the questions.

Hanukkah celebrates the recapturing of the great temple at Jerusalem over 2,000 years ago. Jewish writings describe how the Jews had barely enough lamp oil for one night in the temple, yet the lamp burned for eight days. Today, the menorah is lit in memory of this. Also called the "Festival of Lights," Hanukkah is celebrated in November or December.

Christmas celebrates the birth of Jesus, also called Christ. According to the Bible, Jesus was born in a stable and welcomed with gifts from wise men and shepherds. Christians believe Jesus is their savior. Small stable scenes are often seen at Christmas. It comes on December 25.

Kwanzaa is a yearly African American holiday created in 1966. It celebrates black people and their history. There are seven principles of Kwanzaa. The kinara, or candle holder, holds seven candles, one for each principle. Kwanzaa lasts from December 26 through January 1.

1. Which holiday celebrates African traditions?
2. Which holiday celebrates the birth of Jesus?
3. Which holiday is also called the "Festival of Lights"?

Possessives

To form possessives of
- singular nouns, add an **apostrophe** and **s: baby's**
- plural nouns that end in **s**, add only an
  apostrophe: babies'

■ **STUDY** Say each word. Then read the meaning phrase.

✳
**WATCH OUT FOR
FREQUENTLY
MISSPELLED
WORDS!**

1.	*Dad's*	took a ride on **Dad's** bicycle
2.	*friend's* ✳	listened to a **friend's** troubles
3.	*girl's*	admired the **girl's** self-portrait
4.	*girls'*	joined the **girls'** basketball league
5.	*teacher's*	met his **teacher's** mother
6.	*teachers'*	visited the **teachers'** lounge
7.	*baby's*	got the **baby's** bottle
8.	*babies'*	talked to the **babies'** fathers
9.	*family's*	read my **family's** history
10.	*families'*	talked about our **families'** holidays

11.	*grandma's*	enjoyed her **grandma's** story
12.	*grandpa's*	ate his **grandpa's** scrambled eggs
13.	*brother's*	my younger **brother's** jacket
14.	*brothers'*	my two older **brothers'** rock band
15.	*boy's*	found the **boy's** bicycle
16.	*boys'*	members of the **boys'** soccer team
17.	*aunt's*	my **aunt's** neighbor
18.	*aunts'*	our **aunts'** husbands
19.	*lady's*	shook the **lady's** hand
20.	*ladies'*	heard the **ladies'** voices

CHALLENGE!

someone's
boss's
James's
grandparent's
grandparents'

■ **PRACTICE** Sort the list words by writing
- twelve singular possessive nouns
- eight plural possessive nouns

■ **WRITE** Choose four phrases to rewrite as questions
and answers.

SINGULAR POSSESSIVES Complete each sentence by writing the singular possessive of the underlined word.

1. We found the <u>boy</u> cap under the chair.
2. I enjoyed the <u>girl</u> piano playing very much.
3. I visited my <u>aunt</u> office last Tuesday.
4. I accidently scratched my <u>brother</u> car.
5. I listened to <u>Dad</u> advice.
6. The children loved their <u>grandma</u> lullabies.
7. She always followed her <u>grandpa</u> directions.
8. I stayed the night at my best <u>friend</u> house.

USING CONTEXT CLUES Write the list word that is a form of the word in parentheses to complete each sentence.

9. I found a (lady) ring at the bottom of the pool.
10. That makes five (lady) rings I've found this week!
11. My (family) way of spending free time is to go hiking.
12. Other (family) free time activities may differ from ours.
13. My math (teacher) classroom is full of large posters.
14. The other (teacher) classrooms have smaller posters.
15. I put the (baby) little jacket on a hook in the closet.

PLURAL POSSESSIVES Write the possessive of each word below.

16. brothers
17. boys
18. aunts
19. babies
20. girls

STRATEGIC SPELLING

Building New Words

Write the words that complete the chart.

Singular	Singular Possessive	Plural Possessive
21. father	___	___
22. monkey	___	___

≡	Make a capital.
/	Make a small letter.
∧	Add something.
ℯ	Take out something.
⊙	Add a period.
¶	New paragraph

PROOFREAD AN OPINION Find four misspelled words in this opinion. Write them correctly. Fix two places where the subject and verb don't agree.

PROOFREADING TIP
I take, you take, but it takes. Be sure your subject (It) always agrees with your verb (takes).

Opinion Poll: Should Your TV Watching Be Restricted?

☑ Yes   ☐ No

Comments:

Watching to much TV is bad for you. It take away from the time you'd be doing important stuff. At my friends house, his family watch TV all day! I read, play basball, and help build my grandpas boat instead.

WRITE AN OPINION Do you think that you should restrict the amount of TV you watch? Write the reasons for your opinion. Use list words and personal words.

Word List

brother's	girls'	lady's	babies'
brothers'	aunt's	ladies'	grandma's
boy's	aunts'	family's	grandpa's
boys'	teacher's	families'	Dad's
girl's	teachers'	baby's	friend's

Personal Words   1. ___ 2. ___

Review

CONTEXT CLUES Write the list word that completes each *if...then* sentence.

1. If a teacher owns a house, then it is the ___ house.
2. If your friend is having a party, then it is your ___ party.
3. If some cars are owned by more than one family, then they are the ___ cars.
4. If a baby has a stuffed animal, then it is the ___ stuffed animal.
5. If some computers are owned by more than one teacher, then they are the ___ computers.
6. If two or more girls have lunches, then they are the ___ lunches.
7. If Dad has his own special chair, then it is ___ chair.
8. If a girl has her own telephone, then it is the ___ telephone.
9. If a family has a vegetable garden, then it is the ___ garden.
10. If several babies have blankets, then they are the ___ blankets.

Dad's
friend's
girl's
girls'
teacher's
teachers'
baby's
babies'
family's
families'

Word *Study*

PALINDROMES Anna, Otto, and Ada have something in common. Their first names are **palindromes**. A palindrome is a word that reads the same backward and forward. To complete the puzzle below, you must write palindromes. You will find the names of the Palindrome Kids hiding in the puzzle.

(crossword grid with letters: 1.O 2.M 3.T 4.A 5.P 6.N 7.D 8.A 9.P)

Across
3. the sound made by a horn or whistle
6. 12 o'clock in the daytime
7. something done; a good ___ should be rewarded
8. a girl's name
9. a young dog

Down
1. a boy's name
2. a short word for *mother*
4. a girl's name
5. the sound made by a young bird

159

Easily Confused Words

SPELLING FOCUS

Some words are easily confused because they have similar pronunciations and spellings: **our, are.**

■ **STUDY**   Say each word. Then read the meaning phrase.

*
WATCH OUT FOR FREQUENTLY MISSPELLED WORDS!

1. set — began to **set** the table
2. sit — tried to **sit** on the jagged rocks
3. off * — turned **off** the radio
4. of — a friend **of** mine
5. when * — **when** Grandpa was a child
6. win — didn't **win** the race
7. our * — lost **our** dog
8. are * — **are** going to the museum
9. than — bigger **than** my sister
10. then * — turned, **then** walked away

11. lose — didn't want to **lose** the game
12. loose — shoelaces were coming **loose**
13. were * — if I **were** you
14. we're * — told them **we're** not interested
15. where * — don't know **where** it is
16. quiet — **quiet** in the library
17. quite — not **quite** three years old
18. quit — **quit** a job she hated
19. whose — wondered **whose** bicycle it was
20. who's — asked **who's** going to the game

CHALLENGE!

recent
resent
pedal
petal
diary
dairy

■ **PRACTICE**   First write the groups of words that are confusing for you. Then write the rest of the words.

■ **WRITE**   Choose two phrases to write a rhyme.

ANTONYMS   Write the list word that means the opposite of the underlined word to complete each phrase.

1. not <u>tight</u>, but ____
2. not <u>noisy</u>, but ____
3. not <u>on</u>, but ____
4. not <u>begin</u>, but ____
5. not <u>stand</u>, but ____
6. not <u>find</u>, but ____

CONTEXT SENTENCES   Write the list word that completes each sentence.

7. Yes, ___ all going camping tomorrow.
8. I'm not sure just ___ we will return.
9. No, I haven't ___ finished packing.
10. I can't remember ___ the camp is located.
11. No, I don't know ___ tent we'll use.
12. No, I'm not sure ___ going to drive.
13. Yes, ___ trip should be full of surprises.

*FREQUENTLY MISSPELLED WORDS * FREQUENTLY MISSPELLED WORDS*

Having trouble with **where** and **were**? Just remember, **where** rhymes with **there,** and **we** is part of **were.**

ALPHA PUZZLES   Decide what letter of the alphabet comes between each pair of letters below. Write the letters to make a list word.

14. **n p** + **e g** =
15. **z b** + **q s** + **d f** =
16. **v x** + **d f** + **q s** + **d f** =
17. **s u** + **g i** + **d f** + **m o** =

STRATEGIC SPELLING

Choosing the Best Strategy

18.–20. Write *set, win,* and *than.* Name one strategy that would help you spell all three words. Discuss your choice with a partner. For a list of strategies, see page 142.

Name of Strategy: ____

≡	Make a capital.
/	Make a small letter.
∧	Add something.
℮	Take out something.
⊙	Add a period.
¶	New paragraph

PROOFREAD A SIGN The sign in the photograph below contains a misspelled word. Can you find it? Write the word correctly.

PROOFREADING TIP
Be sure that words you've written with apostrophes really should have them. Read the words without the apostrophe—*who's* as *who is*, for example—to see if it's needed.

RANDY HUGHES   DAVE RIEMER
BLUE FARM
TORTILLA CHIPS
THE CHIP WHO'S TIME HAS COME

CREATE A SIGN Do you have a favorite snack you'd like to tell everyone about? Draw a picture and use a word or two from the word list. Be sure to proofread your writing.

Word List

were	quit	then	sit
we're	off	than	when
where	of	lose	win
quiet	our	loose	whose
quite	are	set	who's

Personal Words 1. ___ 2. ___

Review

WORDS IN CONTEXT Write the boxed words that complete the following note.

set
sit
off
of
when
win
our
are
than
then

> Dear Robert and Carrie,
>   I will be a little late getting home this evening. In case you (1)___ hungry, I (2)___ a bowl of fruit on the kitchen table. I plan to be home about 6:30, and (3)___ we will have (4)___ dinner. Remember, do not (5)___ in front of the television while you are doing your homework. The TV must be turned (6)___ until you have finished your work.
>   Carrie, did your team (7)___ the relay race today? You said your team had faster runners (8)___ the other team. Robert, did you do all right on that math test? I am anxious to see both (9)___ you (10)___ I get home.
>   Love,
>   Mom
>
> P.S. Don't forget to feed Scuffy.

Word *Study*

USING EXACT WORDS *Win* is a perfectly good word to use when describing a victory. But think how boring sportscasts would be if scores from baseball games were read using only *win* or *lose.*

>   Cozy's Cafe had a 10–9 win against Dee's Diner.
>
>   Harold's Hardware lost 3–5 to Main St. Lumber.

When sportscasters use words that are more exact and descriptive, we get a better (and more interesting) picture.

>   Cozy Cafe slapped Dee's Diner with a 10–9 check that was the upset of the season.
>
>   Main St. Lumber hammered away at Harold's Hardware to gain a 5–3 victory.

Use your own words to complete the sportscast below.

1. The Hawks' superior pitching ___ the Pigeons in the first five innings.
2. The Pigeons ___, but couldn't get a hit.
3. The Pigeons were ___ by the Hawks 6–0.

163

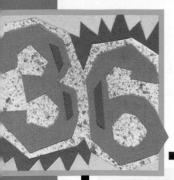

Review

Lesson 31: Vowels with No Sound Clues
Lesson 32: Vowels in Final Syllables
Lesson 33: Capitalization and Abbreviation
Lesson 34: Possessives
Lesson 35: Easily Confused Words

REVIEW WORD LIST

1. animals
2. August
3. buffalo
4. Canada
5. especially
6. favorite
7. giant
8. iron
9. machine
10. moment
11. probably
12. relatives
13. stomach
14. support
15. welcome
16. yesterday
17. angel
18. another
19. broken
20. button
21. common
22. model
23. number
24. oven
25. people
26. Ave.
27. Chinese New Year
28. Dr.
29. Hanukkah
30. Ms.
31. November
32. Rd.
33. Sun.
34. Valentine's Day
35. Wed.
36. baby's
37. boys'
38. Dad's
39. are
40. loose
41. lose
42. of
43. our
44. quit
45. quite
46. set
47. than
48. were
49. we're
50. win

Wed.
Dad s
Rd.
Sun.
Dr.

WEEKLY CALENDAR

Use the list words to complete the calendar.

__(1)__	Visit Arnetta.
Mon.	Board Meeting—21 Oak __(2)__
Tue.	Pick up __(3)__ shirts.
__(4)__	Book Club—7 P.M.
Thurs.	Eye Exam— __(5)__ Fowler 10 a.m.

Offbeat Greetings

baby's August probably
iron Ave. yesterday
loose of

These days, greeting cards say more than just "Happy Birthday" and "Get Well." Supply the missing words in each card below.

Congratulations!
It's your (1) first tooth! Let's hope it stays in there and doesn't get (2) !

HAPPY BIRTHDAY
(in advance)
I know it's July and you were born in (3), but I like to keep ahead (4) things!

Welcome to the Neighborhood!
You have (5) heard the rumors about Maple (6). Well, most of them are true!

DEAR FRIEND,
I'm sorry I didn't call you (7). I had to (8) my best shirt and that takes time. Maybe tomorrow... after I wash my hair.

BEING CATERED TO

Jake and Clare make healthy desserts for people giving parties. Supply the list words missing from their advertising brochure.

favorite
number
we're
especially
stomach
oven
our
quite

- Ja'Clare offers your (1) the healthiest and tastiest dessert it's ever had.
- Our treats come direct from our (2) to you!
- Choose from tarts, pies, custards, mousses, and any (3) of your (4) cakes.
- We work seven days a week and (5) always available for consultations.
- You'll find that (6) desserts are (7) the thing for parties, (8) the masterpiece we call Strawberry Rapture.

Happy Holidays

Use these list words to complete the holiday memories.

Hanukkah   **Chinese New Year**   **Valentine's Day**
angel   **relatives**   **moment**
giant

1. What I love best about Christmas is putting the ___ on the tree.
2. I love the glow of the candles in the menorah on ___ .
3. My favorite memory of Kwanzaa is seeing all my friends and ___ .
4. Memorial Day is a time I like to take a ___ to remember those who have died.
5. I enjoy welcoming in the new year with fireworks and a dragon parade during ___ .
6. We always buy a ___ pumpkin to carve at Halloween. It's great!
7. I like getting those fancy, heart-shaped greetings on ___ .

Canada	**button**
boys	**animals**
machine	**model**
set	

The Russos are packed and ready to move, but they need help labeling all their belongings. Use each list word once.

MOVING OUT

Grandma's (1) collection

Mom's five-speed rowing (2)

Leonardo's (3) airplane kits

Dion's miniature tea (4)

(5) skates—sizes 5 and 6

Jenelle's stuffed (6)

Angela's map of (7)

Where the Buffalo Roam

Read the information below and supply the missing list words.

lose   **buffalo**   **are**   **than**
quit   **were**   **common**

The American bison, also called the (1), once roamed over most of North America. In the 1700s there (2) thirty to sixty million buffalo in North America. A single herd might be twenty miles wide and more (3) fifty miles long. By the 1800s the slaughter of buffalo by the thousands was a (4) occurrence. It looked as though we might (5) the buffalo forever. By 1900 there were only 20 wild bison left in the United States. Laws were passed to ensure that people would (6) hunting them, and there (7) now parks and preserves that protect the buffalo.

Election Time

Lynn Page is running for student council treasurer. Help her finish her campaign slogans.

people
Ms.
support
win
welcome
November
broken
another

If YOU vote for Lynn, we're all sure to (1)! Lend your (2) to one who understands money.

Attention: all (3) of voting age. When you vote in (4), be sure it's for (5) Page.

VOTE FOR LYNN PAGE!

No more (6) promises!! You are all (7) to join LYNN to discuss the issues.

It's time for (8) point of view! Turn to Page!

Vocabulary, Writing, and Reference Resources

Cross-Curricular Lessons

Writer's Handbook

Spelling Dictionary

Writer's Thesaurus

English/Spanish Word List

Cross-Curricular Lessons

Global Grid

location
latitude
parallels
equator
degrees
hemispheres
longitude
meridians
prime meridian
coordinates

Can you find Ecuador on a map? What about Egypt or Finland? Understanding the words in the list can help you find places in the world. Add your own words to the list.

■ GETTING AT MEANING

Locating Places   Look at globes A and B on the next page. Use them to help you complete the sentences.

hemispheres   latitude   equator   parallels

 Globe A

The imaginary east-west lines on a map or globe are used to show (1). They are called (2). The (3) is at 0° latitude. It divides the Earth into two halves, or (4)—the Northern and Southern Hemispheres.

degrees   longitude   meridians   location
prime meridian   coordinates

 Globe B

The imaginary north-south lines that go from pole to pole on a map or globe are used to show (5). They are called (6). The (7) is at 0° longitude. It divides the Earth into the Western and Eastern Hemispheres. Both latitude and longitude are measured in (8). On a globe showing both parallels and meridians, the intersecting lines 20°S, 20°E that go through Africa are called (9). You can find any (10) on a map or globe when you know its coordinates.

A Parallels
Lines of Latitude

B Meridians
Lines of Longitude

■ SPELL WELL

Double Letters   Sometimes double letters can cause spelling problems. Write the words in the list that have double letters. Underline the double letters.

171

oak
dune
evergreens
cactus
needleleaf
moisture
forest
broadleaf
desert
sagebrush

Deserts and Forests

What makes a desert? What makes a forest? How are the two alike or different? Use the pictures below to find out. Add your own words to the list. Use the Spelling Dictionary.

■ GETTING AT MEANING

Using Picture Clues   Look at all of the illustrations. Use words from the list to complete each caption.

cactus	desert	sagebrush	dune	moisture

One-seventh of all the Earth's land is dry, sandy (1). The United States has deserts in the Southwest. Strong, dry winds can blow sand into a mounded (2).

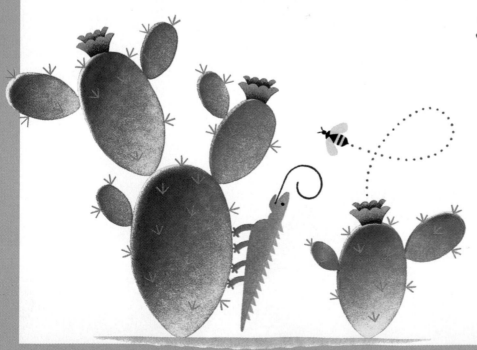

The dry, bushy (3) is found on western plains.

Although all living things require (4) to live, a (5) doesn't need much water. It grows in hot, dry regions.

172

| evergreens | needleleaf | oak | forest | broadleaf |

A (6) is more than just trees. It includes shrubs, mosses, and flowers. The largest ones in the United States are in the North and East.

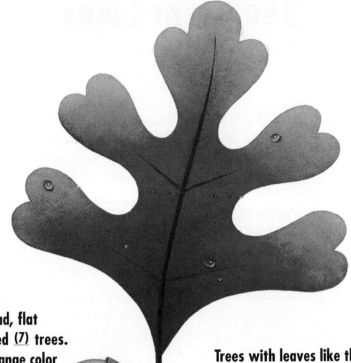

Trees with broad, flat leaves are called (7) trees. Their leaves change color and fall off. The (8) is this kind of tree.

Trees with leaves like thin, sharp needles are called (9) trees. These trees are also called (10) because they stay green all year.

■ SPELL WELL

Divide and Conquer Study long words piece by piece. Draw a line between the two base words in each compound below. Write each word.

11. needleleaf

12. evergreens

CREATE A DIORAMA
Make a three-dimensional desert or forest. First, research your chosen area. What kinds of plants and animals are found there? Next, get a shoe box and pictures, sand, clay, branches, and so on. Create the environment inside the box. Label your diorama.

The Great Lakes

The Great Lakes and the St. Lawrence Seaway are North America's major water highways. Read the list below to learn about them. Add your own words and sentences.

Lake Huron	**Lake Huron** borders Michigan and Canada.
Lake Ontario	**Lake Ontario** borders New York and Canada.
Lake Michigan	**Lake Michigan** borders Wisconsin, Illinois, Indiana, and Michigan.
Lake Erie	**Lake Erie** borders Michigan, Ohio, New York, Pennsylvania, and Canada.
Lake Superior	**Lake Superior** borders Michigan, Wisconsin, Minnesota, and Canada.
St. Lawrence Seaway	**The St. Lawrence Seaway** is a waterway that connects the Great Lakes and the Atlantic Ocean.
Atlantic Ocean	**The Atlantic Ocean** is east of North and South America and west of Europe and Africa.
waterway	A **waterway** is a channel through which boats can navigate.
canal	An artificial waterway for navigation is a **canal.**
lock	An enclosed section of a canal in which the level of water can be changed is called a **lock.**

■ GETTING AT MEANING

Using Written Clues Complete each sentence using either **lock, canal,** or **waterway.**

1. The St. Lawrence Seaway is a major ___.

2. The ship at right is sailing through a ___.

3. The ship at left enters the ___ and the gates are then closed

Labeling a Map Label the Great Lakes, the St. Lawrence Seaway, and the Atlantic Ocean using the map below.

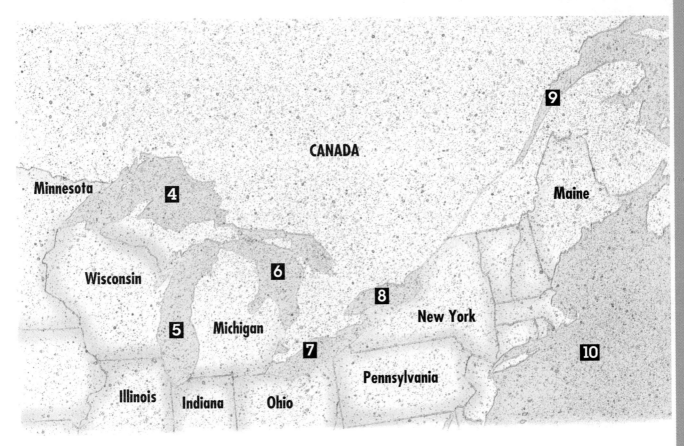

■ SPELL WELL

Divide and Conquer Study the name of each lake syllable by syllable. Then write the names.

11. Lake Su • per • i • or _____

12. Lake On • tar • i • o _____

Look into This

List the names of streams, rivers, lakes, and other bodies of water that influence your environment. Are they natural or made by people? Where do they begin and end? Present your findings in the form of a chart, map, or diagram.

Did You Know?

The first letters of the names of the Great Lakes spell a word that means "places where we live." What is that word? (Once you figure it out, you can use it to help you remember the names of all the Great Lakes!)

Using Natural Resources

Many of our natural resources are very important to our way of living. Read the sentences below to find out why. Add your own related words and phrases to the list.

energy	We use natural resources to create **energy** to do work.
electricity	**Electricity** is energy that powers lights and machines.
hydroelectric	**Hydroelectric** plants use water power to make electricity.
fuels	**Fuels** are resources that are burned to create energy or heat.
oil	**Oil** is our main fuel for running kinds of transportation.
gasoline	By cleaning and breaking down oil, we get **gasoline.**
natural gas	Another fuel, **natural gas,** is used for heating and cooking.
coal	We burn **coal** to create heat.
steel	**Steel** is a product of iron ore and carbon that is formed into sheets, beams, and other shapes.
products	Steel and gasoline are **products** that are made from natural resources.

■ GETTING AT MEANING

Using Context Clues   Use the clues in the sentences above to help you choose the right list word for each blank below.

1. In manufacturing and industry, natural resources are made into finished ___.
2. Melting down the natural resource of iron ore and mixing it with carbon produces ___.
3. Factories may burn coal, oil, or other ___ to produce energy.
4. Burning coal turns water into steam that generates electrical ___.
5. The Earth's mineral fuels, including coal, oil, and ___, may be used up in the next few centuries.

Using Visual Clues Write the list word that best corresponds to each picture below.

6

7

8

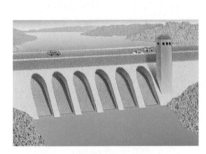

9

10

■ SPELL WELL

Seeing Meaning Connections The word *electric* is related to two list words. Finish each sentence by writing the correct list word.

12. Without ____ I couldn't watch TV.
13. Hoover Dam is a ____ dam.

Constitution
republic
democratic
participate
leaders
elected
represent
local
state
federal

Our Government

What's so special about the United States' government? Plenty! The words in the list will help you find this out. Add more government words to the list. Then do the exercises.

■ GETTING AT MEANING

Context Clues   Use the list words to complete what the people below are saying.

democratic   participate   represent   elected
leaders   republic

America's highest (1) are the President and Vice-President.

Government officials are (2) by citizens when they vote.

All citizens should take part in, or (3) in, elections.

Because the people run our government, we're a (4) country.

We also elect senators and representatives to (5) us in Congress.

We pledge allegiance to the flag and to the (6) for which it stands.

178

State the Facts
Use the list words to answer the questions.

state   federal   local   constitution

What written plan gives Americans their power?

Do governors and lieutenant governors work on the state or local level?

Do the President and Vice-President work on the federal, state, or local level?

10
Do mayors and city council members work on the federal, state, or local level?

■ SPELL WELL

Divide and Conquer   Some long words are easier to study if you sound them out in syllables. Study each word below, saying it syllable by syllable. Then write the words.

11. Con • sti • tu • tion

12. par • tic • i • pate

CLASSMATE CONSTITUTION

What kind of government would work best in your classroom? Work in small groups to author a "Classroom Constitution" that establishes the kind of government you want. Think about the number of leaders, their powers, limitations, and responsibilities, as well as the role of the rights and responsibilities of classroom citizens. Use the Constitution of the United States as your guide.

Did You Know?
The Constitution of the United States is one of the oldest written constitutions. Many other countries have patterned their constitutions after it.

pueblo
adobe
corn
ceremony
pottery
Navajo
hogans
silver
weaving
reservation

Southwest American Indians

Many Southwest American Indians keep the traditions their ancestors kept hundreds of years ago. The list words reflect their past as well as their present life. Add your own words. Use the Spelling Dictionary as you do the exercises.

■ GETTING AT MEANING

Using Picture Clues Look at the illustrations. Complete the sentences using words from the list.

adobe   ceremony   pottery   pueblo   reservation

These American Indians of New Mexico and Arizona get their name from the apartmentlike villages in which they live. Each village is called a (1). The pueblos are made of stone or sun-dried (2) bricks. In one religious (3), the Pueblo pray for harmony and order in the universe. The Pueblo make beautiful clay (4), which they sell to tourists who visit the (5).

silver   hogans   weaving   Navajo   corn

The (6) are also American Indians of the Southwest. Many of them are farmers, growing (7) and raising sheep. Others are gifted at (8) wool into beautiful blankets, while others are engineers, teachers, and technicians. The Navajo are also famous for the artistic turquoise and (9) jewelry they make. A single ring can cost over $20,000. Many Navajo live in (10), shelters made of log frames covered with earth.

■ SPELL WELL

Seeing Meaning Connections   Write the list word that completes each sentence. The underlined word is a clue.

11. That beautiful clay <u>pot</u> is just one of a large (11) collection.
12. A parcel of land <u>reserved</u> exclusively for American Indians is a (12).

Design Your Own Pottery
Each Pueblo village creates pottery using its own special design. Draw a pot and decorate it with your own one-of-a-kind design.

Inuit
seal
whale
walrus
polar bear
caribou
blubber
fur
tundra
kayak

Arctic Life

The Arctic is quite a place! How do people and animals live and travel there? The list words will help you answer these questions. Add your own Arctic words to the list.

■ GETTING AT MEANING

Using Photographs   Use list words to complete the caption for each photograph.

blubber   Inuit   kayak   polar bear   whale

Many of the people who live in the Arctic, such as the (1), zip around in snappy little snowmobiles!

When the ice melts, an easy way to get around is to paddle a (2), a special boat.

The huge, snow-colored (3) looks at us as if to say, "Isn't the Arctic wonderful?"

This leaping (4) has a thick layer of fat called (5) that keeps it warm in cold water.

fur   tundra   walrus   caribou   seal

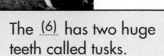

The (6) has two huge teeth called tusks.

A sleek (7) tends to its pup.

The reindeer feeding on the grass is also called a (9)!

This girl will stay warm in a hood trimmed in animal (8).

The caribou stands on the treeless plain, called (10).

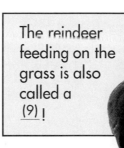

■ SPELL WELL

Rhyming Helpers The rhyming helpers *meal* and *Mary Lou* can help you spell two list words. Write the list word that rhymes with each rhyming helper.

11. The polar bear
Sniffs the air,
Hoping for a meal.
While diving for a codfish,
It sees a lively (11).

12. "What are you doing,
Mary Lou?"
"Reading a book
About (12)."

TRY IT OUT

The Inuit are famous for their sculptures. They use soapstone, whalebone, and other material to carve animals or scenes from their environment. Try it yourself. Use clay or a bar of soap to carve something you see each day.

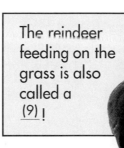

Know Yourself

strengths
appreciate
weaknesses
decision
disagree
tears
result
psychologist
special
appearance

You are one-of-a-kind. The list words celebrate that. Add your own words to the list. Use the Spelling Dictionary for help.

■ GETTING AT MEANING

Talking About You The friends in the comic strip are eager to share their wisdom with you, but the cartoonist left out words. Use the list words to complete their sentences.

strengths · appreciate · special · appearance · tears

The Walkie Talkies

You know, nobody else is quite like you. You are unique. You are (1).

That's right! For instance, your (2)-- what you look like. Your looks are yours alone.

Right! And what about your (3)? What do you do really well? What do people like about you and (4) you for?

Feelings are important too. What makes you smile? What brings (5) to your eyes?

■ SPELL WELL

Problem Parts Some words cause problems because they are not spelled the way they sound. Write *psychologist* and *appreciate*. Underline any letters in these words that you think might cause spelling problems.

decision · psychologist · disagree · result · weaknesses

And what makes you mad? An argument? It's okay to (6) with people. You can't agree all the time.

And, like all of us, you have faults. Be aware of your (7). What needs improvement? Once you've made a (8) to improve a fault, ask family and friends to help.

If a problem is bigger than you can handle, a professional (9) may help you.

The (10) may be a happier, healthier you!

Being Safe

crosswalks
first aid
pedestrians
rescue
reflector
bicycle
hand signal
jaywalking
emergency
helmet

You've heard the phrase "safety first." Understanding the words in the list can help you put safety first in your life. Add your own words to the list. Use the Spelling Dictionary if you need help.

■ GETTING AT MEANING

Labeling Write a list word from the sign that identifies each numbered part of the picture.

reflector
bicycle
helmet
hand signal

Using Context Clues As Sara rides to school, she is reviewing some of the safety rules she knows. Use the list words on the sign to complete Sara's thoughts.

- • People who are walking, or (5), must follow safety rules.

- • Pedestrians should cross streets only at (6), or specially marked places.

- • Not crossing a street at a crosswalk is called (7).

- • If someone is hurt in an accident, call the police and request an ambulance. A paramedic team will come to the (8).

- • When driving a car or riding a bike, always pull over to the right side of the road and stop to allow an (9) vehicle to pass.

- • Stand back and allow the paramedics to provide (10).

jaywalking
pedestrians
first aid
emergency
rescue
crosswalks

DETOUR

Did You Know?

Preventing accidents is the goal of safety engineers. These experts design structures and equipment to keep us safe at home, in school, on the job, and on the road.

■ SPELL WELL

Divide and Conquer Sometimes it helps to study long words piece by piece. Study the following words syllable by syllable. Then write each one.

11. e • mer • gen • cy

12. pe • des • tri • an

bicuspid
cuspid
incisor
molar
enamel
epidermis
dermis
pore
sweat gland
oil gland

Your Body

■ GETTING AT MEANING

There's more to teeth than a dazzling smile, and more to skin than bone covering. Read about them below. Add more words to the list. Use your Spelling Dictionary for help.

Labeling Diagrams   Read about the teeth and skin. Then use list words to write the parts of each diagram.

The Teeth

The word **cuspid** means "tooth with a sharp point." A **bicuspid,** therefore, is a tooth with two sharp points. An **incisor** is a front tooth, and a **molar** is a back tooth. All of our teeth are protected by hard, white **enamel.**

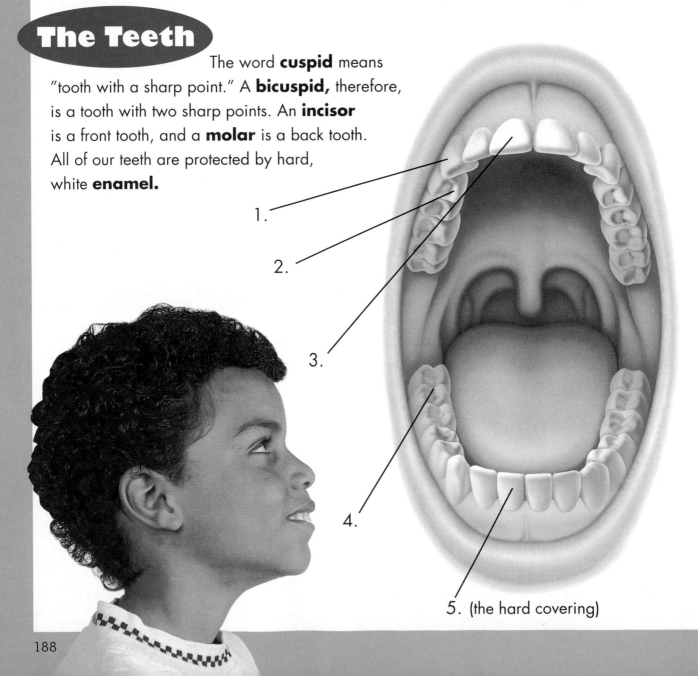

1. _____

2. _____

3. _____

4. _____

5. (the hard covering)

The Skin

The **epidermis** is the outer layer of the skin. The **dermis** is the inner layer. Each tiny opening in the skin is called a **pore.** Sweat is released through the **sweat gland,** and oil is released through the **oil gland.**

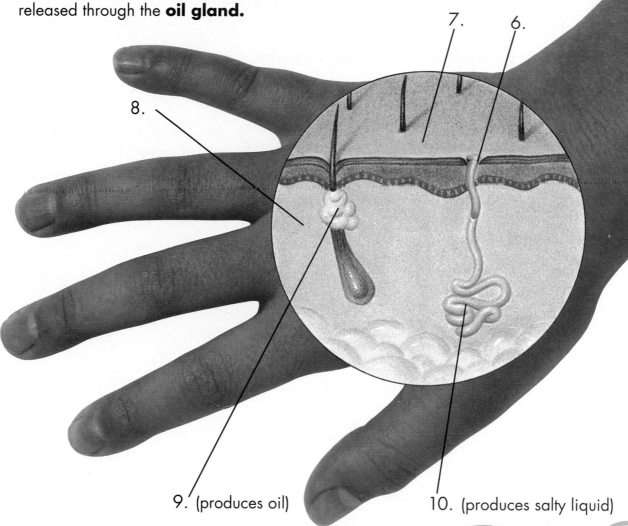

7.
6.
8.
9. (produces oil)
10. (produces salty liquid)

■ SPELL WELL

Root Awareness Some of your list words come from Greek and Latin words. Often, a word is easier to understand and remember if you look at its root, the word it came from. Complete the chart to create two list words.

Prefix	Root Word	List Word
	derm (skin)	11. ____
epi (on, upon)	derm (skin)	12. ____

Try to Talk Without Teeth!

Not only do we need our teeth to eat, we need them to talk. Slowly read this sentence out loud: *The tiny worm sat upon a log.* Write down the words in which your tongue touches your teeth. Next to each word, also jot down where your tongue touches your teeth.

189

SCIENCE

Plant Reproduction

reproduce
seed
conifers
ferns
spores
pollen
stamen
pistil
fertilize
fruit

How do plants reproduce—that is, make other plants?
Use the list words and the diagrams to find the answer.
Add your own words to the list. Use the Spelling Dictionary.

■ **GETTING AT MEANING**

Plants from Seeds   Many plants, like the cherry tree below,
reproduce by means of seeds. The diagram will help you
complete the sentences.

1. This flower will ___ by means of seeds.

2. The tiny grains made by the stamen are called ___ .

3. The flower's ___ makes these tiny grains.

4. Bees and butterflies carry pollen from the stamen to the ___ .

5. The pollen will ___ an egg at the bottom of the flower's pistil.

6. The fertilized ___ will grow inside the plant.

7. The ___ grows around the seed.
   It is the part we eat.

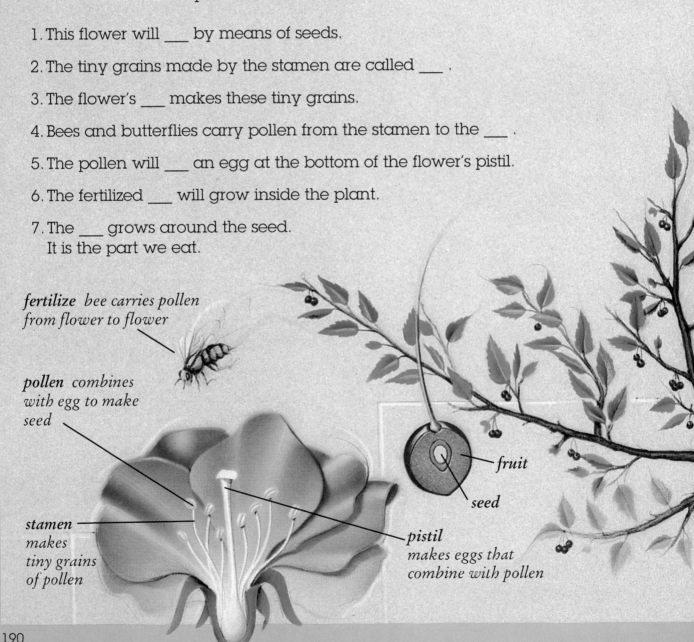

*fertilize bee carries pollen
from flower to flower*

*pollen combines
with egg to make
seed*

*stamen
makes
tiny grains
of pollen*

fruit

seed

*pistil
makes eggs that
combine with pollen*

Plants from Spores and Cones **Ferns** and mosses reproduce by means of **spores**. **Conifers** such as pine trees reproduce by means of cones. The male cone is smaller and softer. The female cone is larger and harder. Use the diagram to complete the sentences.

8. Unlike flowers, mosses and ___ have clusters of tiny cells under their leaves.

9. These cells are called ___ .

10. Spruce and pine are both ___ . They produce cones.

fern

spores on the underside of a fern

■ SPELL WELL

Divide and Conquer

Long words are easy to spell if you divide them into smaller parts. Study each word below, syllable by syllable. Then write each word.

11. fer • ti • lize

12. re • pro • duce

13. con • i • fers

Plants Aplenty

What's your favorite plant? A garden flower? A wildflower? An exotic tree of the rain forest? Draw and paint or color your favorite plant on a big sheet of paper. Cut it out, and with your classmates' plants, create a classroom "botanical garden" on the wall. For fun, label your plant with its name, where it grows, and some interesting facts about it.

Living Together

producers
consumers
herbivore
carnivore
omnivore
food chain
food web
predator
prey
decomposer

Every living thing—plant and animal—depends in some way on other living things. The list words can help you find out how. Can you add others? Use your Spelling Dictionary.

■ GETTING AT MEANING

Looking at Pictures **Producers** make their own food. **Consumers** eat other living things. Look at the picture below. Then answer the questions.

I'm an herbivore~ I eat only plants.

YOUR BACKYARD

I'm an omnivore~ I eat plants and meat.

I'm a decomposer~ I break down dead plants and animals.

I'm a carnivore I eat only mea

1. The dog, boy, and squirrel all eat food. What are they called?

2. Are plants such as lettuce and carrots producers or consumers?

3. What do you call an animal who eats only beef and chicken?

4. What is an animal who eats only leaves, fruit, and nuts called?

5. What is an animal who eats both fish and rice called?

6. What do you call the tiny organism that causes dead plants and animals to crumble and rot?

Seeing Connections Animals that are hunted and eaten are called **prey**. Animals that do the hunting and eating are called **predators**. A **food chain** shows a direct link between an animal and the thing it eats and is eaten by. A **food web** is a complex arrangement of food chains. Label each picture below either **food chain** or **food web**. Answer the questions that follow.

8.

7.

9. Is the mouse in the food chain predator or prey?

10. Is the hawk in the food chain predator or prey?

■ SPELL WELL

Pronouncing Words Carefully We sometimes spell words wrong because we say them wrong. Say each word below. Be sure to pronounce the sounds of the underlined letters. Write the words.

11. her<u>bi</u>vore

12. car<u>ni</u>vore

13. om<u>ni</u>vore

Draw the Food Chain in Your Yard

Take a good look around your schoolyard or yard at home. Sketch some of the plant and animal life you see. Turn your sketches into an illustration of your yard's food chains. Does your yard also have a food web? Illustrate that too!

Electricity and Magnetism

Electricity and magnetism are forces we use every day. The list words tell about each force. Look up unknown words in the Spelling Dictionary. Add other words to the list.

■ GETTING AT MEANING

Using Diagrams Write the words **current, conduct, insulation, series circuit,** and **parallel circuit** to complete the explanation below the diagrams.

Copper is a good conductor of electricity.

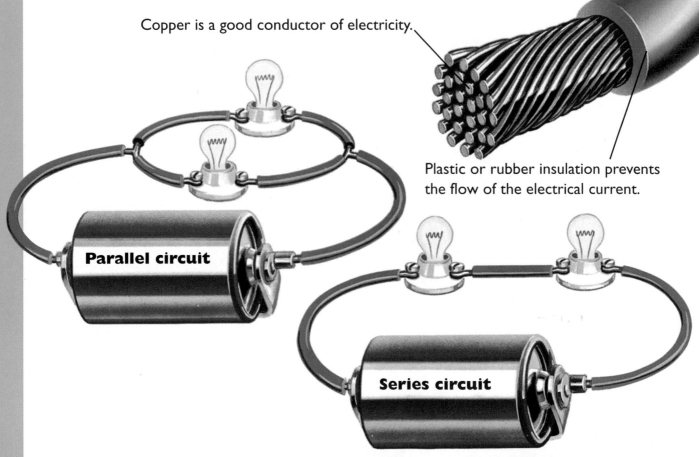

Plastic or rubber insulation prevents the flow of the electrical current.

Parallel circuit

Series circuit

Like a river, electricity flows in a (1). Copper wire is used to (2) the electricity. The wires are wrapped in plastic (3) so that they are safe to touch. When the electricity moves along one path, the circuit is a (4). When the electricity moves along two or more paths, the circuit is a (5).

Using Diagrams Use the words below to complete the sentences.

poles   **magnetic field**   **magnetism**   **compass**   **magnet**

A (6) is any piece of iron or steel that can pull iron or steel things to it. The magnet's power to attract is called (7). The parts of a magnet where the magnetism is the strongest are called the (8). The magnetic force curves out between a magnet's poles creating what is called a (9). A magnetic (10) helps travelers to find directions. The arrow on the compass will point to the north because the north-seeking pole of the needle is attracted to the magnetic north pole of the earth.

Magnet

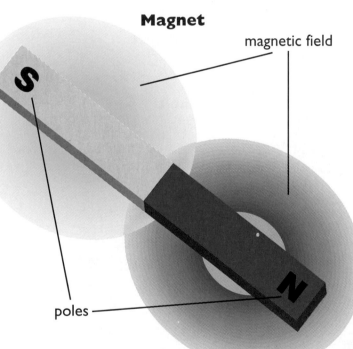

magnetic field

poles

Compass

■ SPELL WELL

Related Words Write the two list words that are related in spelling and meaning to *magnet.*

11. ___

12. ___

Did You Know?

About 500 species of fish send out electric charges. Electric eels are the best known. They stun their prey with a 350–650 volt charge!

meteorologist
forecast
barometer
wind vane
rain gauge
humidity
air mass
front
Fahrenheit
Celsius

SCIENCE

Weather

The weather's "behavior" tells us how to behave. What we wear and do often depends on the weather. The list words name ways we find out about weather. Look up unfamiliar words in the Spelling Dictionary. Add more weather words to the list.

■ GETTING AT MEANING

Weather Report Finish writing the newscaster's and weather forecaster's cue cards by writing these list words. Use the thermometer on the next page to help you.

humidity
meteorologist
forecast
Celsius
Fahrenheit

And now it's time for the weather (1). Here's Channel 2 (2), Connie Yu.

Thanks, Dave. Did you notice how damp the air was today? The (3) was so high! Watch out for the rain tonight— and it could freeze! That's because the temperature might drop to 32 degrees (4). That's the same as 0 degrees (5). Brrr!

Related Words Complete each sentence by writing the list word that is related to the underlined word or term.

6. A ___ measures the <u>barometric</u>, or air, pressure.

7. A ___ measures the amount of <u>rainfall</u>.

8. Both a ___ and a <u>wind sock</u> can show wind direction.

rain gauge

wind vane

barometer

Reading a Weather Map An **air mass** is a large body of air pushing into an area. A **front** is where two different air masses meet. Look at the map key. Then label the symbols on the map for **air mass** and **front**.

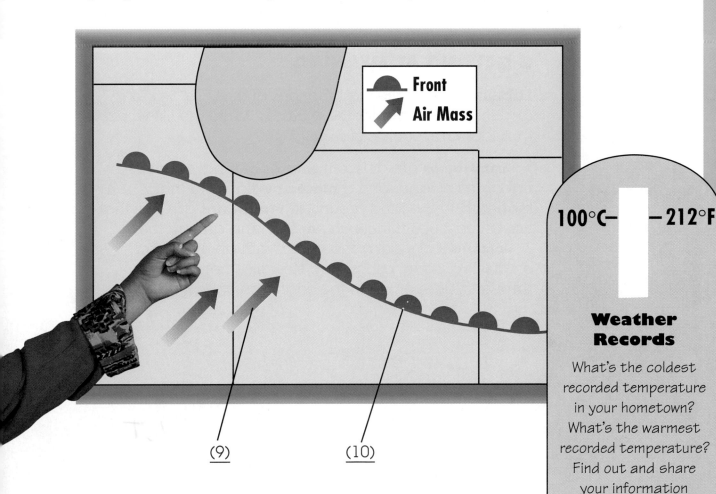

Front

Air Mass

(9)   (10)

100°C— —212°F

Weather Records

What's the coldest recorded temperature in your hometown? What's the warmest recorded temperature? Find out and share your information with your classmates.

0°C — —32°F

■ **SPELL WELL**

Divide and Conquer Study these long words syllable by syllable. Then cover the words and write them.

11. me • te • o • rol • o • gist

12. Fahr • en • heit

197

Landforms

Can you describe your natural surroundings? Are there any mountains or plains nearby? The list words will help you talk about landforms and the forces that cause them. Look up unfamiliar words in the Spelling Dictionary. Add two words of your own.

■ GETTING AT MEANING

Labeling   Read the explanations of these list words and look at the numbered pictures. Write the list word that identifies each picture.

   Landforms are different shapes of land. **Plains** are flat areas of land, and a **plateau** is flat land that is higher than the land around it. **Mountains** are hills that rise at least 600 meters above the land around them. A **volcano** looks like a mountain with an opening on the top. Lava, ashes, and steam sometimes flow through this opening in the earth's crust.

1. ___
2. ___
3. ___
4. ___

5. These four shapes of land are called ___.

Scientific Vocabulary When writers use technical words, they often put clues in the sentences to help you understand what the terms mean. Using the underlined clues, write list words to complete this paragraph about earthquakes.

Earth Notes

When the <u>earth shakes</u>, it is called an
(6). An earthquake is caused by the
shifting of <u>large sections of rock that
make up the earth's surface</u> called (7).
The earth's surface has <u>cracks</u> called (8).
Earthquakes usually begin along these
fault lines. An instrument called a (9)
records how strong the earthquake is by
drawing lines on <u>graph paper</u>. Scientists
report their results using the (10), a
<u>scale of measurement</u> that goes from
zero for the weakest quake, up to 9 for
the very strongest.

■ SPELL WELL

Divide and Conquer Study these
long words syllable by syllable.
Then cover the words and write them.

11. earth • quake

12. seis • mo • graph

pupil
iris
retina
optic nerve
lens
eardrum
ear canal
outer ear
middle ear
inner ear

The Eyes and Ears

Our eyes and ears provide us with two important senses—seeing and hearing. The list words tell about the parts that make up our eyes and ears. Add other related words. Use your Spelling Dictionary for help.

■ GETTING AT MEANING

Labeling Diagrams   Read the paragraphs describing the parts of the eye and the parts of the ear. Write the list word that identifies each numbered part in the diagram.

The Eyes   We can see only certain parts of the eye: the white of the eye and the colored part called the **iris.** The iris has an opening in the middle called the **pupil,** which controls the amount of light that enters the eye. Right behind the iris is the **lens.** The lens works to make sure that the eye gets a sharp picture. The **retina** is the eye's "back wall." The retina changes the light coming in into electric signals. Then the **optic nerve** carries the electric signals to the brain.

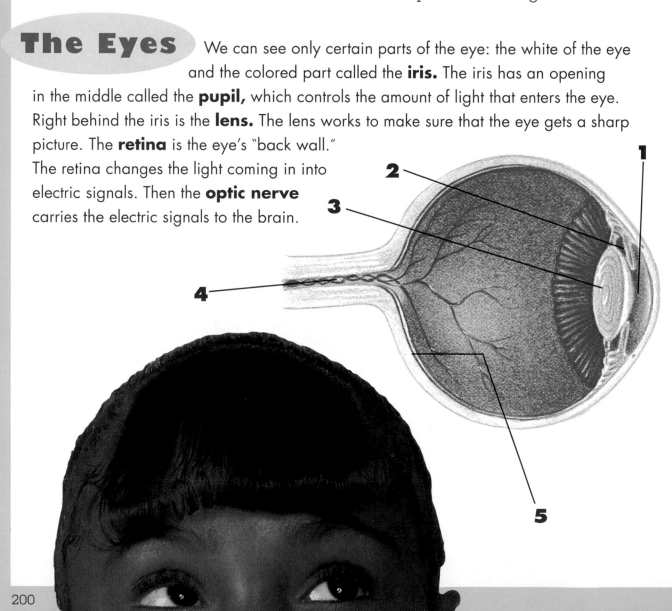

The Ears

Ears are the sense organs that let us hear. The part of the ear on the outside of the head is part of the **outer ear.** The other part of the outer ear is the **ear canal.** This little "tunnel" leads from the outer ear to the **eardrum,** which separates the outer ear from the **middle ear.** Sound waves make the eardrum vibrate. These vibrations move through the middle ear to the inner ear. The middle ear has three tiny bones that link the eardrum to the **inner ear** deep inside the head. The inner ear is the part of the ear that sends messages to the brain. The brain then "hears" the sounds.

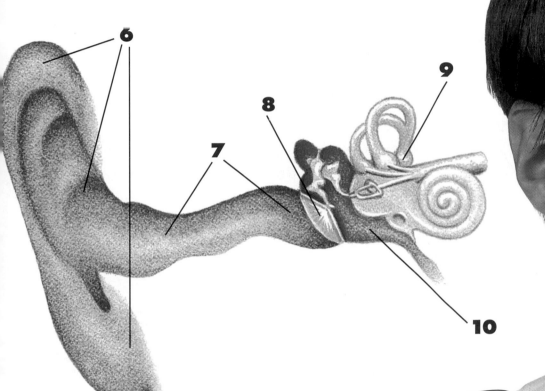

■ SPELL WELL

Pronouncing Words Carefully
Some words are not spelled the way they're pronounced. Exaggerate the sounds of the underlined letters to help you remember them. Write the words.

11. ret_ina

12. pup_il

All Eyes and Ears

The animal kingdom is full of amazing eyes and ears. Check out eagles, owls, cats, insects, or lobsters to learn about their eyes. To learn about animals that "get an earful," check out foxes, bats, dogs, or elephants. Share what you find.

accomplishments
artist
celebrated
humor
confidence
determination
disappointment
expert
strategy
successful

Hopes, Dreams, and Wishes

What goals and achievements do you dream about and wish for? The words in the list will help you understand attitudes and actions that help make dreams come true. Look up unfamiliar words in the Spelling Dictionary. Add your own words to the list.

■ GETTING AT MEANING

Using Context Clues   Write the list words below to complete a recipe for success.

determination

disappointment

accomplishments

humor

expert

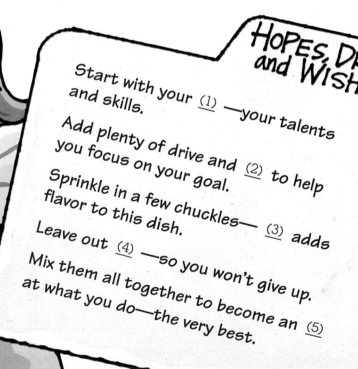

HOPES, DREAM and WISHES

Start with your (1) —your talents and skills.

Add plenty of drive and (2) to help you focus on your goal.

Sprinkle in a few chuckles— (3) adds flavor to this dish.

Leave out (4) —so you won't give up.

Mix them all together to become an (5) at what you do—the very best.

Using Synonyms Write the list word that is similar in meaning to each group of words below.

successful   celebrated   strategy   artist   confidence

(6)
painter, musician, sculptor

(7)
famous, well-known

(8)
method, plan

(9)
self-trust, self-belief

(10)
triumphant, fortunate, well-off

■ SPELL WELL

Double Trouble Double letters can cause spelling problems. Write the words below. Underline the double letters in each word to help you remember them.

11. successful

12. accomplishments

13. disappointment

Did You Know?

Not all dreams come true overnight. Inventors Wilbur and Orville Wright experimented for about seven years before their first successful airplane flight!

Many Ways of Learning

How do we learn new things? We learn in many different ways. The list words name just a few. Use the Spelling Dictionary to look up unknown words. Add your own words.

assignments
collections
counselor
demonstrations
interview
experiment
exhibit
research
librarian
brainstorm

■ GETTING AT MEANING

Labeling Illustrations   Write the list word that identifies each picture.

interview

exhibit

experiment

brainstorm

assignments

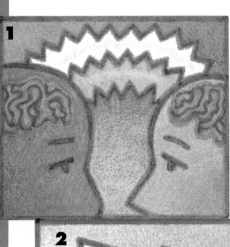

Completing Word Webs   Use the following list words to finish the word webs.

librarian   demonstrations   counselor   research   collections

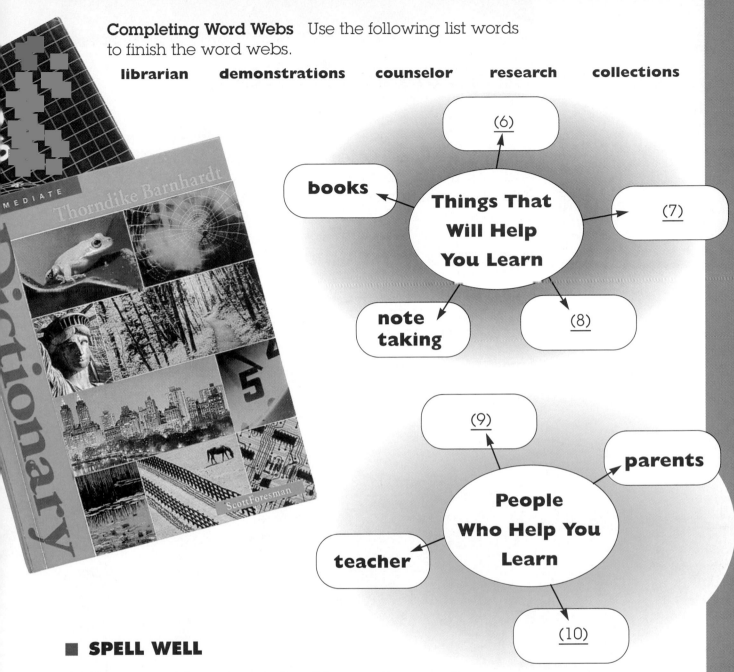

books

Things That Will Help You Learn

(6)

(7)

note taking

(8)

(9)

People Who Help You Learn

parents

teacher

(10)

■ SPELL WELL

Pronouncing Words Carefully   We sometimes spell words wrong because we say them wrong. Say each word carefully. Be sure to pronounce the sound of each underlined letter. Write each word.

11. experiment

12. counselor

Create the Perfect Learning Environment

Suppose you could create the perfect place where you could learn everything you wanted to know. Where would it be? What would it look like? What would you have there? Who would you have there? Draw or write a description of your "perfect learning place."

family
parents
children
home
shared
chores
love
childhood
memories
scrapbook

How Families Matter

What makes families special? Read the list of words, and look up unknown words in the Spelling Dictionary. Add your own family words to the list.

■ GETTING AT MEANING

Labeling Photographs   Everyone's family is different. Using what you know about families, write the list word that describes each photograph in John's scrapbook.

home   **family**   **chores**

parents   **children**

Using Context Clues Use these list words to complete the note that John's parents wrote to him in the front of his scrapbook.

love   shared

memories   scrapbook

childhood

Dear John,

We can't believe that you are nine years old already! Your (6) is going so quickly! For your birthday we would like you to have this (7). It is full of photos, and it holds (8) of many happy times we have (9) together. Happy 9th birthday! We (10) you!

Mom and Dad

Conduct Interviews

Interview the older members of your family. Ask them to tell you about their early memories of childhood. Take notes as they speak. Share these memories with the class.

■ SPELL WELL

Related Words
Write the two list words that are related in spelling and meaning to *child*.

11. ___

12. ___

cafeteria
concert
curtains
furniture
office
library
orchestra
skateboarding
spider web
water fountain

Your Own Universe

The words in the list name just ten of the thousands of things that are part of your universe. Add your own words. Use the Spelling Dictionary if you need help.

■ GETTING AT MEANING

Context Clues   School is a big part of your universe. Look at the bulletin board notices from Maple School. Complete them with list words.

THANK YOU, P.T.A. PARENTS!

Thanks to a generous gift from the P.T.A., students will not go thirsty during recess. Take a sip from the new (1) on the playground.

You're Invited!

Enjoy an evening of music. The band and the (2) will have a combined (3) on Saturday, May 22, at 7:30 P.M.

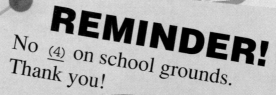

REMINDER!

No (4) on school grounds. Thank you!

HELP WANTED!

We still need help with the fourth-grade play, *Charlotte's Web*. These jobs are still open.

Stage Crew: Responsible for opening and closing the (5) between acts.

Set Design: Responsible for building a (6) for Charlotte the spider.

FOR SALE

Used art table $10.00
File Cabinets $15.00
Money from the sale of the (7) will be used to buy new books for the (8).

$10.⁰⁰ $15.⁰⁰

HOT DOG HEAVEN

The Student Council will be selling hot dog lunches every Wednesday. Tickets are $1.75 each and may be purchased in the principal's (9) before school or in the (10) during the lunch hour.

■ SPELL WELL

Pronouncing for Spelling Some words are not spelled the way they're pronounced. Exaggerate the sounds of the underlined letters in each word below. Then write the words.

11. or<u>ch</u>estra

12. furni<u>t</u>ure

home

music

Take a Look at Your Universe

School is only one part of your universe. Create word webs to show other parts of it—home, sports, hobbies, fashion, and so on. Share your webs with friends or display them on a bulletin board.

nature

sports

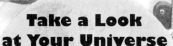

fashion

cathedral
Chartres
church
temple
Parthenon
marble
jewels
tomb
Taj Mahal
honor

Looking at the World in New Ways

Imagine that you are at the Parthenon, the Cathedral of Notre Dame, or the Taj Mahal. What would you notice about it? The list words tell about these three monuments. Add words about other world-famous buildings. Use your Spelling Dictionary for help.

■ GETTING AT MEANING

Using Photographs Complete the caption under each postcard. Use the words in the brick.

The (1) is in Athens, Greece. The ancient Greeks built this beautiful (2) to honor Athena, the goddess of wisdom. The Greeks built the entire structure of white (3). Inside stood a huge gold-and-ivory statue of Athena.

temple   marble
Parthenon

210

cathedral Chartres
church   jewels

The city of (4) in France is world famous for its (5), called the Cathedral of Notre Dame. The great (6) has more than 100 stained-glass windows so richly colored that they shine like (7).

tomb   honor
Taj Mahal

The (8) is in Agra, India. The Indian ruler Shah Jahan had this beautiful (9) built in the mid-1600s. It was constructed in (10) of his wife, Mumtaz Mahal. It has a domed roof and four prayer towers.

■ SPELL WELL

Capital Letters Three of your list words are proper nouns. Write them. Remember to capitalize the words.

11. ___

12. ___

13. ___

Design a Monument

The Parthenon was erected to honor Athena. Farmers in Enterprise, Alabama, erected a monument to the boll weevil in 1919. By destroying their crops, the insect forced them to grow new and different crops. As a result, the farmers became richer. Think of someone you'd like to design a monument to honor. Draw the monument and write an inscription.

211

Tales of Courage

Many situations call for courage. The words in the list bring to mind some sounds, sights, and feelings of such situations. Add some of your own words of courage.

■ GETTING AT MEANING

Using Context Clues Use the list words at the right to complete the phone call.

siren
pressure
emergency
panic
recover

Hi, Aunt Betty! Guess what?

I'm a heroine, but I hardly remember what happened! When I saw Gram fall on the stairs and hit her head, I knew it was an (1). I managed not to (2). I ran to the phone and dialed 911. Giving my name and address helped me (3) my control. But until I heard the (4) and saw the paramedics pull up in the fire truck, I really felt the (5). I couldn't do anything for Gram—just wait and hold her hand. Anyhow, the doctor said I saved her life. And our newspaper gave me a commendation. Say hello to Uncle Jack.

Bye for now!

More Context Clues Complete the paragraph with these list words. The underlined words may help you.

debris   compassionate   extraordinary   tremendous   devastate

A powerful earthquake can <u>destroy</u>, or (6), a city. The <u>awesome</u>, (7) force of the earth moving can topple buildings. <u>Building materials,</u> <u>crushed automobiles, broken pipes,</u> and other (8) can block the streets. At times like this, <u>ordinary</u> citizens show (9) courage to help their neighbors. And <u>concerned</u> people from all over the country show their (10) nature by sending food, clothing, and money to aid the victims of an earthquake.

■ SPELL WELL

Divide and Conquer Study the words below syllable by syllable. Then cover them and write them.

11. com • pas • sion • ate

12. ex • traor • di • nar • y

Did You Know?

Courage comes from a Latin word that means "heart."

operation key
number keys
display
memory recall
memory plus
memory minus
key sequence
error
clear key
equals key

The Calculator

Do you, your parents, or your friends use calculators? The words in the list tell all about these small, remarkable machines. Add your own words. Use the Spelling Dictionary for help.

■ GETTING AT MEANING

Understanding a Calculator Read the paragraphs below. Then write list words to complete the sentences.

The **number keys** and each **operation key** are used to give information to the calculator. The order in which you press the keys is the **key sequence.** The answer to the problem appears in the **display** after you press the **equals key.**

Press the **clear key** once if you make a mistake entering numbers. An "E" will appear in the display if you make an **error** like trying to divide by zero.

Marta wanted to add the number of muffins she sold on Monday and Tuesday. She pressed the (1) 3 and 5, and the number 35 appeared in the (2). She pressed the "+" (3) before she entered 27. When 24 appeared in the display, she realized that she had pressed the 4 by mistake. She pressed the (4) once and then entered the correct numbers. The answer appeared after she pressed the (5). 35 ⊞ 27 ⊟ is the (6) Marta entered to solve her problem. If the answer to her problem had been greater than eight digits long, or she had tried to divide by zero, an "E" in the display would have told her that she had made an (7).

214

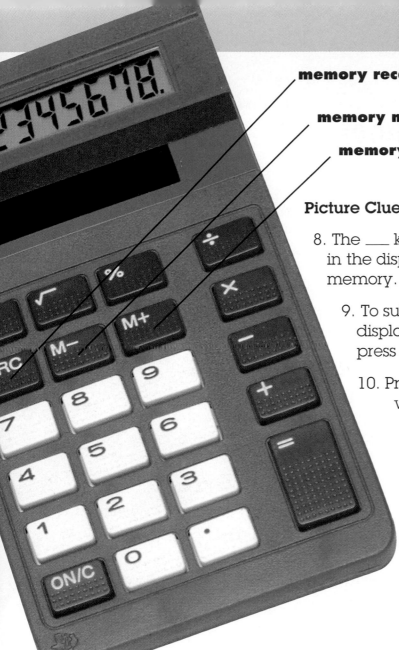

memory recall

memory minus

memory plus

Picture Clues Complete the sentences below.

8. The ___ key adds the number shown in the display to what is in the memory.

9. To subtract the number in the display from the memory, press the ___ key.

10. Press the ___ key, and the display will show what is in the memory.

■ SPELL WELL

Pronouncing Words Correctly We sometimes spell words wrong because we say them wrong. Write each word below. Then say each word. Be sure to pronounce the sound of the underlined letter.

11. mem<u>o</u>ry plus

12. mem<u>o</u>ry minus

13. mem<u>o</u>ry recall

Did You Know?

Estimation is an important math skill. You should estimate the answer to a problem when you use a calculator. If your answer isn't close to your estimate, you may have entered some numbers incorrectly.

length
width
height
weight
capacity
volume
area
perimeter
distance
temperature

Measurement

How would you describe the size and shape of a soccer field? Words of measurement, like the ones in the word list, help you describe places or objects.

■ GETTING AT MEANING

Context Clues Complete each sentence with the correct list word from those given in parentheses.

1. In youth soccer, the field is usually 100 yards in length and 50 yards in _____. **(width, length)**

2. The _____ of the field is divided by a halfway line. **(width, length)**

3. The _____ from one goal to the other is 100 yards. **(distance, area)**

4. The entire _____ of the field covers about 5,000 square yards. **(distance, area)**

5. White lines are drawn around the _____ of the field. **(perimeter, volume)**

6. Modern soccer shoes are light in _____ . **(height, weight)**

7. In soccer, the _____ and weight of a player are not as important as the player's speed and fitness. **(height, width)**

8. Soccer can be played outside whether the _____ is warm or cool. **(volume, temperature)**

Understanding Measurements Study the figure to the right. Complete each sentence with the correct list word.

9. To measure volume, multiply length x width x height. The ___ of the box is 27 cubic feet.

10. When the box is filled to its ___ it holds about ten soccer balls.

3 ft.

volume

capacity

3 ft.

3 ft.

SPELL WELL

Pronouncing Words Correctly We sometimes spell words wrong because we say them wrong. Write each word below. Then say each word. Be sure to pronounce the sound of the underlined letter.

11. temperature

12. width

Measure Up

With a partner, measure the size of your classroom. Measure to the nearest foot. On a separate sheet of paper, write your measurements on a chart like the one below. Assume the height is 9 feet.

length: _____ feet

width: _____ feet

height: __9__ feet

area (length x width): _____ square feet

volume (length x width x height): _____ cubic feet

Division

family of facts
grouping
number sentence
divide
dividend
divisor
division
quotient
remainder
divisible

Division is one of the four basic math operations. Read the list of words that talk about division and add your own words. Look up unfamiliar words in the Spelling Dictionary.

■ GETTING AT MEANING

Understanding Math Terms When you have 12 tennis balls and want to put them into groups of 3, you **divide** to find the number of groups you can make. You may show the **division** problem in two ways.

$$3\overline{)12}^{\,4}$$

$$\text{divisor}\overline{)\text{dividend}}^{\,\text{quotient}}$$

$$12 \div 3 = 4 \qquad \text{dividend} \div \text{divisor} = \text{quotient}$$

A **family of facts** can be used to represent the groupings of the tennis balls. Each **number sentence** in a family of facts tells about the **grouping.** Two of the number sentences show related multiplication facts and two of the number sentences show the related division facts.

Write the list word that describes each item.

A number is **divisible** by another if it can be divided by that number with no remainder. When a number cannot be divided exactly by another number, the number left over is called a **remainder.**

Look at the examples below. Complete the sentences with list words.

$$2 \overline{\smash{)}8} \quad \overset{4}{}$$

$$2 \overline{\smash{)}5} \quad \overset{2R1}{}$$

7. Eight is ___ by two.

8. One is the ___ in the second problem.

9. When you ___ eight by two, the quotient is four.

10. The symbol ÷ represents the operation of ___ .

■ SPELL WELL

Problem Parts Say the words below. Notice that the last syllables of the two words sound alike but are spelled differently. Write each word and underline the last two letters.

11. divis<u>or</u>

12. remaind<u>er</u>

Did You Know?
Division is repeated subtraction. To find how many groups of 3 are in 12 you can subtract 3 from 12 until your answer is zero. You can subtract 4 times, so there are 4 groups of 3 in 12.

Geometry

angle
vertex
endpoint
intersecting
line
parallel
point
ray
segment
perpendicular

Geometry is the branch of mathematics that studies and measures lines, angles, and shapes. The words in the list will tell you about geometry. Look up unknown words in the Spelling Dictionary. Add more words.

■ GETTING AT MEANING

Picture Clues Use the illustrations to help you write the list words that complete the sentences.

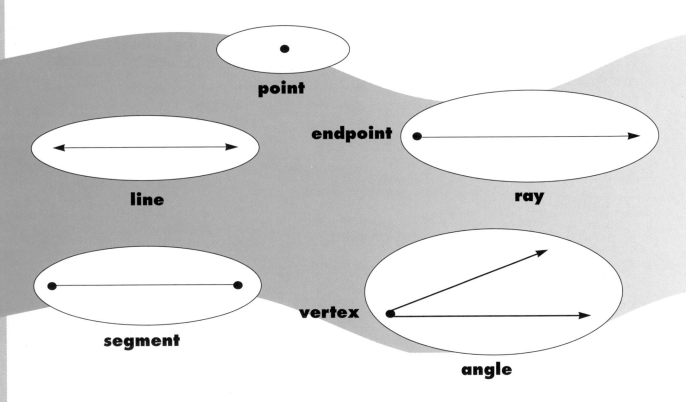

point

line

endpoint

ray

segment

vertex

angle

A (1) continues without end in both directions.

A (2) is part of a line. It has two endpoints.

A (3) is part of a line that has one (4) and goes on and on in one direction.

An (5) is formed by two rays with the same endpoint. The endpoint is its (6).

The sharpened end of your pencil could be thought of as a (7).

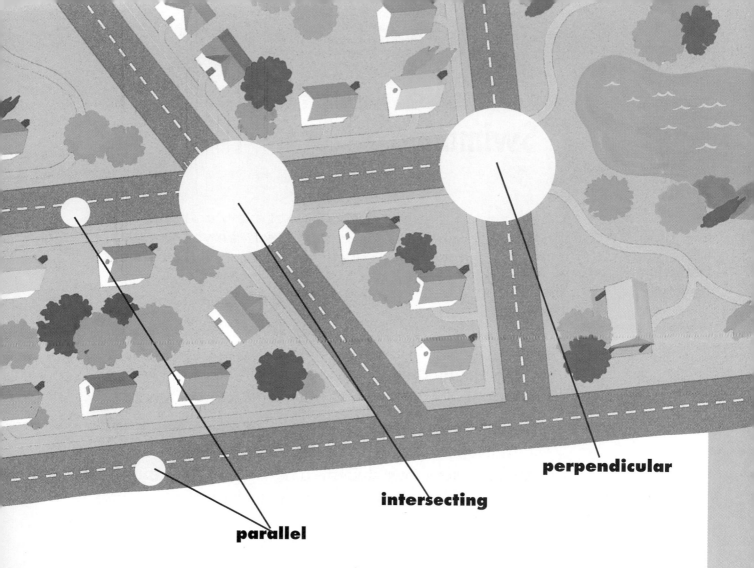

perpendicular

intersecting

parallel

Sometimes lines meet, or intersect. Two lines that cross each other at one point are __(8)__ lines.

Lines that do not meet and remain the same distance apart are called __(9)__ lines.

Intersecting lines that form square corners are called __(10)__ lines.

■ SPELL WELL

Divide and Conquer Long words are easier to spell when they are divided into syllables. Say the syllables in each word. Then write the words.

11. par • al • lel

12. in • ter • sect • ing

Did You Know?

The word *geometry* comes from two ancient Greek words that mean "to measure" and "earth." The ancient Egyptians used geometry to figure out the boundaries of their farms every year after the Nile River's flooding washed away or covered landmarks!

kicks
stroke
breathe
floats
treads
dive
dog paddle
backstroke
butterfly
freestyle

Swimming

Swimming is a sport that people of every age enjoy. What swimming skills do you have? Which are you working on? Add your own words about swimming to the list. Check unknown words in the Spelling Dictionary.

■ GETTING AT MEANING

Using Picture Clues Look at the illustration. Complete the sentences using list words.

treads   floats   stroke   kicks   breathe   dog paddle

Jamal is practicing (1), moving his legs and feet.

An instructor shows students a new (2) with his arms.

As Sal raises his arm, he brings his head out of the water to (3).

Mailee does the (4) . Just like a swimming dog, she keeps her head above water and moves her arms in circles.

Robert (5) quietly nearby.

Julie (6) water by moving her feet up and down as if she were walking underwater!

freestyle   dive   butterfly   backstroke

A good (7) will give Alma a super start.

Janice likes the (8) because it's easy to breathe swimming on her back.

Abe works on his (9) stroke. Moving both arms and legs together is tough!

Abe, Janice, and Alma compete in (10) meets. In these races swimmers are free to choose any swimming style.

7

8

9

■ **SPELL WELL**

Double Consonants The double consonants in the words below have only one sound. Remember to include both consonants when you write these words.

11. butterfly

12. dog paddle

Did You Know?
American swimmer Mark Spitz has won more Olympic medals in swimming events than any other swimmer. Spitz has eleven medals: nine gold, one silver, and one bronze. He won seven of his nine gold in 1972.

Basketball

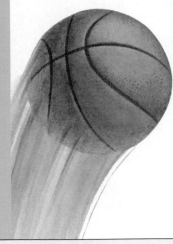

Basketball is a fun, fast, and entertaining game. Knowing the list words can help you enjoy the game more. Read the sentences below. Add your own related words to the list. Check unknown words in the Spelling Dictionary.

backboard	A **backboard** with a basket hangs over each end of the court.
rim	A basket is made of a net hung from a metal **rim**.
dribble	Players can **dribble** the ball on the floor past an opponent.
rebound	A **rebound** is a ball that bounces off the backboard or rim.
foul	Hitting or pushing another player is a **foul**.
free throw	A player shoots a **free throw** from behind a free throw line.
field goal	A player can score a **field goal** from anywhere on the court.
lay-up	A player close to the basket can shoot a **lay-up** to score.
jump shot	A player jumps straight up to shoot a **jump shot**.
slam-dunk	In a **slam-dunk,** a player slams the ball through the basket from above.

■ GETTING AT MEANING

Rhyming Clues   Complete these rhyming basketball cheers with list words.

Just (1) that basketball down the floor!
Make a (2) for two points more!

The ball bounces off the (3)
And rolls around the (4).
Get that (5) and put it in!

We'll all howl
If you (6).

Picture Clues What kind of shot is each player trying to make? Write the list word that matches each picture.

lay-up   **slam-dunk**   **jump shot**   **free throw**

■ SPELL WELL

Divide and Conquer It helps to study some words piece by piece. Study the words syllable by syllable. Then cover them and write them.

11. re • bound

12. drib • ble

Did You Know?
The first game of basketball was played with two peach baskets and a soccer ball.

Reporter

Newspapers and magazines employ thousands of reporters. Knowing the list words will help you understand a reporter's job. Use your Spelling Dictionary to learn the exact meaning of the words or to find other words to add to the list.

■ GETTING AT MEANING

Using Picture Clues Look at the illustration below to help you finish each sentence with the correct list word.

Newspapers and magazines contain many (1) about important events and people.

A (2) in big, dark print tells about the article in a few words.

Many articles have a (3) that gives the writer's name.

byline   headline   articles

W A L K E R ★ S C H O O L NEWS

Who's That Shaggy-Looking New Kid?

by Erin Gates

Ms. Maggie Sullivan's kindergarten had an unusual visitor last week. New student Eliot Greenwald's dog Dexter decided to follow him to schoo. Dexter ran behind the school bus all the way to Walker S Then he wouldn't stay outs on the playground. Ms. Su kindly allowed Dexter to in the kindergarten room Eliot until Mr. Greenwal dog and

Just Reuse It!

by Jason Nevin

Walker School students have joined the community effort to recycle. First of all, the entire student body has pledged to carry their lunches in reusable bags or lunch b

bring from home. A bins have been place cafeteria for collectir cartons, aluminum ca aluminum foil.

In addition, recyclir paper products have b in each class

Using Definitions Use the definitions to help you complete
the news article on the computer screen.

details   the facts of a news story that give more information
                 about the news
editors   people who often write the headlines and add
                 or rewrite the details of articles
sources   people, places, or written materials where reporters
                 and editors get information
lead   the opening paragraph of a news story
verify   to be sure that a fact is true
interview   to ask people about their activities or opinions
deadline   latest time by which articles must be finished

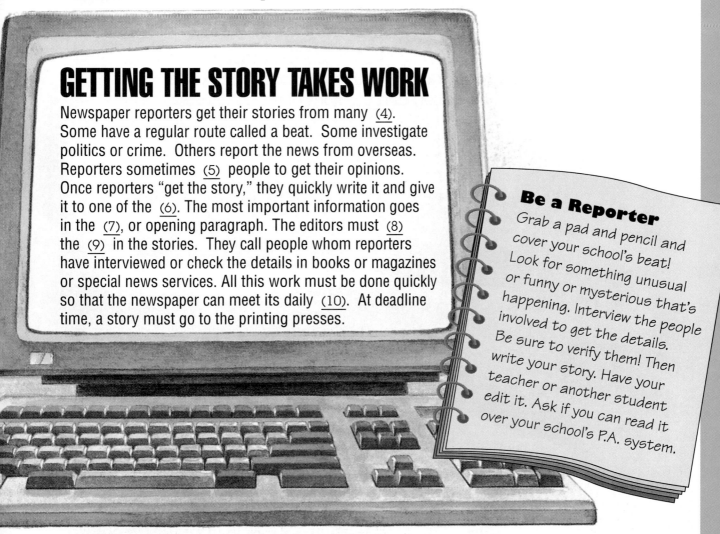

GETTING THE STORY TAKES WORK

Newspaper reporters get their stories from many (4).
Some have a regular route called a beat. Some investigate
politics or crime. Others report the news from overseas.
Reporters sometimes (5) people to get their opinions.
Once reporters "get the story," they quickly write it and give
it to one of the (6). The most important information goes
in the (7), or opening paragraph. The editors must (8)
the (9) in the stories. They call people whom reporters
have interviewed or check the details in books or magazines
or special news services. All this work must be done quickly
so that the newspaper can meet its daily (10). At deadline
time, a story must go to the printing presses.

Be a Reporter
Grab a pad and pencil and
cover your school's beat!
Look for something unusual
or funny or mysterious that's
happening. Interview the people
involved to get the details.
Be sure to verify them! Then
write your story. Have your
teacher or another student
edit it. Ask if you can read it
over your school's P.A. system.

■ SPELL WELL

Problem Parts Sometimes the vowel sounds you hear in a word
give you no clue as to its spelling. Pay special attention to the
underlined letters below. Then write the words.

11. articles   12. editors

Photography

camera
film
lens
shutter
focus
portrait
snapshot
develops
negative
print

Photographs surround us everywhere we go. In newspapers, in magazines, on billboards, and in brochures, photographs give us glimpses of people, places, and events. The list words tell about photography. Look up unfamiliar words in the Spelling Dictionary. Add your own related words.

■ GETTING AT MEANING

Diagrams Complete the sentences with words from the labels and captions of the diagram.

film

Load **film** here.

camera

shutter   **lens**

1. A ___ is a photographer's tool.
2. The glass ___ is the camera's "eye." You see your subject through the lens.
3. The lens also helps to ___ the picture so that it will appear sharp and clear.
4. The ___ opens to let light through the lens. The shutter works like an eyelid.
5. As the shutter clicks, a picture is recorded on the ___ inside.

Use the lens to **focus** the picture.

Analogies Use the words in dark type in the following sentences to finish the analogies.

- A special process **develops** the photographs on film.
- A **negative** photograph is developed first. A negative shows dark objects as light and light objects as dark.
- A **print** is made from each negative.
- A **portrait** is a photograph of a person's face.
- A **snapshot** is a photograph taken quickly with a small camera.

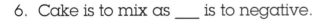

6. Cake is to mix as ___ is to negative.

7. Pattern is to sewing as ___ is to photograph.

8. Fingerprint is to finger as ___ is to face.

9. Sketch is to drawing as ___ is to photography.

10. Bakes is to cake mix as ___ is to film.

■ SPELL WELL

Divide and Conquer Some words are easier to study in smaller parts. Study each word syllable by syllable. Then cover the words and write them.

11. cam • er • a

12. neg • a • tive

Writer's Handbook

INTRODUCTION

You can speak and even read well without knowing how to spell. However, knowing how to spell well is a skill that every good writer needs. This handbook will help you with some of the other skills good writers need.

CONTENTS

The Writing Process

This section answers questions that you might ask about the five steps of the writing process: prewriting, drafting, revising, proofreading, and presenting.

1. PREWRITING

What should I do before I start to write?

Think about and plan your writing before you actually put sentences on paper. Time you spend prewriting is time well spent. Follow these steps and suggestions.

- **Select a topic** by listing ideas; by browsing through books, magazines, or newspapers for ideas; or by reviewing a personal journal or diary.
- **Determine your purpose and audience.** Your purpose may be to express feelings, describe or explain, give or get information, persuade, or tell a story. Your audience could be classmates, your aunt in Tennessee, or a friend.
- **Narrow your topic.** To focus on one specific idea, you might brainstorm questions about the topic, create a word web or cluster, or list and classify key words to explore.
- **Find details** about your topic from a variety of sources and make notes. Make personal observations, interview people, or look up information in books and magazines.
- **Organize your information** to best accomplish your purpose for writing. Use time order, spatial order, or order of importance.

2. DRAFTING

How do I actually begin to write the paper?

Take your writing materials and prewriting notes to a comfortable, well-lighted place. Plan on writing for at least twenty minutes. Try some of these strategies to get started.

- **Ignore** distractions like the telephone, and television.
- **Set a goal.** Decide how much that you *will* write now.
- **Review** your notes to find an idea for the first paragraph.
- **Start** with a direct, interesting sentence that states the main idea of the composition. Then let your ideas flow.
- **Push ahead** without worrying about perfect spelling, punctuation, or capitalization.

3. REVISING

How do I start revising?

Revising means to review what you've written and find ways to improve it. To begin, you might do the following:

- **Read your draft to yourself** to catch obvious errors such as unclear sentences.
- **Have a conference** with other students or your teacher.

What kinds of changes should I make?

You might do any or all of the following:

- **Add** words or ideas.
- **Take out** unnecessary words, sentences, or paragraphs.
- **Move** words, sentences, or paragraphs.
- **Substitute** words or ideas to improve your draft.

What kinds of questions should I ask myself?

The questions you'll ask depend on your purpose, audience, and type of writing. Here are some basic questions:

Ask yourself these questions!

- Did I say what I wanted to say?
- Are my details in the best possible order?
- Do I have a clear beginning, middle, and end?
- Does each paragraph have a topic sentence and stick to one idea?
- Can I take out extra words or choose better ones?
- Are all facts and figures correct?

≡	Make a capital.
/	Make a small letter.
∧	Add something.
ℓ	Take out something.
⊙	Add a period.
¶	New paragraph

4. PROOFREADING

Why should I proofread, and when and how should I do it?

Proofreading a paper means reading it carefully to find any mistakes in grammar, punctuation, and spelling. Proofread after you have completed revising your first draft to be sure that you have included all corrections. Proofread your final copy too.

Use proofreading symbols such as those at the right to clearly mark the corrections that are needed.

What kinds of things should I look for when I proofread?

Use the following questions as a proofreading checklist:

- Do subjects and verbs agree?
- Is each sentence correctly punctuated?
- Have I avoided fragments and run-on sentences?
- Did I capitalize the first word of each sentence?
- Did I capitalize proper nouns and adjectives?
- Did I check spelling and meaning of unfamiliar words?
- Is my handwriting clear and easy to read?

Check for these possible errors!

5. PRESENTING

How should I present my final work?

Publishers have certain guidelines for writers. Teachers do too. The guidelines will vary depending on the assignment.

Here are some suggestions for **regular assignments.**

- Write neatly on the front side only of white lined paper. If you're typing your final copy on a computer, use plain white paper.
- Put your name, the class, and the date in the top right-hand corner of the first page.
- Center the title of your composition on the second line.
- Leave a one-inch margin on the sides of the paper and leave the last line blank.

Special ways to present writing include displaying it on a bulletin board, sharing it in a young author's conference, binding it in an illustrated book, publishing it in a newspaper, and reading it aloud.

Taking Writing Tests

Writing under pressure can be difficult. Improve your performance on writing tests by following these guidelines.

GENERAL GUIDELINES FOR WRITING TESTS

- **Listen carefully to test instructions.** Note how much time you have. Listen for whether to use pen or pencil.
- **Read the assignment and identify the key words.** Be certain that you are writing the correct type of answer. Look for key words like these and know what they mean.

Categorize or *Classify:* Sort ideas or facts into groups.
Compare or *Contrast:* Point out similarities (compare) or differences (contrast).
Defend: Give evidence to show why a view is right.
Define: Tell what something is or means.
Describe: Create a word picture with details and examples.
Discuss: State your ideas about what something means.
Evaluate: Give your opinion, with support, on whether an idea is good or bad, right or wrong.
Explain: Make something clear by giving reasons, examples, or steps.
Summarize: State main points, or retell important parts of a story or article.

Look for these key words!

- **Plan how you'll use your time.** Allow time for prewriting activities, actual writing, and revision.
- **Write a strong opening** to catch your reader's attention. It should address the topic directly.
- **Use specific facts, details, or incidents** to develop your topic.
- **Write an interesting conclusion** that sums up your ideas or brings your story to a satisfying end.

WRITING A PERSONAL NARRATIVE

When you write about something you did or something that happened to you, you are writing a personal narrative.

KEY WORDS IN ASSIGNMENTS

- "Tell **what happened** to you. . ."
- "Write about how you **felt** when. . ."
- "What did you **do** when. . ."

SAMPLE ASSIGNMENTS

- Write about an experience you had when you were a child. Tell what you did and how you felt about your experience.
- Write about something you have done that makes you feel proud of yourself. Be sure to tell where you were when it happened and why it made you feel proud.

A PLAN OF ATTACK

- For both assignments, choose an occasion to write about that will be interesting and entertaining for the reader. If your topic seems too broad, narrow it.
- Jot down the details describing the event you are writing about. Think of strong verbs and colorful adjectives and adverbs to use to relate your story.
- Organize your story in **time order.** Make notes on what happened at the beginning, middle, and end of your experience. Then, when you write, use your time-order notes and list of details as a guide.

FOLLOW-UP CHECKLIST

- Did you tell your story in time order, from beginning to end?
- Did you tell both what happened and how you felt about what happened?
- Did you leave your readers with a clear sense of what kind of person you are?
- Is all capitalization, punctuation, and spelling correct?

WRITING A DESCRIPTION

Descriptive writing allows a reader to experience a scene by appealing to the senses of sight, sound, smell, touch, and taste.

KEY WORDS IN ASSIGNMENTS

- "**Tell** what you **see (**or **hear, smell, feel, taste).** . ."
- "**Describe** what it **looks (**or **sounds, smells, feels, tastes) like**. . ."

SAMPLE ASSIGNMENTS

- Thanksgiving is an American holiday celebrated with a traditional dinner. Describe a Thanksgiving dinner.
- Many people wear uniforms for their jobs. Visualize yourself wearing a uniform for a job you might enjoy. Describe what you are wearing.

A PLAN OF ATTACK

- Know exactly what you must write about. In the first assignment describe the sights, sounds, smells, and tastes of a Thanksgiving dinner. In the second, tell only about the uniform, not the job itself.
- Jot down specific details that tell about the color, shape, feel, sounds, smells, and tastes. Think of colorful, precise words. What comparisons can you use?
- Choose an order to use to describe details. You might use **time order** for the first assignment, describing the first course through dessert. Many descriptions use **spatial order.** You might describe the uniform from top to bottom.

FOLLOW-UP CHECKLIST

- Does the topic sentence state what you're describing in an interesting way?
- Do all the details focus on your topic?
- Do you follow the order you've decided upon?
- Does your ending tie your description together?
- Is all capitalization, punctuation, and spelling correct?

WRITING INSTRUCTIONS

Instructions tell a reader how to do or make something. Good instructions are written in step-by-step order.

KEY WORDS IN ASSIGNMENTS

- "**Explain how to. . .**"
- "**Describe the steps** you would take to. . ."
- "**Tell how you would**. . ."

SAMPLE ASSIGNMENTS

- Mmmm good! Explain how to make the best-ever ice cream sundae.
- Recycle it! Describe the steps you would take to make a book cover from a brown paper grocery bag.

A PLAN OF ATTACK

- Before you write, list the materials needed and the steps in the process.
- Organize the steps in time order, beginning with the first step and ending with the last.
- When you write, use time-order words like *first, next, then,* and *last* to show the correct order of steps.

FOLLOW-UP CHECKLIST

- Does the topic sentence state what the reader will learn to make or do?
- Are the steps arranged in correct order, and are all the steps there?
- Have you stuck to the topic—or have you put in extra information that you ought to get rid of?
- Are time-order words used to help the reader understand the order of the steps?
- Is all capitalization, punctuation, and spelling correct?

WRITING A FABLE

A fable is a very short story. The characters are usually animals, and the story states a moral, or lesson.

KEY WORDS IN ASSIGNMENTS

- "Write a modern **fable**. . ."
- "Choose a **moral,** or **lesson,** to **illustrate**. . ."

SAMPLE ASSIGNMENTS

- Choose a moral from this list. Then write a modern fable to illustrate it.

    Think how you will get out before you get in.
    Better safe than sorry.
    One good turn deserves another.

- We sometimes think of animals as having human traits—the fox as sly, the owl as wise, and so on. Choose several animals. What morals or lessons might they teach by their actions? Write an original fable that features one or more of these animals.

A PLAN OF ATTACK

- For either assignment, think carefully until you choose or decide upon the moral you will develop into a fable. Visualize animal characters that will teach the lesson well.
- Develop the plot of the fable. List what happens in the beginning, the middle, and the end. Organize the details of the plot in time order.
- Jot down possible dialogue that the animals might use to develop the story and to show character traits.
- End your fable with your moral.

FOLLOW-UP CHECKLIST

- Have you told your story in time order, with a beginning, a middle, and an ending?
- Are the animal characters well-chosen to teach the lesson you've chosen to illustrate?
- Does your fable really teach the moral that ends it?
- Is all capitalization, punctuation, and spelling correct?

WRITING COMPARISON/CONTRAST

Comparison tells a reader how two or more people or things are alike. Contrast tells how two or more things are different from each other.

KEY WORDS IN ASSIGNMENTS

- "**Compare** (or **contrast**) these two things (or people, places, ideas, and so on)."
- "Describe the **similarities** (or **differences**) between. . ."
- "How are . . . **alike?** How are . . .**different?**"

SAMPLE ASSIGNMENTS

- Like mother, like daughter. Like father, like son. Write a paragraph explaining how you and one of your family members are alike.
- What's that you're reading? Contrast the differences between reading for pleasure and reading a textbook.

A PLAN OF ATTACK

- Know the purpose of your paragraph. In the first assignment, you will tell about likenesses. In the second, you will tell about differences.
- List the likenesses or differences. Think of vivid, descriptive words to use for the comparison or contrast.
- Decide what order you will use to describe details. You may want to use **order of importance**—from the most important likeness or difference to the least important. If you are making a physical comparison or contrast, you may want to use **spatial order**—from head to toe, for example.

FOLLOW-UP CHECKLIST

- Does the topic sentence state what things are being compared or contrasted?
- Are the points of comparison or contrast arranged in the order you planned?
- Are words like *same* and *different* used to signal comparisons and contrasts?
- Is all capitalization, punctuation, and spelling correct?

WRITING A PERSUASIVE PARAGRAPH

When you write a persuasive paragraph, your goal is to make the reader agree with your opinion. To do this, you must support your opinion with good reasons.

KEY WORDS IN ASSIGNMENTS

- "**Persuade** your parents. . ."
- "Write a paragraph to **convince** your principal. . ."

SAMPLE ASSIGNMENTS

- You have been eyeing the iguana in the pet store for months, and you are sure it would be a perfect pet. Write a paragraph for your parents to persuade them to let you buy it.
- Your home town's baseball team is playing in a championship game in a nearby town. Convince your teacher to allow your class to watch the championship game, which will be played on a school day.

A PLAN OF ATTACK

- Clearly state the opinion you intend to support.
- List at least three good reasons to support your opinion.
- Organize your reasons in **order of importance.** Usually writers save their strongest reason for last.
- Jot down convincing words to use to persuade your reader.

FOLLOW-UP CHECKLIST

- Does the topic sentence clearly state your opinion?
- Are the supporting reasons organized from least important to most important?
- Are the reasons logical and sensible?
- Does the conclusion summarize the opinion and reasons?
- Is all capitalization, punctuation, and spelling correct?

Models and Guidelines

FRIENDLY LETTER FORM

Study the five parts of the friendly letter below. Notice the capitalization and punctuation in the greeting and the closing. If you know the person you are writing well, omit your address from the heading, but include the date.

> 21 Juneway Terrace
> Glenview, IL 60025
> February 13, 19—
>
> Dear Julie,
>
>   Thanks for inviting me to your Mardi Gras party! I'm really upset that I can't be there. We're going to be out of town that weekend. Take pictures so I can see all the costumes. Maybe we can get together over summer vacation.
>
>   Your friend,
>
>   Lizzie

Heading

Greeting

Body

Closing

Signature

State abbreviations:

AL (Alabama)	LA (Louisiana)	OH (Ohio)
AK (Alaska)	ME (Maine)	OK (Oklahoma)
AZ (Arizona)	MD (Maryland)	OR (Oregon)
AR (Arkansas)	MA (Massachusetts)	PA (Pennsylvania)
CA (California)	MI (Michigan)	RI (Rhode Island)
CO (Colorado)	MN (Minnesota)	SC (South Carolina)
CT (Connecticut)	MS (Mississippi)	SD (South Dakota)
DE (Delaware)	MO (Missouri)	TN (Tennessee)
FL (Florida)	MT (Montana)	TX (Texas)
GA (Georgia)	NE (Nebraska)	UT (Utah)
HI (Hawaii)	NV (Nevada)	VT (Vermont)
ID (Idaho)	NH (New Hampshire)	VA (Virginia)
IL (Illinois)	NJ (New Jersey)	WA (Washington)
IN (Indiana)	NM (New Mexico)	WV (West Virginia)
IA (Iowa)	NY (New York)	WI (Wisconsin)
KS (Kansas)	NC (North Carolina)	WY (Wyoming)
KY (Kentucky)	ND (North Dakota)	

CAPITALIZATION

Besides letter parts, capitalize the following:

Names, initials, and titles used with names:

Dr. Martin S. Alvarez, Jr.   Lieutenant Ann Jones

Proper adjectives:

Midwestern values   Canadian bacon   African art

The pronoun *I*:

Laura and I will interview the principal.

Names of cities, states, countries, continents:

Glenview   Utah   Mexico   Australia

Names of lakes, rivers, mountains, structures:

Fish Lake   Po River   Ural Mountain   Navy Pier

Names of streets and street abbreviations:

Fir Street   Locust Ave.   Crown Rd.   East Spruce

Days, months, holidays, special events:

Monday   Wed.   June   Dec.

Labor Day   Olympics

First, last, and all important words in movie, book, story, play, and TV show titles:

Tom Sawyer   The Cat in the Hat   "The Gold Bug"

First word in a sentence:

We'll try harder.

First word inside quotation marks:

Marcus said, "He's allergic to cats."

PUNCTUATION

Use **periods**

- to end declarative and imperative sentences:

  Susan likes sunflowers.   Please listen carefully.

- after most **abbreviations**:

  Ms.   Jan.   Sat.   Jr.   Ave.   P.M.   Dr.

Use **exclamation marks**

- after sentences that show strong feeling:

    We won the championship!

Use **question marks**

- after interrogative sentences:

    Where are the stamps?

Use **commas**

- between the day and the year in a date:

    April 15, 1994

- between the name of a city and state:

    Mendocino, California

- between series of words in a sentence:

    Mr. Lee grows tomatoes, peppers, and beans.

- before the word that joins a compound sentence:

    The sun is out, and the air is warm.

- to separate a noun after a direct address:

    Mom, where's my key?   It's on the desk, Amy.

- before quotation marks or inside the end quotation marks:

    Bob said, "I like soup."   "I prefer salads," said Zoe.

Use **quotation marks**

- around the exact words someone used when speaking:

    Vera asked, "What time is it?"

- around titles of stories, poems, and songs:

    "The Cat's in the Cradle"   "The Pit and the Pendulum"

Underline titles of books and movies:

    Anne of Green Gables   Aladdin

Use **apostrophes**

- to form the possessive of a noun:

    nurse's   brothers'   men's

- in contractions in place of dropped letters:

    wasn't (was not)   don't (do not)   I'm (I am)

Use **colons** between hours and minutes to indicate time:

    2:20   4:45

Spelling Dictionary

Parts of a Dictionary Entry

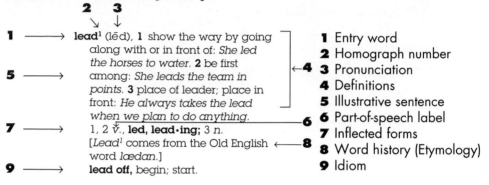

2   **3**

1 ⟶ **lead**[1] (lēd), **1** show the way by going along with or in front of: *She led the horses to water.* **2** be first among: *She leads the team in points.* **3** place of leader; place in front: *He always takes the lead when we plan to do anything.*

5 ⟶

⟵**4**

7 ⟶ 1, 2 *v.*, **led, lead·ing;** 3 *n.* [*Lead*[1] comes from the Old English word *lædan*.] ⟵**8**

6

9 ⟶ **lead off,** begin; start.

1 Entry word
2 Homograph number
3 Pronunciation
4 Definitions
5 Illustrative sentence
6 Part-of-speech label
7 Inflected forms
8 Word history (Etymology)
9 Idiom

Full Pronunciation Key

a	hat, cap	**i**	it, pin	**p**	paper, cup	**v**	very, save
ā	age, face	**ī**	ice, five	**r**	run, try	**w**	will, woman
ä	father, far			**s**	say, yes	**y**	young, yet
âr	care, hair	**j**	jam, enjoy	**sh**	she, rush	**z**	zero, breeze
		k	kind, seek	**t**	tell, it	**zh**	measure
b	bad, rob	**l**	land, coal	**th**	thin, both		seizure
ch	child, much	**m**	me, am	**ŦH**	then, smooth		
d	did, red	**n**	no, in			**ə**	represents:
		ng	long, bring	**u**	cup, butter		a in about
e	let, best			**u̇**	full, put		e in taken
ē	equal, be	**o**	hot, rock	**ü**	rule, move		i in pencil
ėr	term, learn	**ō**	open, go				o in lemon
		ȯ	all, saw				u in circus
f	fat, if	**ô**	order, store				
g	go, bag	**oi**	oil, voice				
h	he, how	**ou**	house, out				

Spellings of English Sounds*

Symbol	Spellings	Symbol	Spellings
a	at, plaid, half, laugh	ng	long, ink, handkerchief, tongue
ā	able, aid, say, age, eight, they, break, vein, gauge, crepe, beret	o	odd, honest
ä	father, ah, calm, heart, bazaar, yacht, sergeant	ō	open, oak, toe, own, home, oh, folk, though, bureau, sew, brooch, soul
âr	dare, aerial, fair, prayer, where, pear, their, they're	ȯ	all, author, awful, broad, bought, walk, taught, cough, Utah, Arkansas
b	bad, rabbit	ô	order, board, floor, tore
ch	child, watch, future, question	oi	oil, boy
d	did, add, filled	ou	out, owl, bough, hour
e	end, said, any, bread, says, heifer, leopard, friend, bury	p	pay, happy
		r	run, carry, wrong, rhythm
ē	equal, eat, eel, happy, cities, vehicle, ceiling, receive, key, these, believe, machine, liter, people	s	say, miss, cent, scent, dance, tense, sword, pizza, listen
		sh	she, machine, sure, ocean, special, tension, mission, nation
ėr	stern, earth, urge, first, word, journey	t	tell, button, two, Thomas, stopped, doubt, receipt, pizza
f	fat, effort, laugh, phrase		
g	go, egg, guest, ghost, league	th	thin
		ŦH	then, breathe
gz	example, exhaust	u	up, oven, trouble, does, flood
h	he, who, jai alai, Gila monster	ů	full, good, wolf, should
hw	wheat	ü	food, junior, rule, blue, who, move, threw, soup, through, shoe, two, fruit, lieutenant
i	it, England, ear, hymn, been, sieve, women, busy, build, weird		
ī	I, ice, lie, sky, type, rye, eye, island, high, eider, aisle, height, buy, coyote	v	very, have, of, Stephen
		w	will, quick
		y	yes, opinion
j	jam, gem, exaggerate, schedule, badger, bridge, soldier, large, allegiance	yü	use, few, cue, view, vacuum
k	coat, kind, back, echo, ache, quit, account, antique, excite, acquire	z	zero, has, buzz, scissors, xylophone
		zh	measure, garage, division
l	land, tell	ə	alone, complete, moment, authority, bargain, April, cautious, circus, pageant, physician, oxygen, dungeon, tortoise
m	me, common, climb, solemn, palm		
n	no, manner, knife, gnaw, pneumonia		

*Not all English spellings of these sounds are included in this list.

A

a·bil·i·ty (ə bil/ə tē), **1** power to do some special thing; skill: *He has great ability in making jewelry.* **2** special natural gift; talent: *Musical ability often shows itself early in life. n., pl.* **a·bil·i·ties.**

a·ble (ā/bəl), having enough power, skill, or means to do something; capable: *A cat is able to see in the dark. adj.*

ac·ci·dent (ak/sə dənt), something harmful or unlucky that happens: *automobile accidents. n., pl.* **ac·ci·dents.**

ac·com·plish·ment (ə kom/plish mənt), something that has been done with knowledge, skill, or ability; achievement: *The teachers were proud of their pupils' accomplishments. n., pl.* **ac·com·plish·ments.**

ac·tion (ak/shən), process of acting; doing something: *The quick action of the firemen saved the building from being burned down. n.*

a·do·be (ə dō/bē), **1** brick made of sun-dried clay. **2** building made of sun-dried clay. **3** built or made of adobe. 1,2 *n.,* 3 *adj.* [*Adobe* was borrowed from Spanish *adobe,* which came from Arabic *at-tūb,* meaning "the brick."]

ad·van·tage (ad van/tij), anything that is in one's favor, or is a benefit; a help in getting something desired: *Good health is always a great advantage. n.*

a·gain (ə gen/), another time; once more: *Come again to play. Say that again. adv.*

air mass (âr/ mas/), a large amount of air with the same temperature and humidity.

aisle (īl), passage between rows of seats in a hall, theater, school, etc.: *The teacher walked down the aisle between the rows of desks. n.*

a·lign (ə līn/), bring into line; arrange in a straight line: *The mechanic aligned the front wheels of our car. v.*

al·ley (al/ē), a narrow back street in a city or town. *n., pl.* **al·leys.**

al·low·ance (ə lou/əns), a sum of money given or set aside for expenses: *a household allowance for groceries of $50 a week. My weekly allowance is $1. n.*

al·mond blos·som (ä/mənd blos/əm), flower, especially of a plant that produces a peachlike fruit from a tree growing in Israel. *n.*

al·most (ȯl/mōst), very near to; all but; nearly: *It is almost ten o'clock. I almost missed the train. adv.*

a lot (ə lot/), **1** a great deal; much: *I feel a lot better.* **2** often, a great many: a great deal: *a lot of books.*

al·pha·bet (al/fə bet), the letters of a language arranged in their usual order, not as they are in words. *n.* [*Alphabet* can be traced back to the names of the first two letters of the Greek alphabet: *alpha* A and *beta* B.]

al·ways (ȯl/wāz or ȯl/wiz), at all times; every time: *Night always follows day. adv.*

a·mus·ing (ə myü/zing), causing laughter or smiles: *an amusing joke. adj.*

an·a·con·da (an/ə kon/də), a very large South American snake related to the boa that crushes its prey in its coils. Anacondas live in tropical forests and rivers and are the longest snakes in America, sometimes over 30 feet (9 meters). *n., pl.* **an·a·con·das.**

an·gel (ān/jəl), **1** messenger from God. **2** person as good or as lovely as an angel. **3** a replica used as a statue on a tree. *n.*

an·gle (ang/gəl), **1** the space between two lines or surfaces that meet. **2** the figure formed by two such lines or surfaces. *n.*

an·gry (ang/grē), feeling or showing anger: *I was angrier when you disobeyed me again. adj.,* **an·gri·er, an·gri·est.**

an·i·mal (an/ə məl), any living thing that is not a plant. Most animals can move about, feed upon other animals or plants, and have a nervous system. A dog, a bird, a fish, a snake, a fly, and a worm are animals. *n., pl.* **an·i·mals.**

adobe (definition 3)
an **adobe** village

almond blossom
The **almond blossom** is the national flower of Israel.

an·nounce (ə nouns′), give public or formal notice of: *The teacher announced that there would be no school tomorrow. v.,* **an·nounced, an·nounc·ing.**

an·nounce·ment (ə nouns′mənt), what is announced or made known: *The principal made two announcements. The announcement was published in the newspapers. n.*

an·oth·er (ə nuŦH′ər), **1** one more: *Have another glass of milk (adj.), I ate a candy bar and then asked for another (pron.).* **2** a different: *Show me another hat.* **1,2** *adj.,* **1** *pron.*

an·ten·na (an ten′ə), one of the long, slender feelers on the head of an insect, scorpion, lobster, etc. *The antennas of the grasshopper can be long or short. n., pl.* **an·ten·nae** (an ten′ē) or **an·ten·nas.**

an·y·way (en′ē wā), in any case; at least: *I am coming anyway, no matter what you say. adv.*

an·y·where (en′ē hwer), in, at, or to any place: *I'll meet you anywhere you say. adv.*

a·pol·o·gize (ə pol′ə jīz), make an apology; say one is sorry; offer an excuse: *I apologized for being late.* *v.* **a·pol·o·gized, a·pol·o·giz·ing.**

a·pos·tro·phe (ə pos′trə fē), sign (') used: **1** to show the omission of one or more letters in contractions. **2** to show the possessive forms of nouns or indefinite pronouns. **3** to form plurals of letters and numbers. *n.*

ap·pear·ance (ə pir′əns), outward look: *a pleasing appearance. n.*

ap·point·ment (ə point′mənt), meeting with someone at a certain time and place; engagement: *an appointment to see the doctor at four o'clock. n.*

ap·pre·ci·ate (ə prē′shē āt), think highly of; recognize the worth or quality of; value; enjoy: *Almost everyone appreciates good food. v.* **ap·pre·ci·at·ed, ap·pre·ci·at·ing.**

A·pril (ā′prəl), the fourth month of the year. It has 30 days. *n.*

are (är; *unstressed* ər), form of the verb **be** used with *we, you,* and *they* and any plural noun to indicate the present tense. *We are ready. You are next. They are waiting. v.*

ar·e·a (âr′ē ə), amount of surface; extent of surface: *The area of this floor is 600 square feet. n., pl.* **ar·e·as.**

ar·gue (är′gyü), discuss with someone who disagrees: *He argued with his sister about who should wash the dishes. v.* **ar·gued, ar·gu·ing.**

ar·rive (ə rīv′), come to; reach: *You should arrive at school before nine o'clock. v.* **ar·rived, ar·riv·ing.**

ar·thri·tis (är thrī′tis), inflammation of a joint or joints of the body. *n.*

ar·ti·cle (är′tə kəl), a written composition on a special subject, complete in itself, but forming part of a magazine, newspaper, or book: *This newspaper has a good article on gardening. n., pl.* **ar·ti·cles.**

art·ist (är′tist), person who is skilled in any of the fine arts, such as sculpture, music, or literature. *n.*

ash·es (ash′iz), what remains of a thing after it has thoroughly burned: *Ashes have to be removed from the fireplace to make room for more wood. n. pl.*

ask (ask), try to find out by words; inquire: *Why don't you ask? She asked about our health. Ask the way. v.*

antenna

Snails have slender **antennae.**

a	hat	ī	ice	u̇	put	ə *stands for*	
ā	age	o	not	ü	rule	a	in about
ä	far, calm	ō	open	ch	child	e	in taken
âr	care	ȯ	saw	ng	long	i	in pencil
e	let	ô	order	sh	she	o	in lemon
ē	equal	oi	oil	th	thin	u	in circus
ėr	term	ou	out	ŦH	then		
i	it	u	cup	zh	measure		

astronaut

An **astronaut** is trained to travel in space.

as·sign (ə sīn′), **1** appoint (to a post or duty): *We were assigned to decorate the room for the party.* **2** name definitely; fix; set: *The judge assigned a day for the trial.* v.

as·sign·ment (ə sīn′mənt), something assigned, especially a piece of work to be done: *Today's assignment in arithmetic consists of ten examples. n., pl.* **as·sign·ments.**

as·tro·naut (as′trə nȯt), pilot or member of the crew of a spacecraft. *n.*

At·lan·tic O·cean (at lan′tik ō′shən), ocean east of North and South America, west of Europe and Africa.

at·tack (ə tak′), **1** use force or weapons against; set upon to hurt; begin fighting: *The dog attacked the cat. The enemy attacked at dawn.* **2** act harmfully on: *Locusts attacked the crops. v.*

Au·gust (ȯ′gəst), the eighth month of the year. It has 31 days. *n.*

aunt (ant), **1** sister of one's father or mother. **2** wife of one's uncle. *My aunt's name is Sarah. n.*

au·to·graph (ȯ′tə graf), **1** a person's signature: *Many people collect the autographs of celebrities.* **2** write one's name in or on: *The movie star autographed my program.* **1** *n.,* **2** *v.*

Ave. or **ave.,** Avenue; avenue.

a·while (ə hwīl′), for a short time: *Stay awhile. adv.*

barometer

A **barometer** predicts changes in weather.

B

ba·by (bā′bē), **1** child too young to walk or speak; infant: *The babies' mothers took them to the park.* **2** the youngest of a family or group. *n., pl.* **ba·bies.**

back·board (bak′bôrd′), (in basketball) the upright, rectangular surface of wood, glass, or plastic, to which the basket is fastened. *n.*

back·pack (bak′pak′), a pack, often supported by a frame, that is worn on the back by hikers and campers to carry food, clothes, and equipment. *n.*

back·stroke (bak′strōk′), a swimming stroke made by a swimmer lying on his back. *n.*

ba·con (bā′kən), salted and smoked meat from the back and sides of a hog. *n.* **bring home the bacon,** succeed; win; earn a living.

band (band), group of musicians performing together, especially on wind and percussion instruments: *The school band played several marches. n.*

bare·foot (bâr′fút′), without shoes and stockings on: *A barefoot child played in the puddles (adj.). If you go barefoot, watch out for broken glass (adv.). adj., adv.*

ba·rom·e·ter (bə rom′ə tər), instrument for measuring the pressure of air, used in determining height above sea level and in predicting probable changes in the weather. *n.*

bar·rel (bar′əl), container with a round, flat top and bottom and sides that curve out slightly. Barrels are usually made of boards held together by hoops. *n.*

base·ball (bās′bȯl′), **1** game played with bat and ball by two teams of nine players each, on a field with four bases. A player who touches all the bases, under the rules, scores a run. **2** ball used in this game. *n.*

bas·ket·ball (bas′kit bȯl′), **1** game played with a large, round ball by two teams of five players each. The players try to toss the ball through a ring into a net shaped like a basket but open at the bottom. **2** ball used in this game. *n.*

beach (bēch), an almost flat shore of sand or pebbles over which water washes when high. *n., pl.* **beach·es.**

beat (bēt), **1** stroke or blow made again and again: *the beat of a drum.* **2** get the better of; defeat; overcome: *Their team beat ours by a huge score.* **3** mix by stirring rapidly with a fork, spoon, or other utensil: *I helped make the cake by beating the eggs.* 1 *n.*, 2,3 *v.*, **beat, beat·en** (bēt'n) or **beat, beat·ing.**

beau·ti·ful (byü'tə fəl), very pleasing to see or hear; delighting the mind or senses. *adj.*

be·cause (bi kóz'), for the reason that; since: *Because we were late, we ran the whole way home. conj.*

beet (bēt), the thick, fleshy root of a garden plant. Red beets and their green leaves are eaten as vegetables. Sugar is made from white beets. *n.*

be·gin (bi gin'), do the first part; make a start: *begin on one's work. When shall we begin? Begin at the third chapter. v.*, **be·gan** (bi gan'), **be·gun** (bi gun'), **be·gin·ning.**

be·go·nia (bi gō'nyə), a tropical plant often grown for its large, richly colored leaves and waxy flowers. *n.*, *pl.* **be·go·nias.** [*The begonia was named after Michel Bégon, 1638-1710, a French patron of botany.*]

be·hav·ior (bi hā'vyər), manner of behaving; way of acting: *Her sullen behavior showed that she was angry. n.*

be·hind (bi hīnd'), **1** not on time; late: *The class is behind in its work.* **2** farther back: *The rest of the bikers are still behind. adv.*

be·lieve (bi lēv'), **1** think (somebody) tells the truth: *Her friends believe her.* **2** think; suppose: *I believe I will go. v.*, **be·lieved, be·liev·ing.**

bev·y (bev'ē), a small group or flock: *a bevy of quail. n.*, *pl.* **bev·ies.**

bib (bib), cloth worn under the chin, especially by babies and small children, to protect clothing during meals. *n.*

bi·cus·pid (bī kus'pid), a double-pointed tooth that tears and grinds food. Adult human beings have eight bicuspids. *n.*

bi·cy·cle (bī'sik'əl), a lightweight vehicle with two wheels, one behind the other, that support a metal frame on which there is a seat. The rider pushes two pedals and steers with handlebars. *n.*

big (big), great in amount or size; large: *a big room, a big book. Making automobiles is a big business. An elephant is a big animal. adj.* **big·ger, big·gest.**

blan·ket (blang'kit), a soft, heavy covering woven from wool, cotton, nylon, or other material, used to keep people or animals warm. *n.*

bleach·ers (blē'chərz), section of wooden or plastic benches for spectators at baseball or other outdoor events. Bleachers are not roofed, and are the lowest priced seats. *n. pl.*

bliss·ful (blis'fəl), very happy; joyful: *blissful memories of a summer vacation. adj.*

block (blok), space in a city or town enclosed by four streets; square. *n.*

bloom·ers (blü'mərz), loose trousers, gathered at the knee, formerly worn by women and girls for physical training: *In the old days girls wore bloomers when playing sports. n. pl.* [*Bloomers were named for Amelia J. Bloomer, 1818-1894, an American magazine publisher who popularized their use.*]

blub·ber (blub'ər), fat of whales and some other sea animals. The oil obtained from whale blubber was formerly burned in lamps. *n.*

bicycle
riding **bicycles** in the park

a	hat	**ī**	ice	**u̇**	put	**ə** *stands for*	
ā	age	**o**	not	**ü**	rule	**a**	in about
ä	far, calm	**ō**	open	**ch**	child	**e**	in taken
âr	care	**ȯ**	saw	**ng**	long	**i**	in pencil
e	let	**ô**	order	**sh**	she	**o**	in lemon
ē	equal	**oi**	oil	**th**	thin	**u**	in circus
ėr	term	**ou**	out	**ṯh**	then		
i	it	**u**	cup	**zh**	measure		

bridge
a **bridge** over the bay

broccoli
two stalks of **broccoli**

Blvd., boulevard.

bo·lo·gna (bə lō′nē), a large sausage usually made of beef, veal, and pork. *n., pl.* **bo·lo·gnas.** [*Bologna* was named for *Bologna*, Italy, where it was first made.]

boom (büm), a deep hollow sound like the roar of cannon or of big waves: *The big bell tolled with a loud boom. n.*

bor·row (bor′ō), get (something) from another person with the understanding that it must be returned: *I borrowed his book and promised to return it in a week. v.*

boss (bȯs), person who hires workers or watches over or directs them; foreman; manager: *It was the boss's decision to hire the new construction worker. n., pl.* **boss·es.**

bot·tle (bot′l), container for holding liquids, made of glass, plastic, etc. Bottles often have narrow necks fitted with caps or stoppers: *drink a bottle of milk. n.*

bow¹ (bou), **1** to stoop; bend: *The old man was bowed by age.* **2** submit; yield: *She bowed to her parents' wishes. v.*
bow out, withdraw.
take a bow, accept praise or applause for something done.

bow² (bō), **1** weapon for shooting arrows. A bow usually consists of a strip of flexible wood bent by a string. **2** a slender rod with horsehairs stretched on it, for playing a violin, cello, etc. *n.*

bow³ (bou), the forward part of a ship, boat, or aircraft. *n.*

boy (boi), a male child from birth to about eighteen. *n.*

brain·storm (brān′stôrm′), INFORMAL. a sudden idea or inspiration. *n.*

brake¹ (brāk), **1** anything used to slow or stop the motion of a wheel or vehicle by pressing or scraping or by rubbing against. **2** slow or stop by using a brake: *The driver braked the speeding car and it slid to a stop.* 1 *n.,* 2 *v.,* **braked, brak·ing.**

brake² (brāk), a thick growth of bushes; thicket. *n.*

break (brāk), **1** come apart or make come apart; smash: *The plate broke into pieces when it fell on the floor.* **2** fail to keep; act against: *to break a promise. People who break the law are punished. v.,* **broke, bro·ken, break·ing.**

breathe (brēᴛʜ), stop for breath; rest; allow to rest and breathe. *v.,* **breathed, breath·ing.**

breath·less (breth′lis), out of breath: *Running upstairs very fast made me breathless. adj.*

bridge (brij), something built over a river, road, railroad, or other obstacle, so that people, cars, trains, etc., can get across. *n.*

bright (brīt), lively or cheerful: *There was a bright smile on his face. adj.* —**bright′ly,** *adv.* —**bright′ness,** *n.*

bring (bring), come with or carry (a thing or person) from another place; take along to a place or person: *The bus brought us home. Bring me a clean plate. v.,* **brought, bring·ing.**

broad·leaf (brȯd′lēf′), of or about a type of tree with broad, flat leaves. An oak is a broadleaf tree. *adj.*

broc·co·li (brok′ə lē), vegetable with green branching stems and flower heads. It belongs to the cabbage family. *n., pl.* **broc·co·li.** [*Broccoli* comes from Italian *broccoli,* meaning "sprouts."]

broke (brōk), See **break.** *I broke my watch. v.*

bro·ken (brō′kən), separated into parts by a break; in pieces: *a broken leg, a broken cup. adj.*

brook (brůk), a small stream; creek. *n.*

broth·er (bruᴛʜ′ər), son of the same parents. A boy is a brother to the other children of his parents. *I knocked on my brother's door. n.*

brought (brȯt), See **bring.** *I brought my lunch yesterday. They were brought to school in a bus. v.*

bruise (brüz), injury to the body, caused by a fall or a blow, that breaks blood vessels without breaking the skin: *The bruise on my arm turned black and blue. n.*

bub·ble (bub/əl), **1** a thin, round film of liquid enclosing air or gas. The surface of boiling water is covered with bubbles. **2** plan or idea that looks good, but soon falls apart. *n.*

buf·fa·lo (buf/ə lō), the bison of North America. *n., pl.* **buf·fa·loes, buf·fa·los,** or **buf·fa·lo.**

build (bild), make by putting materials together; construct: *People build houses, bridges, and machines. Birds build nests. v.,* **built** (bilt), **build·ing.**

bunch (bunch), group of things of the same kind growing, fastened, placed, or thought of together: *a bunch of grapes, a bunch of flowers, a bunch of sheep. n., pl.* **bunch·es.**

bush (bush), a woody plant smaller than a tree, often with many separate branches starting from or near the ground. *n., pl.* **bush·es.**

bus·y (biz/ē), having plenty to do; working; active; not idle: *a busy person. adj.,* **bus·i·er, bus·i·est.**

busi·ness (biz/nis), thing that one is busy at; work; occupation: *A carpenter's business is building. n.*

butch·er (buch/ər), person who cuts up and sells meat. *n.*

but·ter·fly (but/ər flī/), **1** an insect with a slender body and two pairs of large, often brightly colored, overlapping wings. **2** a swimming stroke, a type of breast stroke, in which both arms are pulled upward out of the water and forward while the feet are kicking up and down. *n., pl.* **but·ter·flies.**

but·ton (but/n), **1** a round, flat piece of metal, bone, glass, or plastic, fastened on garments to hold them closed or to decorate them. **2** fasten the buttons of; close with buttons: *Button your coat.* 1 *n.,* 2 *v.*

by-line (bī/līn/), line at the beginning of a newspaper or magazine article giving the name of the writer. *n.*

C

cab·i·net (kab/ə nit), piece of furniture with shelves or drawers, used to hold articles for use or display: *a medicine cabinet, a filing cabinet for letters. We keep our very best dishes in the china cabinet. n.*

ca·ble (kā/bəl), an insulated bundle of wires which carries an electric current. *n.*

cac·tus (kak/təs), plant with a thick, fleshy stem that usually has spines but no leaves. Most cactuses grow in very hot, dry regions of America and often have brightly colored flowers. *n., pl.* **cac·tus·es, cac·ti** (kak/tī).

caf·e·ter·i·a (kaf/ə tir/ē ə), restaurant where people serve themselves. *n., pl.* **caf·e·ter·i·as.**

cam·er·a (kam/ər ə), machine for taking photographs or motion pictures. A camera lens focuses light rays through the dark inside part of the camera onto film which is sensitive to light. *n.*

Can·a·da (kan/ə də), country in the N part of North America, consisting of ten provinces and two territories and extending from the Atlantic to the Pacific. *Capital:* Ottawa. *n.*

ca·nal (kə nal/), waterway dug across land for ships or small boats to go through or to carry water to places that need it. *n.*

ca·noe (kə nü/), **1** a light boat pointed at both ends and moved with a paddle. **2** paddle a canoe; go in a canoe. 1 *n.,* 2 *v.,* **ca·noed, ca·noe·ing.**

butterfly (definition 1)
three colorful
butterflies

a	hat	ī	ice	u̇	put		ə *stands for*
ā	age	o	not	ü	rule	a	in about
ä	far, calm	ō	open	ch	child	e	in taken
âr	care	ȯ	saw	ng	long	i	in pencil
e	let	ô	order	sh	she	o	in lemon
ē	equal	oi	oil	th	thin	u	in circus
ėr	term	ou	out	ŦH	then		
i	it	u	cup	zh	measure		

catcher

a **catcher** kneeling

behind home plate

ca·pac·i·ty (kə pas′ə tē), amount of room or space inside; largest amount that can be held by a container. *n., pl.* **ca·pac·i·ties.**

care (kãr), **1** a troubled state of mind because of fear of what may happen; worry: *Few people are completely free from care.* **2** be concerned; feel interest. 1 *n.,* 2 *v.,* **cared, car·ing.**
take care of, watch over; be careful with: *Take care of your money.*

care·ful (kãr′fəl), showing care; done with thought or effort; exact; thorough: *Arithmetic requires careful work. adj.* —**care′ful·ly,** *adv.*

care·less (kãr′lis), not thinking what one says; not watching what one does; not careful: *I was careless and broke the cup. adj.*

car·i·bou (kar′ə bü), the North American reindeer. *n., pl.* **car·i·bous** or **car·i·bou.**

car·ni·vore (kär′nə vôr), any animal that feeds chiefly on flesh. Carnivores have large, strong teeth with sharp cutting edges. *n.*

cash (kash) money in the form of coins and bills. *n.*

cat (kat), a small, furry, flesh-eating mammal, often kept as a pet or for catching mice and rats: *The cat meowed for food. n.*

catch (kach), **1** grab or seize (something in flight): *Catch the ball with both hands.* **2** come upon suddenly; surprise; *Mother caught me just as I was hiding her birthday present. v.,* **caught, catch·ing.**

catch·er (kach′ər), a baseball player positioned behind the batter to catch the ball thrown by the pitcher. *n.*

ca·the·dral (kə thē′drəl), a large or important church. *n.*

cat·tle·ya or·chid (kat′lē ə ôr′kid), a tropical South American plant with showy flowers. [The *cattleya orchid* was named for William *Cattley,* died 1832, English patron of botany.]

caught (kot), See **catch.** *I caught the ball. v.*

cause (kóz), **1** person, thing, or event that makes something happen: *The flood was the cause of much damage.* **2** make happen; make do; bring about: *The fire caused much damage.* 1 *n.,* 2 *v.,* **caused, caus·ing.**

cel·e·brat·ed (sel′ə brā′tid), much talked about; famous; well-known: *a celebrated author. adj.*

cel·er·y (sel′ər ē), vegetable related to parsley, with long, crisp stalks. Celery is eaten either raw or cooked. *n.*

Cel·si·us (sel′sē əs), of, based on, or according to the Celsius scale; centigrade. *adj.* [The *Celsius* scale was named for Anders *Celsius,* 1701-1744, a Swedish astronomer who invented it in 1742.]

ce·ment (sə ment′), a fine, gray powder made by burning clay and limestone. Cement is used to make concrete and mortar. *n.*

cer·e·mo·ny (ser′ə mō′nē), a special act or set of acts to be done on special occasions such as weddings, funerals, graduations, or holidays: *The graduation ceremony was held in the gymnasium. n., pl.* **cer·e·mo·nies.**

cer·tain (sėrt′n) without a doubt; sure: *It is certain that 2 and 3 do not make 6. I am certain that these are the facts. adj.*

chalk·board (chok′bôrd′), a smooth, hard surface, used for writing or drawing on with crayon or chalk. *n.*

cham·pi·on (cham′pē ən), person, animal, or thing that wins first place in a game or contest: *He is the swimming champion of our school. n.*

change (chānj), **1** make or become different: *She changed the room by painting the walls green. The wind changed from east to west.* **2** change one's clothes; *After swimming we went to the cabin and changed. v.,* **changed, chang·ing.**

Cha·nu·kah (hä′nə kə), Hanukkah. *n.*

cattleya orchid

The **cattleya orchid** is

the national flower of

Costa Rica.

chap·ter (chap/tər), main division of a book or other writing, dealing with a particular part of the story or subject. *n.*

charge (chärj), **1** put down as a debt to be paid: *We charged the entire dinner, so the restaurant will send a bill for it.* **2** a task, a responsibility: *The charge of the baby was given to my sister.* 1 *v.*, **charged, charg·ing;** 2 *n.*

Char·tres (shär/trə), city in N France. Its Gothic cathedral is over 700 years old. *n.*

chase (chās), run or follow after to catch or kill: *The cat chased the mouse.* *v.*, **chased, chas·ing.**

check (chek), stop suddenly. *v.*

cheer·ful (chir/fəl), full of cheer; joyful; glad: *She is a smiling, cheerful girl.* *adj.*

child (chīld), **1** a young boy or girl: *games for children.* **2** son or daughter: *Parents love their children.* *n., pl.* **chil·dren** (chil/drən).

child·hood (chīld/hùd), time during which one is a child. *n.*

Chi·nese New Year (chī/nēz nü/ yir/), a yearly event that begins between the dates of January 21 and February 19. It lasts four days, and on the last day people dress as dragons.

choc·o·late (chȯk/lit or chȯk/ə lit), **1** candy made of chocolate. **2** made of or flavored with chocolate: *chocolate cake.* 1 *n.,* 2 *adj.*

chop (chop), cut by hitting with something sharp: *You can chop wood with an ax. We chopped down the dead tree.* *v.*, **chopped, chop·ping.**

chore (chôr), an odd job; small task: *Feeding the dog is my daily chore.* *n., pl.* **chores.**

Christ·mas (kris/məs), the yearly celebration of the birth of Christ; December 25. *n., pl.* **Christ·mas·es.**

church (chėrch), building for public Christian worship. *n.*

cin·na·mon (sin/ə mən), spice made from the dried inner bark of a small tree of the East Indies: *Put cinnamon into the apple cider and heat it up.* *n.*

cir·cus (sėr/kəs), a traveling show of acrobats, clowns, horses, riders, and wild animals. The performers who give the show and the performances they give are both called the circus. *n., pl.* **cir·cus·es.**

cit·i·zen (sit/ə zən), person who by birth or by choice is a member of a nation. A citizen owes loyalty to that nation and is given certain rights by it. *Many immigrants have become citizens of the United States.* *n.*

class (klas), group of students taught together: *The art class meets in room 202.* *n., pl.* **class·es.**

class·mate (klas/māt/), member of the same class in school. *n.*

class·room (klas/rüm/), room in which classes are held. *n.*

clat·ter (klat/ər), a confused noise like that of many plates being struck together: *The clatter in the cafeteria made it hard for us to hear one another talk.* *n.*

clear key (klir/ kē/), the computer key that enables the user to remove the number in the display window from the calculator's memory.

climb (klīm), **1** go up, especially by using the hands or feet, or both; ascend: *She climbed the stairs quickly.* **2** go in any direction, especially with the help of hands: *climb over a fence, climb down a ladder.* *v.*

cinnamon
different forms of the
spice **cinnamon**

a	hat	**ī**	ice	**u̇**	put	**ə** *stands for*	
ā	age	**o**	not	**ü**	rule	**a**	in about
ä	far, calm	**ō**	open	**ch**	child	**e**	in taken
âr	care	**ȯ**	saw	**ng**	long	**i**	in pencil
e	let	**ô**	order	**sh**	she	**o**	in lemon
ē	equal	**oi**	oil	**th**	thin	**u**	in circus
ėr	term	**ou**	out	**ŦH**	then		
i	it	**u**	cup	**zh**	measure		

collection
a baseball card
collection

compass
Compasses show
directions.

close¹ (klōz), bring together or move the parts of so as to leave no opening; shut: *Close the door. The sleepy child's eyes are closing. v.*, **closed, clos·ing.**

close² (klōs), intimate; dear: *We are close friends. adj.*, **clos·er, clos·est.**

clos·et (kloz/it), a small room for storing clothes or household supplies. *n.*

clothes (klōz or klōᴛʜz), coverings for a person's body: *I bought some new clothes for my trip. n. pl.*

cloud (kloud), **1** mass of tiny drops of water, water vapor, or ice particles floating in the air high above the earth. Clouds may be white, rounded heaps, streamers, or dark, almost black, masses. **2** mass of smoke or dust in the air. *n.*

coal (kōl), a black mineral that burns and gives off heat, composed mostly of carbon. It is formed from partly decayed vegetable matter under great pressure in the earth. Anthracite and bituminous coal are two kinds of coal. *n.*

col·lapse (kə laps/), fall in; shrink together suddenly: *Sticking a pin into the balloon made it collapse. v.*, **col·lapsed, col·laps·ing.**

col·lec·tion (kə lek/shən), group of things gathered from many places and belonging together: *Our library has large collections of books. n., pl.* **col·lec·tions.**

co·logne (kə lōn/), a fragrant liquid, not so strong as perfume. *n.*

col·o·ny (kol/ə nē), group of animals or plants of the same kind, living or growing together: *a colony of ants. Coral grows in colonies. n., pl.* **col·o·nies.**

col·or (kul/ər), any color except black, white, or gray; red, yellow, blue, or any combination of them. The color green is a mixture of yellow and blue. *n.*

comb (kōm), take out tangles with a comb. *v.*

come (kum), move toward: *Come this way. v.*, **came** (kām), **come, com·ing.**

com·mer·cial (kə mėr/shəl), **1** having to do with trade or business: *a store or other commercial establishment.* **2** an advertising message on radio or television, broadcast between or during programs. **1** *adj.,* **2** *n.*

com·mon (kom/ən), **1** from all; by all; to all; general: *By common consent of the class, she was chosen president.* **2** often met with; ordinary; usual. *adj.*

com·mute (kə myüt/), **1** travel regularly to and from work by train, bus, automobile, etc. **2** the distance or trip ordinarily traveled by a commuter: *a long commute, an easy commute.* **1** *v.,* **com·mut·ed, com·mut·ing;** **2** *n.*

com·pass (kum/pəs), instrument for showing directions, especially one consisting of a needle that points to the North Magnetic Pole. *n., pl.* **com·pass·es.**

com·pas·sion·ate (kəm pash/ə nit), wishing to help those that suffer; sympathetic; pitying. *adj.*

com·plete (kəm plēt/), **1** with all the parts; whole; entire: *We have a complete set of garden tools.* **2** make whole or entire; make up the full number or amount of: *I completed the set of dishes by buying the cups and saucers.* **1** *adj.,* **2** *v.,* **com·plet·ed, com·plet·ing.** —**com·plete/ly,** *adv.*

com·pose (kəm pōz/), **1** make up; form: *The ocean is composed of salt water.* **2** put together. To compose a story or poem is to construct it from words. To compose a piece of music is to invent the tune and write down the notes. *v.,* **com·posed, com·pos·ing.**

com·po·si·tion (kom/pə zish/ən), thing composed. A symphony, poem, a school exercise, or painting is a composition. *n.*

con·cert (kon/sərt), a musical performance in which several musicians or singers take part: *The school orchestra gave a concert last night. n.*

con·duct (kən dukt/), transmit; be a channel for: *Those pipes conduct steam to the radiators upstairs. v.*

con·fes·sion (kən fesh′ən), act of confessing; owning up; telling one's mistakes or sins. *n.*

con·fi·dence (kon′fə dəns), firm belief in oneself; self-confidence: *Years of work at school have given her great confidence. n.*

con·fuse (kən fyüz′), 1 throw into disorder; mix up; bewilder: *So many people talking to me at once confused me.* 2 be unable to tell apart; mistake (one thing or person for another): *People often confuse this girl with her twin sister. v.*, **con·fused, con·fus·ing.**

con·i·fer (kon′ə fər or kō′nə fər), plant that bears cones. The pine, fir, spruce, hemlock, and larch are conifers. *n., pl.* **con·i·fers.**

con·scious·ness (kon′shəs nis), condition of being conscious; awareness: *The injured woman did not regain consciousness for two hours. n.*

con·sti·tu·tion (kon′stə tü′shən or kon′stə tyü′shən), 1 way in which a person or thing is organized; nature; makeup: *A person with a good constitution is strong and healthy.* 2 system of fundamental principles according to which a nation, state, or group is governed: *The United States has a written constitution.* 3 the Constitution, the written set of fundamental principles by which the United States is governed. *n.*

con·sum·er (kən sü′mər), person who uses food, clothing, or anything grown or made by producers: *A low price for wheat should reduce the price of flour to the consumer. n., pl.* **con·sum·ers.**

con·test (kon′test *for 1,2;* kən test′ *for 3*), 1 trial of skill to see which can win. A game or race is a contest.

2 a fight, struggle, or dispute. 3 argue against; dispute about: *The decision was not contested.* 1,2 *n.,* 3 *v.*

con·test·ant (kən tes′tənt), person who takes part in a contest: *My sister was a contestant in the 100-yard dash. n.*

cool (kül), somewhat cold; more cold than hot: *a cool, cloudy day. adj.*

co·or·di·nate (kō ôrd′n it), any of a set of numbers that give the position of a point by reference to fixed lines or axes. *n., pl.* **co·or·di·nates.**

corn (kôrn), kind of grain that grows on large ears; Indian corn. *n.*

cor·rect (kə rekt′), 1 free from mistakes; right: *give the correct answer.* 2 change to what is right; remove mistakes or faults from: *Correct any misspellings that you find.* 1 *adj.,* 2 *v.*

cor·rec·tion (kə rek′shən), a change to correct an error or mistake: *Write in your corrections neatly. n.*

couch (kouch), a long seat, usually upholstered and having a back and arms; sofa: *She sat on the couch and read the newspaper. n., pl.* **couch·es.**

could've (kůd′əv), could have.

coun·se·lor or **coun·sel·lor** (koun′sə lər), person who gives advice; adviser. *The counselor helped my brother select some courses for college. n.*

cou·ple (kup′əl), 1 INFORMAL. a small number; a few: *Give me a couple of those apples—about four of them.* 2 man and woman who are married, engaged, partners in a dance, etc. *n.*

constitution
(definition 3)
the **Constitution** of
the United States

a	hat	ī	ice	ů	put	ə *stands for*	
ā	age	o	not	ü	rule	a	in about
ä	far, calm	ō	open	ch	child	e	in taken
âr	care	ȯ	saw	ng	long	i	in pencil
e	let	ô	order	sh	she	o	in lemon
ē	equal	oi	oil	th	thin	u	in circus
ėr	term	ou	out	ᴛʜ	then		
i	it	u	cup	zh	measure		

cou·ra·geous (kə rā′jəs), full of courage; brave; fearless. *adj.*

course (kôrs), **1** regular order: *the course of nature.* **2** a series of studies in a school, college, or university. A student must complete a certain course in order to graduate: *Biology is the course I will take to become a science teacher. n.*

court (kôrt), place marked off for a game: *a tennis court, a basketball court. n.*

court·room (kôrt′rüm′), room where a court of law is held. *n.*

courtroom

hearing a case in the

courtroom

cous·in (kuz′n), son or daughter of one's uncle or aunt. First cousins have the same grandparents; second cousins have the same great-grandparents. *n.*

cov·er (kuv′ər), **1** put something over: *I covered the child with a blanket.* **2** anything that covers. Books have covers. A box, can, or jar usually has a cover. A blanket is a cover. **3** be enough for; provide for: *My allowance covers my lunch at school.* 1,3 *v.,* 2 *n.*

cov·er·let (kuv′ər lit), a covering, especially a covering for a bed. *n.*

cov·ey (kuv′ē), a small flock of partridges, quail, etc. *n., pl.* **cov·eys.**

cow·ard (kou′ərd), person who lacks courage or is easily made afraid; person who runs from danger, trouble, etc. *n.*

crash (krash) a sudden, loud noise like many dishes falling and breaking: *The lightning was followed by a crash of thunder. n., pl.* **crash·es.**

cra·zy (krā′zē), unwise or senseless; foolish: *It was a crazy idea to jump out of such a high tree. adj.,* **cra·zi·er, cra·zi·est.**

crocodile

A **crocodile** is a large

reptile.

cred·it (kred′it), a trust in a person's ability and intention to pay: *This store will extend credit to you by opening a charge account in your name. n.*

cried (krīd), See **cry.** *The baby cried until its mother picked it up. v.*

croc·o·dile (krok′ə dīl), a large, lizardlike reptile with thick skin, similar to the alligator, but having a long narrow head and webbed feet. Crocodiles live in the rivers and marshes of the warm parts of Africa, Asia, Australia, and America. *n.*

cross·walk (krós′wok′), area marked with lines, used by pedestrians in crossing a street. *n., pl.* **cross·walks.**

crowd (kroud) a large number of people together: *A crowd gathered at the scene of the fire. n.*

cruise (krüz), **1** sail about from place to place on pleasure or business; sail over or about: *Freighters and tankers cruise the oceans of the world.* **2** a voyage from place to place for pleasure: *We went for a cruise on the Great Lakes last summer.* 1 *v.,* **cruised, cruis·ing;** 2 *n.*

crumb (krum), a very small piece of bread, cake, etc., broken from a larger piece: *I fed crumbs to the birds. n.*

crum·ble (krum′bəl), fall to pieces; decay: *The old wall was crumbling away at the edges. v.,* **crum·bled, crum·bling.**

crutch (kruch), a support to help a lame or injured person walk. It is a stick with a padded crosspiece at the top that fits under a person's arm and supports part of the weight in walking. *n., pl.* **crutch·es.**

cry (krī), call loudly; shout: *"Wait!" she cried from behind me. v.,* **cried, cry·ing.**

cuck·oo clock (kü′kü klok′), clock with a little toy bird that makes a sound like that of the European cuckoo to mark intervals of time.

cue card (kyü′ kärd′), words written out as to what to do or when to act: *He held up the cue cards to the actor so he could continue the play. n., pl.* **cue cards.**

cur·few (kėr′fyü), rule requiring certain persons to be off the streets or at home before a fixed time: *There is a 10 p.m. curfew for children in our city. n.*

cur·rent (kėr′ənt), **1** flow of electricity through a wire, etc.: *The current went off when lightning hit the power lines.* **2** of the present time: *We discuss current events in social studies class.* 1 *n.*, 2 *adj.*

cur·tain (kėrt′n), the fall or closing of the curtain at the end of an act or scene. *n., pl.* **cur·tains.**

cush·ion (kush′ən), a soft pillow or pad used to sit, lie, or kneel on: *I rested my head on a cushion. n.*

cus·pid (kus′pid), the kind of tooth with a sharp point used to tear food. Adults have four cuspids. *n.*

cute (kyüt), pretty and dear: *a cute baby. adj.,* **cut·er, cut·est.**

D

dad (dad), INFORMAL. father: *Dad's new car is green. n.*

dahl·ia (dal′yə), a tall plant with large, showy flowers of many colors and varieties that bloom in autumn. It is related to the aster. *n., pl.* **dahl·ias.** [The *dahlia* was named for Anders *Dahl,* 1751-1789, a Swedish botanist.]

dai·ly (dā′lē), done, happening, or appearing every day, or every day but Sunday, day by day: *a daily newspaper, a daily visit. adj.*

dair·y (dâr′ē), room or building where milk and cream are kept and made into butter and cheese. *n., pl.* **dair·ies.**

dance (dans), move in rhythm, usually in time with music: *She can dance very well. v.,* **danced, danc·ing.**

dan·ger (dān′jər), chance of harm; nearness to harm; risk; peril: *The trip through the jungle was full of danger. n.*

dark (därk), **1** absence of light; darkness: *Don't be afraid of the dark.* **2** night; nightfall: *The dark comes on early in the winter. n.* —**dark′ness,** *n.*

dead·line (ded′līn′), the latest possible time to do something: *The teacher made Friday afternoon the deadline for handing in all book reports. n.*

deal (dēl), distribute playing cards: *It's your turn to deal. v.,* **dealt, deal·ing.**

dealt (delt), See **deal.** *The cards have been dealt. v.*

de·bris (də brē′), scattered fragments; ruins; rubbish: *The street was covered with debris from the explosion. n.*

Dec., December.

De·cem·ber (di sem′bər), the 12th and last month of the year. It has 31 days. *n.*

de·cide (di sīd′), make up one's mind; resolve: *She decided to be a scientist. v.,* **de·cid·ed, de·cid·ing.**

de·ci·sion (di sizh′ən), **1** a making up of one's mind; deciding: *I have not yet come to a decision about buying the property.* **2** judgment reached or given: *The jury brought in a decision of not guilty. n.*

de·com·pos·er (dē′kəm pō′zər), a consumer that puts materials from dead plants and animals back into soil, air, and water. *n.*

deed (dēd), thing done; act; action: *a good deed. Deeds, not words, are needed. n.*

deep (dēp), **1** going a long way down from the top or surface: *the deepest well. The pond is deeper in the middle.* **2** in depth: *a tank 8 feet deep. adj.,* **deep·er, deep·est.**

dance
dancing in a ballet

a	hat	**ī**	ice	**u̇**	put	**ə** stands for	
ā	age	**o**	not	**ü**	rule	**a**	in about
ä	far, calm	**ō**	open	**ch**	child	**e**	in taken
âr	care	**ȯ**	saw	**ng**	long	**i**	in pencil
e	let	**ô**	order	**sh**	she	**o**	in lemon
ē	equal	**oi**	oil	**th**	thin	**u**	in circus
ėr	term	**ou**	out	**ᴛʜ**	then		
i	it	**u**	cup	**zh**	measure		

desert¹
exploring the dry
desert

diary
A **diary** is for writing personal thoughts.

de·gree (di grē′), **1** unit for measuring temperature: *The freezing point of water is 32 degrees (32°) Fahrenheit, or 0 degrees (0°) Celsius.* **2** unit for measuring an angle or an arc of a circle. A degree is ¹/₉₀ of a right angle or ¹/₃₆₀ of the circumference of a circle. 45 degrees (45°) is half a right angle. *n., pl.* **de·grees.**

de·lay (di lā′), **1** put off till a later time: *We will delay the party for a week and hold it next Saturday.* **2** a putting off till a later time: *The delay upset our plans.* **3** be late; go slowly; stop along the way: *Do not delay on this errand.* 1,3 *v.,* 2 *n., pl.* **de·lays.**

de·liv·er·y (di liv′ər ē), a carrying and giving out of letters, goods, etc.: *There is one delivery of mail a day in our city. n., pl.* **de·liv·er·ies.**

dem·o·crat·ic (dem′ə krat′ik), of a democracy; like a government run by the people who live under it. *adj.*

dem·on·stra·tion (dem′ən strā′shən), a showing or explaining something by carrying out experiments or by using samples: *A compass was used in a demonstration of the earth's magnetism. n., pl.* **dem·on·stra·tions.**

den·im (den′əm), a heavy, coarse cotton cloth with a diagonal weave, used for overalls, sports clothes, etc. *n.* [*Denim* comes from French *serge de Nimes,* meaning "serge from Nimes," a town in France where the fabric was made.]

der·mis (dėr′mis), the sensitive layer of skin beneath the outer skin; derma. *n.*

de·scrip·tion (di skrip′shən) a telling in words how a person, place, thing, or an event looks or behaves; describing: *The reporter's description of the hotel fire made me feel as if I were right at the scene. n.*

des·ert¹ (dez′ərt), a dry, barren region that is usually sandy and without trees. The Sahara Desert is a great desert in northern Africa. *n.*

de·sert² (di zert′), go away and leave a person or a place, especially one that should not be left; forsake: *She deserted her old friends when she became famous. v.*

de·sign (di zīn′), **1** arrangement of details, form, and color in painting, weaving, building, etc.: *a wallpaper design in tan and brown.* **2** make a first sketch of; arrange form and color of; draw in outline: *design a dress.* 1 *n.,* 2 *v.*

de·tail (di tāl′ or dē′tāl), a small or unimportant part: *Her report was complete; it didn't leave out a single detail. n., pl.* **de·tails.**

de·ter·mi·na·tion (di tėr′mə nā′shən), great firmness in carrying out a purpose; fixed purpose: *His determination was not weakened by the difficulties he met. n.*

de·ter·mine (di tėr′mən), make up one's mind very firmly; resolve: *He determined to become the best player on the team. v.*

dev·as·tate (dev′ə stāt), lay waste; destroy; ravage: *A long war devastated the country. v.,* **dev·as·tat·ed, dev·as·tat·ing.**

de·vel·op (di vel′əp), **1** come into being or activity; grow: *Plants develop from seeds.* **2** treat (a photographic film or plate) with chemicals to bring out the picture: *A photographer develops film and makes prints.* **3** make or become known: *The lawyer's investigation did not develop any new facts. v.*

di·ar·y (dī′ər ē), a book for writing down each day of what has happened to one, or what one has done or thought, during that day. *n., pl.* **di·ar·ies.**

dic·tion·ar·y (dik′shə ner′ē), book that explains the words of a language or of some special subject. It is arranged alphabetically. You can use this dictionary to find out the meaning, spelling, or pronunciation of a word. *n., pl.* **dic·tion·ar·ies.**

did·n't (did′nt), did not: *I didn't hear you.*

dif·fer·ent (dif′ər ənt), **1** not alike; not like: *People have different names. A boat is different from an automobile.* **2** not like others or most others; unusual. *adj.*

di·rect (də rekt′ or dī rekt′). have authority or control over; manage or guide: *The teacher directs the work of the class.* *v.*

di·rec·tion (də rek′shən or dī rek′shən), a directing; managing or guiding: *the direction of a play or movie. The school is under the direction of the principal.* *n.*

dirt·y (dėr′tē) soiled by dirt; not clean: *Children playing in the mud get dirty. adj.*

dis·a·gree (dis′ə grē′), have unlike opinions; differ: *Doctors sometimes disagree about the proper method of treating a patient. Your account of the accident disagrees with hers.* *v.*, **dis·a·greed, dis·a·gree·ing.**

dis·ap·pear (dis′ə pir′), pass from sight; from existence; stop being seen: *The dog disappeared around the corner. When spring comes, the snow disappears.* *v.*

dis·ap·point·ment (dis′ə point′mənt), a being disappointed; the feeling you have when you do not get what you expected or hoped for: *When she did not get a new bicycle her disappointment was very great.* *n.*

dis·cov·er (dis kuv′ər), see or learn of for the first time; find out: *discover a new drug, discover a secret.* *v.*

dis·hon·est (dis on′ist), ready to cheat; not upright: *A person who lies or steals is dishonest. adj.*

dis·like (dis līk′), not like; object to; have a feeling against: *He dislikes studying and would rather play football.* *v.*, **dis·liked, dis·lik·ing.**

dis·o·be·di·ence (dis′ə bē′dē əns), refusal to obey; failure to obey: *The child was punished for disobedience. n.*

dis·play (dis plā′), a showing of information in visual form, as on the screen of a computer or calculator. *n.*

dis·tance (dis′təns), space in between: *The distance from the farm to the town is five miles. n.*

dis·trust (dis trust′), have no confidence in; not trust; be suspicious of; doubt: *Many people distrust statements made in advertisements. v.*

dive (dīv), **1** plunge headfirst into water. **2** act of diving: *The crowd applauded the girl's graceful dive.* **1** *v.*, **dived** or **dove** (dōv), **dived, div·ing;** **2** *n.*

di·vide (də vid′), to find how a total amount can be separated into an equal number of groups, or into groups of equal size. *v.*, **di·vid·ed, di·vid·ing.**

div·i·dend (div′ə dend), number or quantity to be divided by another: *In 728 ÷ 16, 728 is the dividend. n.*

di·vis·i·ble (də viz′ə bəl), able to be divided without leaving a remainder: *12 is divisible by 1, 2, 3, 4, 6, and 12. adj.*

di·vi·sion (də vizh′ən), operation of dividing one number by another: *26 ÷ 2 = 13 is a simple division. n.*

di·vi·sor (də vī′zər), number or quantity by which another is to be divided: *In 728 ÷ 16, 16 is the divisor. n.*

doc·tor (dok′tər), person trained in treating diseases or injuries. Physicians, surgeons, dentists, and veterinarians are doctors. *n.*

does·n't (duz′nt), does not.

dive (definition 1)

a	hat	ī	ice	u̇	put	ə *stands for*	
ā	age	o	not	ü	rule	a	in about
ä	far, calm	ō	open	ch	child	e	in taken
âr	care	ȯ	saw	ng	long	i	in pencil
e	let	ô	order	sh	she	o	in lemon
ē	equal	oi	oil	th	thin	u	in circus
ėr	term	ou	out	ᵺ	then		
i	it	u	cup	zh	measure		

dog pad·dle (dòg′ pad′l), a downward swimming stroke in which the arms and legs stay under the water and each limb paddles by turns, first one and then the other: *The child did the dog paddle in the pool.*

dol·phin (dol′fən) a sea mammal related to the whale, but smaller. It has a beaklike snout and remarkable intelligence. *n.*

don·key (dong′kē) a small animal somewhat like a horse but with longer ears and a shorter mane. *n., pl.* **don·keys.**

door·bell (dôr′bel′), bell that a caller may ring by pressing a button or pulling a handle on the outside of a door to a house. *n.*

down·stairs (doun′stârz′), on or to a lower floor: *Look downstairs for my glasses (adv.) The downstairs rooms are dark (adj.).*

Dr., Doctor.

drib·ble (drib′əl), **1** move (a ball) along by bouncing it or giving it short kicks: *dribble a basketball, dribble a soccer ball.* **2** act of dribbling a ball. 1 *v.,* **drib·bled, drib·bling;** 2 *n.*

dried (drīd), See **dry.** *I dried my hands. The dishes have already been dried. v.*

drive (drīv), **1** go or carry in an automobile or carriage: *We want to drive through the mountains on the way home. She drove us to the station.* **2** (in sports) hit very hard and fast: *drive a golf ball.* **3** make by drilling, boring: *drive a well. v.,* **drove, driv·en** (driv′ən), **driv·ing.**

drive·way (drīv′wā′), a privately owned road to drive on, usually leading from a house or garage to the road. *n.*

drove (drōv), See **drive.** *We drove two hundred miles today. v.*

drown (droun), die under water or other liquid because of lack of air to breathe: *We almost drowned when our sailboat suddenly overturned. v.,* **drowned, drown·ing.**

dolphin

a **dolphin** enjoying

the water

dry (drī), make or become dry: *We washed and dried the dishes after dinner. Clothes dry in the sun. v.,* **dried, dry·ing.**

dry cleaner (drī′ klē′nər), person or business that does dry cleaning.

dry dock (drī′ dok′), dock built watertight so that the water may be pumped out or kept high. Dry docks are used for building or repairing ships.

dry run (drī′ run′), a practice test or session.

dud (dud), shell or bomb that fails to explode. *n.*

dune (dün or dyün), mound or ridge of loose sand heaped up by the wind. *n.*

dur·ing (dùr′ing or dyùr′ing), through the whole time of; throughout: *The children played inside during the storm. prep.*

E

ear (ir), part of the body by which people and animals hear. It consists of the external ear, the middle ear, and the inner ear. *n.* **be all ears,** INFORMAL. listen eagerly; pay careful attention: *The children were all ears while their teacher read them the exciting story.* **play by ear,** play (a piece of music or a musical instrument) without using written music: *She can't read notes but she can play any tune on the piano by ear.*

ear ca·nal (ir′ kə nal′), tunnel sound travels through to the eardrum.

ear·drum (ir′drum′), a thin membrane across the middle ear that vibrates when sound waves strike it. *n.*

ear·ring (ir′ring′), ornament for the ear. *n., pl.* **ear·rings.**

earth·quake (ėrth′kwāk′), a shaking or sliding of a portion of the earth's crust. It is caused by the sudden movement of masses of rock far beneath the earth's surface. Earthquakes are often related to volcanic activity. *n.*

e·del·weiss (ā′dl vīs), a small plant that grows in high places, such as the mountains in Austria and Switzerland. It has heads of very small, white flowers in the center of star-shaped leaf clusters. *n., pl.* **e·del·weiss** or **e·del·weiss·es.**

edge (ej), **1** line or place where something ends or begins; side: *This page has four edges. We walked to the edge of the water.* **2** rim; brink: *The stag stood on the edge of the cliff. n.*

ed·i·tor (ed′ə ter), person who edits. *She is the editor of our school paper. n., pl.* **ed·i·tors.**

e·lect (i lekt′), choose or select for an office by voting: *We elect our class officers every autumn. v.,* **elect·ed, elect·ing.**

e·lec·tion (i lek′shən), a choosing or selecting for an office by vote: *In our city we have an election for mayor every four years. n.*

e·lec·tric·i·ty (i lek′tris′ə tē), form of energy which can produce light, heat, motion, and magnetic force. Electricity makes light bulbs shine, televisions play, and cars start. *n.*

el·e·phant (el′ə fənt), a huge, heavy mammal, the largest living land animal, with ivory tusks and a long, muscular snout called a trunk. *n.*

e·lev·en (i lev′ən), **1** one more than ten; 11. **2** a football or cricket team. 1,2 *n.,* 1 *adj.*

e·mer·gen·cy (i mėr′jən sē), **1** a sudden need for immediate action: *I keep a box of tools in my car for use in an emergency.* **2** for a time of sudden need: *The surgeon did an emergency operation.* 1 *n., pl.* **e·mer·gen·cies;** 2 *adj.*

e·nam·el (i nam′əl), the smooth, hard, glossy outer layer of the teeth. *n.*

end·point (end′point′), the point at the end of a line segment or ray. *n., pl.* **end·points.**

en·e·my (en′ə mē), a force, nation, army, fleet, or air force that opposes another; person, ship, etc., of a hostile nation. *n., pl.* **en·e·mies.**

en·er·gy (en′ər jē), capacity for doing work, such as lifting or moving an object. Light, heat, and electricity are different forms of energy: *A steam engine changes heat into mechanical energy. n., pl.* **en·er·gies.**

en·er·vate (en′ər vāt), lessen the vigor or strength of; weaken: *A hot, damp climate enervates people who are not used to it. v.,* **en·er·vat·ed, en·er·vat·ing.**

en·gine (en′jən), machine that changes energy from fuel, steam, water pressure, etc., into motion and power. An engine is used to apply power to some work, such as a car engine. *n.*

Eng·lish (ing′glish), the language of England. English is also spoken in the United States, Canada, Australia, New Zealand, the Republic of South Africa, and many other countries. *n. sing.*

e·nough (i nuf′), quantity or number needed or wanted; sufficient amount: *I had enough to eat. n.*

ep·i·der·mis (ep′ə dėr′mis), the outer layer of the skin. *n.*

ep·i·gram (ep′ə gram), a short, pointed or witty saying. EXAMPLE: "Speech is silver, but silence is golden." *n.*

e·qual (ē′kwəl), **1** the same in amount, size, number, value, or rank: *Ten dimes are equal to one dollar. All persons are considered equal before the law.* **2** the same throughout; even; uniform: *equal pieces. adj.*

edelweiss
The **edelweiss** is the national flower of Austria.

elephant
The **elephant** is the largest four-footed animal.

a	hat	ī	ice	u̇	put	ə stands for	
ā	age	o	not	ü	rule	a	in about
ä	far, calm	ō	open	ch	child	e	in taken
âr	care	ȯ	saw	ng	long	i	in pencil
e	let	ô	order	sh	she	o	in lemon
ē	equal	oi	oil	th	thin	u	in circus
ėr	term	ou	out	ᵺ	then		
i	it	u	cup	zh	measure		

evergreen
the majestic **evergreen**

e·qual·ly (ē′kwə lē), in equal shares; in an equal manner: *Divide the pie equally. My sister and brother are equally talented. adv.*

e·quals key (ē′kwəlz kē′), key that supplies a result of a calculator's next calculation.

e·qua·tion (i kwā′zhən), statement of the equality of two quantities. EXAMPLES: $(4 \times 8) + 12 = 44$. $C = 2\pi r$. *n.*

e·qua·tor (i kwā′tər), an imaginary circle around the middle of the earth, halfway between the North Pole and the South Pole. The United States is north of the equator; Australia is south of it. *n.*

Er·ie (ir′ē), **Lake,** one of the five Great Lakes that borders Ohio, Pennsylvania, New York, and Canada. *n.*

er·ror (er′ər), a message that appears on a calculator when more digits are generated than can be displayed. *n.*

e·rup·tion (i rup′shən) a bursting or throwing forth: *There was an eruption of glowing melted rock from the mountain top. n.*

es·cape (e skāp′), get out and away; get free: *The bird escaped from its cage. v.*, **es·caped, es·cap·ing.**

es·pe·cial·ly (e spesh′ə lē), more than others; specially; particularly; principally; chiefly. *adv.*

etc., et cetera. *Etc.* is usually read "and so forth." *Etc.* shows that the definition applies to many similar items in addition to the ones mentioned.

eve (ēv), the evening or day before a holiday or some other special day: *New Year's Eve, Christmas Eve, the eve of my birthday. n.*

experiment
working on an
experiment with light

eve·ning (ēv′ning), the last part of day and early part of night; time between sunset and bedtime. *n.*

ev·er·green (ev′ər grēn′), a plant that has green leaves or needles all year round. *n.*, *pl.* **ev·er·greens.**

eve·ry·bod·y (ev′rē bud′ē or ev′rē bod′ē), every person; everyone: *Everybody likes the principal. pron.*

eve·ry·one (ev′rē wun or ev′rē wən), each one; everybody: *Everyone in the class is here. pron.*

ex·act·ly (eg zakt′lē), accurately; precisely; just so; quite right. *adv.*

ex·cel·lent (ek′sə lənt), of unusually good quality; better than others; superior: *Excellent work deserves high praise. adj.*

ex·cept (ek sept′) leaving out; other than: *He works every day except Sunday. prep.*

ex·cess (ek ses′ or ek′ses), part that is too much; more than enough: *The tailor trimmed off the excess from the cloth being measured for the two sleeves. n.*

ex·cite (ek sīt′), **1** stir up the feelings of: *News of the wedding excited the entire family.* **2** arouse: *Plans for a field trip excited the students' interest. v.*, **ex·cit·ed, ex·cit·ing.**

ex·cuse (ek skyüs′ or ek′ses), reason, real or pretended, that is given; explanation: *Sickness was his excuse for being absent from school. n.*

ex·hib·it (eg zib′it), an exhibiting; public showing: *The village art exhibit drew 10,000 visitors. n.*

ex·pect (ek spekt′), think something will probably come or happen; look forward to: *I expect to take a vacation in May. v.*

ex·per·i·ment (ek sper′ə mənt), trial or test to find out something: *a chemistry experiment. Scientists test out theories by experiments. n.*

ex·pert (ek′spért′), a very skillful person; person who knows a great deal about some special thing: *She is an expert at fishing. n.*

ex·plain (ek splān′), make plain or clear; tell the meaning of: *The teacher explained long division to the class. Will you explain this poem to me? v.*

ex·plo·sion (ek splō′zhən), a bursting with a loud noise; a blowing up: *The explosion shook the whole neighborhood. n.*

ex·tra (ek′strə), beyond what is usual, expected, or needed; additional: *extra fare, extra pay, extra favors.* *adj.* [*Extra* was probably shortened from *extraordinary.*]

ex·traor·di·nar·y (ek strôr′də ner′ē), beyond what is ordinary; very unusual; very remarkable: *Eight feet is an extraordinary height for a person.* *adj.*

eye (ī), the organ of the body by which people and animals see. *n.*
an eye for an eye, punishment as severe as the injury.
catch one's eye, attract one's attention: *The bright red sign caught my eye.*
see eye to eye, agree entirely: *My parents and I do not see eye to eye on my weekly allowance.*

eye·lash (ī′lash′), **1** one of the hairs on the edge of the eyelid. **2** fringe of such hairs. *n., pl.* **eye·lash·es.**

F

Fahr·en·heit (far′ən hīt), a scale for measuring temperature on which 32 degrees marks the freezing point of water and 212 degrees marks the boiling point. *adj.* [The *Fahrenheit* scale was named for Gabriel D. *Fahrenheit*, 1686-1736, the German physicist who introduced it.]

fair·ness (fâr′nis), a being fair: *Our teacher is known for fairness in grading pupils.* *n.*

fam·i·ly (fam′ə lē), **1** a father, mother, and their children: *Our town has about a thousand families.* **2** all of a person's relatives: *His family's reunion is an annual event.* *n., pl.* **fam·i·lies.**

family of facts, (fakts), related number sentences for addition and subtraction (or multiplication and division) that contain all the same numbers.

fat (fat), **1** having much flesh; fleshy; plump; well-fed: *a fat baby, a fat pig.* **2** large or larger than usual: *a fat contract, a fat salary.* *adj.,* **fat·ter, fat·test.**

fa·ther (fä′THər), a male parent. *n.*

fault (fôlt), a break in the earth's crust, with the mass of rock on one side of the break pushed up, down, or sideways. *n., pl.* **faults.**

fa·vor·ite (fā′vər it), liked better than others. *adj.*

fear·less (fir′lis), without fear; afraid of nothing; brave; daring. *adj.*

Feb., February.

Feb·ru·ar·y (feb′rü er′ē or feb′yü er′ē), the second month of the year. It has 28 days except in leap years, when it has 29. *n.*

fed·er·al (fed′ər əl), formed by an agreement between states establishing a central government to handle their business while the states keep separate their own affairs: *Switzerland and the United States both became nations by federal union.* *adj.*

feel·ing (fē′ling), **1** emotion. Joy, sorrow, fear, and anger are feelings. *The loss of the ball game stirred up much feeling.* **2** feelings, *pl.* tender or sensitive side of one's nature: *You hurt my feelings when you yelled at me.* *n., pl.* **feel·ings.**

fence (fens), railing, wall, put around a yard, garden, field, farm, etc., to show where it ends or to keep people or animals out or in. Most fences are made of wood, wire, or metal. *n.*

Fahrenheit
The **Fahrenheit** scale is used on these thermometers.

a	hat	ī	ice	u̇	put	ə stands for	
ā	age	o	not	ü	rule	a	in about
ä	far, calm	ō	open	ch	child	e	in taken
âr	care	ȯ	saw	ng	long	i	in pencil
e	let	ô	order	sh	she	o	in lemon
ē	equal	oi	oil	th	thin	u	in circus
ėr	term	ou	out	ᴛʜ	then		
i	it	u	cup	zh	measure		

fern
two Boston **ferns**

fern (fėrn), kind of plant that has roots, stems, and feathery leaves, but does not have flowers or seeds. The plant reproduces by means of spores which grow in little brown clusters on the backs of the leaves. *n., pl.* **ferns.**

fer·ti·lize (fėr′tl īz), unite with (an egg cell) in fertilization; impregnate. *v.,* **fer·ti·lized, fer·ti·liz·ing.**

few (fyü), not many: *Few people attended the meeting. adj.*

field (fēld), piece of land used for crops or for pasture. *n.*

field goal (fēld′ gōl′), (in basketball) a basket scored while the ball is in play, counting two points.

fil·i·gree (fil′ə grē), very delicate, lacelike, ornamental work of gold or silver wire. *n.*

film (film), roll or sheet of thin, flexible material covered with a coating that is sensitive to light, used in taking photographs. *n.*

fi·nal·ly (fī′nl ē), at the end; at last. *adv.*

fin·ger (fing′gər), one of the five slender divisions that end the hand, especially the four besides the thumb. *n.*
put one's finger on, point out exactly: *The inspector was able to put his finger on the weak point in the suspect's alibi.*

fire·proof (fir′prüf′), very resistant to fire; almost impossible to burn: *A building made entirely of steel and concrete is fireproof. adj.*

first (fėrst), **1** coming before all others: *She is first in her class.* **2** person, thing, place, etc., that is first: *We were the first to get here.* 1 *adj.,* 2 *n.*

first aid (fėrst′ ād′), emergency treatment given to an injured or sick person before a doctor sees the person.

flash·light (flash′līt′), a portable electric light, operated by batteries. *n.*

flaw (flȯ), defective area: *There is a flaw in this shirt. n.*

football (definition 2)

flawed (flȯd), having a defect: *a flawed diamond. adj.*

float (flōt), stay on top of or be held up by air, water, or other liquid. A cork will float, but a stone sinks. *v.*

Flo·ri·da (flôr′ə də), one of the southeastern states of the United States. *Abbreviation:* Fla. or FL *Capital:* Tallahassee. *n.*

flow·er (flou′ər), part of a plant that produces the seed; blossom. It has modified leaves called petals. Flowers are often beautifully colored or shaped. *n., pl.* **flow·ers.**

fly (flī), any of a large group of insects that have two wings and make a buzzing sound, especially the housefly. *n., pl.* **flies.**

fo·cus (fō′kəs), bring (rays of light, heat, etc.) to a focus: *The lens focused the sun's rays on a piece of paper. v.* **fo·cused, fo·cus·ing,** or **fo·cussed, fo·cus·sing.**

food chain (füd′ chān′), several kinds of living things that are linked because each uses another as food. Cats, birds, caterpillars, and plants eat the one named next.

food web (füd′ web′), the flow of energy and materials through connected food chains.

foot (fůt), the end part of a leg; part that a person, animal, or thing stands on. *n., pl.* **feet** (fēt).
put one's best foot forward, INFORMAL. do one's best.

foot·ball (fůt′bȯl′), **1** game played with an inflated leather ball by two teams of eleven players each, on a field with a goal at each end. A player scores by carrying the ball over the goal line by a run or pass, or by kicking it through the goal posts. **2** ball used in this game. *n.*

fore·cast (fôr′kast′), what is coming; prophecy; prediction: *What is the forecast for the weather today? n.* —**fore′cast·er,** *n.*

fo·rest (fôr′ist), a large piece of land covered with trees; thick woods. *n.*

for·get (fər get′), fail to think of; fail to do, take, notice, etc.: *I forgot to call the dentist. v.,* **for·got, for·got·ten** (fər got′n) or **for·got, for·get·ting.**

for·got (fər got′), See **forget.** *She was so busy that she forgot to eat her lunch.* v.

form (fôrm), **1** be formed; take shape: *Clouds form in the sky.* **2** piece of printed paper with blank spaces to be filled in: *We filled out a form to get a license for our dog.* 1 v., 2 n.

foul (foul), **1** (in football, basketball, etc.) an unfair play; thing done against the rules. **2** make an unfair play against. 1 n., 2 v.

four·teen (fôr′tēn′), four more than ten; 14. n., adj.

fourth (fôrth), next after the third; last in a series of 4. adj., n.

Fourth of July, Independence Day.

fran·tic (fran′tik), very much excited; wild with rage, fear, pain, or grief. adj.

freck·le (frek′əl), a small, light-brown spot on the skin, often caused by exposure to the sun. n., pl. **freck·les.**

free·style (frē′stīl′), a freestyle race or figure-skating contest. n.

free throw (frē′ thrō′), (in basketball) an unblocked shot from a line **(free-throw line)** about 15 feet (4.5 meters) away from the basket, awarded to a player fouled by a member of the opposing team, and worth one point.

friend (frend), **1** person who knows and likes another. *My friend's companionship is priceless.* **2** person who favors and supports: *She was a generous friend to the poor.* n.

front (frunt), the line where two air masses meet. n.

fruit (früt), a juicy or fleshy product of a tree, bush, shrub, or vine which consists of the seed and its covering and is usually sweet and good to eat. Apples and pears are fruits. n.

fuch·sia (fyü′shə), shrub with handsome pink, red, or purple flowers that droop from the stems. n., pl. **fuch·sias.** [The *fuchsia* was named for Leonhard *Fuchs,* 1501-1566, a German botanist.]

fudge (fuj), a soft candy made of sugar, milk, chocolate, butter, etc. n.

fu·el (fyü′əl), **1** anything that can be burned to produce useful heat or power. Coal, wood, and oil are fuels. **2** supply with fuel. **3** get fuel: *The ship will have to fuel at the nearest port.* 1 n., pl. **fu·els,** 2,3 v.

fun·ny (fun′ē), **1** causing laughter; amusing: *The clown's funny jokes and antics kept us laughing.* **2** INFORMAL. strange; queer; odd. adj., **fun·ni·er, fun·ni·est.**

fur (fėr), **1** the soft hair covering the skin of many animals. **2** skin with such hair on it. Fur is used to make, cover, trim, or line clothing. n.

fur·ni·ture (fėr′nə chər), movable articles needed in a room or house. Beds, chairs, tables, and desks are furniture. n.

fruit
Fresh **fruit** is good for your health.

G

gag (gag), **1** something put in a person's mouth to prevent talking or crying out. **2** INFORMAL. joke; amusing remark or trick. n.

gal·lant (gal′ənt), noble in spirit or in conduct; brave: *King Arthur was a gallant knight.* adj.

gal·lon (gal′ən), measure for liquids equal to 4 quarts. n.

gang (gang), group of people acting or going around together: *A whole gang of us went swimming.* n.

gallon
a **gallon** of milk

a	hat	ī	ice	u̇	put		ə stands for
ā	age	o	not	ü	rule	a	in about
ä	far, calm	ō	open	ch	child	e	in taken
âr	care	ȯ	saw	ng	long	i	in pencil
e	let	ô	order	sh	she	o	in lemon
ē	equal	oi	oil	th	thin	u	in circus
ėr	term	ou	out	‡H	then		
i	it	u	cup	zh	measure		

giraffe
Giraffes are the tallest animals in the world.

grasshopper
a **grasshopper** and its surroundings

gas·o·line (gas′ə lēn′ or gas′ə lēn′), a colorless, liquid mixture of hydrocarbons which evaporates and burns very easily. It is made from petroleum or from gas formed in the earth and is used as a fuel to run automobiles, airplanes, etc. *n.*

gen·tle (jen′tl), not severe, rough, or violent; mild and soft: *a gentle tap. a gentle sound. adj.*, **gen·tler, gen·tlest.**

ghost (gōst), spirit of a dead person, supposed to appear to living people as a pale, dim, shadowy form: *A ghost was said to haunt the house. n.*

gi·ant (jī′ənt), like a giant; huge: *a giant potato. adj.*

gi·gan·tic (jī gan′tik), very large; huge: *a gigantic elephant. adj.*

gi·raffe (jə raf′), a large African mammal that chews its cud and has hoofs, a very long neck, long legs, and a spotted skin. Giraffes are the tallest living animals. *n.*

girl (gėrl), **1** a female child from birth to about eighteen: *The girl's face was young and pretty.* **2** a young, unmarried woman. *n.*

girl·friend (gėrl′frend′), INFORMAL. **1** boy's sweetheart or steady female companion. **2** a female friend. *n.*

glass (glas), **1** container to drink from made of glass: *I filled the glass with water.* **2 glasses,** *pl.* eyeglasses. *n., pl.* **glass·es.**

go (gō), move along. *v.* **went, gone** (gon), **going.**

good·ness (gùd′nis), a being good; kindness. *n.*

grand·ma (grand′mä′ or gram′ə), INFORMAL. grandmother: *My grandma's cookies are delicious. n.*

grand·pa (grand′pä′ or gram′pə), INFORMAL. grandfather: *My grandpa's stories are very funny. n.*

grand·par·ent (grand′pâr′ent or grand′par′ənt), grandfather or grandmother: *Both sets of grandparents' letters arrived today. n.*

grass·hop·per (gras′hop′ər), a winged insect with strong hind legs for jumping. Locusts and katydids are grasshoppers. *n.*

grate·ful (grāt′fəl), feeling kindly because of a favor received; wanting to do a favor in return: *I am grateful for your help. adj.*

great·ness (grāt′nis), great mind or character. *n.*

group (grüp), number of persons or things together: *A group of children were playing tag. n.*

group·ing (grü′ping), putting a known number of objects into each group and making as many groups as you can. *v.*

guess (ges), form an opinion of something without really knowing. *v.*, **guessed, guess·ing.**

guest (gest), person who is received and entertained at another's home or staying at a hotel or motel. *n.*

H

ham·burg·er (ham′bėr′gər), ground beef, usually shaped into round, flat cakes and fried or broiled and placed in a roll or bun. *n.* [*Hamburger* comes from a German word meaning "of Hamburg."]

ham·mer (ham′ər), hit again and again. *v.*

ham·ster (ham′stər), a small rodent with a short tail and large cheek pouches. Hamsters are used in scientific research and are often kept as pets. *n.*

hand (hand), the end part of the arm, below the wrist, which takes and holds objects. Each hand has four fingers and a thumb. *n.*
at first hand, from direct knowledge or experience.
by hand, by using the hands, not machinery: *embroidered by hand.*
lend a hand, help.
wash one's hands of, have no more to do with; refuse to be responsible for: *I washed my hands of that job when I discovered what I had done.*

hand sig·nal (hand′ sig′nəl), help giving a sign, a notice, warning, or pointing out something: *The girl gave a hand signal when she turned.*

Ha·nuk·kah (hä′nə kə), a yearly Jewish festival celebrated in November or December. Candles are lighted on each of the eight days of Hanukkah. *n.* Also, **Chanukah.**

hap·pen (hap′ən), **1** come about; take place; occur: *What happened at the party yesterday?* **2** be or take place by chance: *Accidents will happen. v.,* **hap·pened, hap·pen·ing.**

hap·pen·ing (hap′ə ning), something that happens; event; occurrence: *The evening newscast reviewed the happenings of the day. n.*

hap·py (hap′ē), feeling as you do when you are well and are having a good time; glad; pleased; contented: *She is happy in her new work. adj.,* **hap·pi·er, hap·pi·est.**

head (hed), the top part of the human body containing the brain, eyes, nose, ears, and mouth. *n.* **lose one's head,** get excited; lose one's self-control.

head·line (hed′līn′), words printed in heavy type at the top of a newspaper article telling what it is about. *n.*

head·phone (hed′fōn′), earphone held against one or both ears by a band over the head. *n., pl.* **head·phones.**

heal (hēl), **1** make whole, sound, or well; bring back to health; cure. **2** become whole or sound; get well; return to health; be cured: *My cut healed in a few days. v.*

health (helth), condition of body or mind: *be in excellent health. n.*

hear (hir), **1** take in a sound or sounds through the ear: *We couldn't hear in the back row.* **2** receive news or information: *I heard from my parents. v.,* **heard** (hėrd), **hear·ing.**

heart (härt), **1** the part of the body that pumps the blood. **2** the part that feels, loves, hates, and desires: *a heavy heart, a kind heart.* **3** figure shaped like this: ♥ *n.*

heart·bro·ken (härt′brō′kən), crushed by sorrow or grief. *adj.*

he'd (hēd), **1** he had: *He'd had an accident.* **2** he would: *He'd come if he could.*

height (hīt), measurement from top to bottom; how tall a person is; how high a thing is; how far up a thing goes: *the height of a mountain. n.*

he'll (hēl), he will: *He'll tell us the story tomorrow afternoon.*

hel·met (hel′mit), covering made of steel, leather, plastic, or some other sturdy material, worn to protect the head. *n.*

help·less (help′lis), not able to help oneself: *A baby is helpless. adj.*

hem·i·sphere (hem′ə sfir), half of a sphere or globe, half of the earth's surface. The earth has four hemispheres: western, eastern, northern, and southern. *n., pl.* **hem·i·spheres.**

her·bi·vore (hėr′bə vôr), any animal that feeds mainly on plants. *n.*

her·self (hər self′), form of *she* or *her* used to make a statement stronger: *She did it herself. pron.*

hide (hīd), put or keep out of sight; conceal: *Hide it where no one else will find it. v.,* **hid** (hid), **hid·den** (hid′n) or **hid, hid·ing.**

high·way (hī′wā′), a main public road or route. *n.*

headphone
listening to music through the **headphones**

herbivore
A rabbit is a **herbivore.**

a	hat	**ī**	ice	**ù**	put	**ə** stands for		
ā	age	**o**	not	**ü**	rule	**a**	in about
ä	far, calm	**ō**	open	**ch**	child	**e**	in taken
âr	care	**ò**	saw	**ng**	long	**i**	in pencil
e	let	**ô**	order	**sh**	she	**o**	in lemon
ē	equal	**oi**	oil	**th**	thin	**u**	in circus
ėr	term	**ou**	out	**ŦH**	then		
i	it	**u**	cup	**zh**	measure		

hippopotamus

hip·po·pot·a·mus (hip/ə pot/ə məs), a huge, thick-skinned, almost hairless mammal found in and near the rivers of Africa that eats plants and can stay under water for a long time. *n., pl.* **hip·po·pot·a·mus·es, hip·po·pot·a·mi** (hip/ə pot/ə mī).

hob·by (hob/ē), something a person especially likes to work at or study which is not the person's main business or occupation; favorite pastime. *n., pl.* **hob·bies.**

hock·ey (hok/ē), game played by two teams on ice or on a field. The players hit a puck or ball with curved sticks to drive it across a goal. *n.*

ho·gan (hō/găn/), dwelling used by the Navajos. Hogans are built with logs and covered with earth. *n., pl.* **ho·gans.** [*Hogan* was borrowed from a Navajo word.]

hol·i·day (hol/ə dā), **1** day when one does not work; day of pleasure and enjoyment: *Labor Day and the Fourth of July are holidays in the United States.* **2** Often, **holidays,** *pl.* vacation. *n.*

home (hōm), place where a person or family lives; one's own house; where a person was born or brought up. *Her home is at 25 South Street. n.*

home·less (hōm/lis), without a home: *a stray, homeless dog. adj.* —**home/less·ness,** *n.*

hon·ey (hun/ē), a thick, sweet, yellow or golden liquid that bees make out of the nectar they collect from flowers. *n.*

hon·or (on/ər), great respect; high regard; *held in honor. n.*

hope·ful (hōp/fəl), feeling and giving or showing hope; expecting to receive what one desires: *a hopeful attitude. adj.* —**hope/ful·ly,** *adv.*

hope·less (hōp/lis), feeling or giving no hope: *He was disappointed so often that he became hopeless. adj.*

horn (hôrn), a hard, hollow, permanent growth, usually curved and pointed and in pairs, on the heads of cattle, sheep, goats, and certain other animals. *n.* **blow one's own horn** or **toot one's own horn,** INFORMAL, praise oneself; boast.

hos·pi·tal (hos/pi təl), place for the care of the sick or injured. *n.*

hot (hot), having much heat; very warm: *Fire is hot. The sun is hot today. adj.,* **hot·ter, hot·test.**

ho·tel (hō tel/), house or large building that supplies rooms and food for pay to travelers and others. *n.*

house (hous), building in which people live. *n., pl.* **hous·es** (hou/ziz).

how·ev·er (hou ev/ər), in spite of that; nevertheless; yet: *We were very late for dinner; however, there was plenty left for us. adv.*

huge (hyüj), very big; extremely large or great: *A whale is a huge animal. adj.*

hu·mid·i·ty (hyü mid/ə tē), moisture in the air: *On a hot, sultry day the humidity is high. The humidity today is worse than the heat. n.*

hu·mor (hyü/mər), funny or amusing quality: *I see no humor in your tricks. n.*

hu·mor·ous (hyü/mər əs), full of humor; funny: *We all laughed at the humorous story. adj.*

Hur·on (hyür/ən), **Lake,** one of the five Great Lakes that borders Michigan and Canada. *n.*

hy·dro·e·lec·tric (hī/drō i lek/trik), developing electricity from water power. *adj.*

hogan
A **hogan** is a type of house.

I

I'd (īd), **1** I would: *I'd enjoy a vacation right now.* **2** I had: *I'd just finished dinner when she called.*

ig·nore (ig nôr/), pay no attention to; disregard: *The driver ignored the traffic light and almost hit another car. v.,* **ig·nored, ig·nor·ing.**

i·gua·na (i gwä/nə), a large tropical American lizard having a spiny crest along its back. *n., pl.* **i·gua·nas.**

I'll (īl), I will: *I'll call you tomorrow.*

I'm (īm), I am: *I'm going to the concert tonight.*

i·mag·ine (i maj′ən), suppose; guess: *I cannot imagine what you mean.* v., **i·mag·ined, i·mag·in·ing.** —**i·mag·i·na·ble,** adj.

im·pos·si·ble (im pos′ə bəl), not capable of being, being done, or happening; not possible: *It is impossible for two and two to be six.* adj.

in·ac·tive (in ak′tiv), not active; idle; slow: *Bears are inactive during the winter.* adj.

in·ci·sor (in sī′zər), tooth having a sharp edge for cutting; one of the front teeth between the canine teeth in either jaw. Humans have eight incisors. n.

in·com·plete (in′kəm plēt′), not complete; lacking some part; unfinished. adj.

in·con·ven·ient (in′kən vē′nyənt), not convenient; causing trouble, difficulty, or bother; troublesome: *Shelves that are too high to reach easily are inconvenient.* adj.

in·cor·rect (in′kə rekt′), containing errors or mistakes; not correct; wrong: *Today's local newspaper gave an incorrect account of the accident.* adj.

in·cred·i·ble (in kred′ə bəl), hard to believe; seeming too extraordinary to be possible; unbelievable: *The racing car rounded the curve with incredible speed.* adj.

in·de·pend·ent (in′di pen′dənt), **1** not influenced by others; thinking or acting for oneself: *an independent voter, an independent thinker.* **2** person who is independent in thought or behavior. **1** adj. **2** n.

in·jur·y (in′jər ē), hurt or loss caused to or endured by a person or thing; harm; damage: *She escaped from the train wreck without injury.* n., pl. **in·jur·ies.**

inner ear (in′ər ir′), the fluid-filled part of the ear that sends messages to the brain.

in·stru·ment (in′strə mənt), **1** a mechanical device that is portable, and usually operated by hand; tool: *a dentist's instruments.* **2** device for producing musical sounds: *wind instruments.* n.

in·su·late (in′sə lāt), keep from losing or transferring electricity, heat, sound, etc., especially by covering, packing, or surrounding with a material that does not conduct electricity, heat, etc.: *Telephone wires are often insulated by a covering of rubber.* v., **in·su·lat·ed, in·su·lat·ing.**

in·ten·si·ty (in ten′sə tē), extreme degree; great vigor; violence: *intensity of thought, intensity of feeling.* n., pl. **in·ten·si·ties.**

in·ter·est·ing (in′tər ə sting *or* in′tə res′ting), arousing interest; holding one's attention: *Stories about travel and adventure are interesting.* adj.

in·ter·sect·ing (in′tər sekt′ing), crossing each other at a point: *intersecting lines.* adj.

in·ter·view (in′tər vyü), a meeting between a reporter and a person from whom information is sought for publication or broadcast. n.

in·to (in′tü; *before consonants often* in′tə), to the inside of; toward and inside: *Come into the house. We drove into the city. I will look into the matter.* prep.

In·u·it (in′ü it *or* in′yü it), the people living mainly in the arctic regions of the world; the Eskimo people. n.

instrument
(definition 2)
types of brass
instruments

a	hat	**ī**	ice	**u̇**	put		**ə** *stands for*	
ā	age	**o**	not	**ü**	rule		**a**	in about
ä	far, calm	**ō**	open	**ch**	child		**e**	in taken
âr	care	**ȯ**	saw	**ng**	long		**i**	in pencil
e	let	**ô**	order	**sh**	she		**o**	in lemon
ē	equal	**oi**	oil	**th**	thin		**u**	in circus
ėr	term	**ou**	out	**ᴛʜ**	then			
i	it	**u**	cup	**zh**	measure			

jai alai

playing the game of

jai alai

jewel

This **jewel** is a sapphire.

in·vade (in vād′), enter with force or as an enemy; attack: *Soldiers invaded the country to conquer it.* v., **in·vad·ed, in·vad·ing.**

in·va·sion (in vā′zhən), an invading; entering by force or as an enemy; attack. n.

in·ven·tion (in ven′shən), something new, thing invented: *Television is a modern invention.* n.

in·vis·i·ble (in viz′ə bəl), not visible; not capable of being seen: *Thought is invisible. Germs are invisible to the naked eye.* adj.

in·vite (in vīt′), ask (someone) politely to come to some place or to do something: *I invited some friends to a party. We invited them to join our club.* v., **in·vit·ed, in·vit·ing.**

i·ris (ī′ris), the colored part of the eye around the pupil. n., pl. **i·ris·es.**

i·ron (ī′ərn), **1** a silver-gray, easily shaped, heavy metallic element. Iron is the most useful metal and is used to make steel. **2** smooth or press (cloth, etc.) with a heated iron. 1 n., 2 v.

is·land (ī′lənd), body of land smaller than a continent and completely surrounded by water: *Cuba is a large island.* n.

is·sue (ish′ü), send out; put forth: *This magazine is issued every week.* v., **is·sued, is·su·ing.**

it'll (it′l), it will: *It'll be better soon.*

it's (its), **1** it is: *It's my turn.* **2** it has: *It's been a beautiful day.*

J

jai a·lai (hī′ lī′), game similar to handball, played on a walled court with a hard ball. The ball is caught and thrown with a kind of curved wicker basket fastened to the arm.

James (jāmz), a boy's name. *James's house is next door to mine.* n.

Jan·u·ar·y (jan′yü er′ē), the first month of the year. It has 31 days. n.

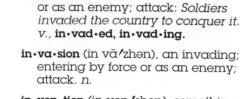

jay·walk (jā′wȯk′), walk across a street without paying attention to traffic rules. v. —**jay·walk·ing,** n.

jer·sey (jėr′zē), a close-fitting, pullover sweater made of this cloth. n. [*Jersey* gets its name from the island of *Jersey*, where this cloth had been made for a long time.]

jew·el (jü′əl), a precious stone; gem. n., pl. **jew·els.**

juice (jüs), the liquid part of fruits, vegetables, and meats: *the juice of a lemon, meat juice.* n.

Ju·ly (jü lī′), the seventh month of the year. It has 31 days. n.

jum·bo (jum′bō), INFORMAL. a big person, animal, or thing; something unusually large of its kind: *a jumbo ice-cream cone.* adj. [*Jumbo* comes from the name of a large circus elephant.]

jump shot (jump′ shot′), (in basketball) shot made while jumping, especially at the highest point of the jump.

June (jün), the sixth month of the year. It has 30 days. n.

jur·y (jur′ē), group of persons chosen to give a judgment in a court of law or to decide who is the winner in a contest: *The jury gave her poem the first prize.* n., pl. **jur·ies.**

K

Kan·sas (kan′zəs), one of the midwestern states of the United States. *Abbreviation:* Kans. or KS *Capital:* Topeka. n.

kay·ak (kī′ak), an Eskimo canoe made of skins stretched over a light frame of wood or bone with an opening in the middle for a person. n. Also, **kaiak.**

key se·quence (kē′ sē′kwəns), a connected series of keys on a calculator used in order to obtain a result.

kick (kik), strike out with the foot: *The boy kicked the soccer ball.* v.

kin·der·gar·ten (kin′dər gärt′n), school or class for children from about 4 to 6 years old that educates them by games, toys, and pleasant occupations. *n.* [*Kindergarten* is from German *Kindergarten*, which comes from *Kinder*, meaning "children," and *Garten*, meaning "garden."]

kitch·en (kich′ən), room or area where food is cooked. *n.* [*Kitchen* comes from Old English *cycene*, and can be traced back to Latin *coquere*, meaning "to cook."]

knee (nē), the joint between the thigh and the lower leg. *n.*

kneel (nēl), go down on one's knee or knees: *She knelt down to pull a weed. He kneels in prayer. v.,* **knelt** (nelt) or **kneeled, kneel·ing.**

knit (nit), make (cloth or an article of clothing) by looping yarn or thread together with long needles, or by machinery which forms loops instead of weaving: *knit a pair of socks. v.,* **knit·ted** or **knit, knit·ting.**

knob (nob), handle on a door, drawer, etc.: *the knob on the dial of a television set. n.*

knot (not), **1** a fastening made by tying or twining together pieces of one or more ropes, cords, strings, etc.: *a square knot, a slip knot.* **2** tie or twine together in a knot: *He knotted two ropes together.* **3** group; cluster: *A knot of students stood talking outside the classroom.* 1,3 *n.,* 2 *v.,* **knot·ted, knot·ting.**

know (nō), have knowledge, have facts: *I know from experience how to drive on icy roads. She knows the poem. v.,* **knew** (nü), **known, know·ing.**

known (nōn), See **know.** *George Washington is known as the father of his country. v.*

Kwan·zaa or **Kwan·za** (kwän′zə), a yearly African American celebration celebrating various African festivals. It lasts from December 26 to January 1. *n.* [*Kwanzaa* is from Swahili *Kwanza*, originally meaning "first (fruits)," which comes from *kuanza*, meaning "to begin."]

Kwanzaa
a family celebrating
Kwanzaa

L

la·crosse (lə krós′), game played on a field with a ball and long-handled, loosely strung rackets by two teams, usually of 10 players each. The players carry the ball in the rackets, trying to send it into the other team's goal. *n.*

la·dy (lā′dē), **1** woman of good family and high social position: *a lady by birth.* **2** a well-bred woman: *I borrowed the lady's umbrella.* **3** a polite term for any woman. "Ladies" is often used in speaking or writing to a group of women: *They went to the ladies' room.* **4** woman who has the rights and authority of a lord. *n., pl.* **la·dies.**

lamb (lam), a young sheep. *n.*

land·form (land′fôrm′), a physical feature of the earth's surface. Plains, plateaus, hills, and mountains are landforms. *n., pl.* **land·forms.**

large (lärj), of more than the usual size, amount, or number; big: *America is a large country. A hundred thousand dollars is a large sum of money. adj.,* **larg·er, larg·est.**

la·sa·gna (lə zä′nyə), dish consisting of chopped meat, cheese, and tomato sauce, baked with layers of wide noodles. *n.*

lasagna
lasagna topped with
grated cheese

a	hat	**ī**	ice	**ů**	put	**ə** *stands for*	
ā	age	**o**	not	**ü**	rule	**a**	in about
ä	far, calm	**ō**	open	**ch**	child	**e**	in taken
âr	care	**ȯ**	saw	**ng**	long	**i**	in pencil
e	let	**ô**	order	**sh**	she	**o**	in lemon
ē	equal	**oi**	oil	**th**	thin	**u**	in circus
ėr	term	**ou**	out	**ᴛʜ**	then		
i	it	**u**	cup	**zh**	measure		

library (definition 2)
gathering information at
the **library**

lion
A **lion** can be 3 feet
high at the shoulder.

late·ly (lāt′lē), a little while ago; not long ago; recently: *He has not been looking well lately. adv.*

lat·i·tude (lat′ə tüd *or* lat′ə tyüd), distance north or south of the equator, measured in degrees. A degree of latitude is about 69 miles (111 kilometers). *n.*

laugh (laf), make the sounds and movements of the face and body that show one is happy or amused: *We all laughed at the joke. v.,* **laughed, laugh·ing.**

lay-up (lā′up′), (in basketball) a shot from close under the basket. *n.*

la·zy (lā′zē), not willing to work or be active: *He lost his job because he was lazy. adj.,* **la·zi·er, la·zi·est.**

lead (lēd), the opening paragraph in a newspaper or magazine article. A lead often summarizes the information in the body of the article. *n.*

lead·er (lē′dər), person who leads, or is well fitted to lead: *an orchestra leader. That girl is a born leader. n., pl.* **lead·ers.**

least (lēst), less than any other; smallest; slightest: *Ten cents is a little money; five cents is less; one cent is least. I have the least work. adj.*

leg (leg), one of the limbs on which people and animals stand and walk. *n.*
on one's last legs, about to fail, collapse, or die.
pull one's leg, INFORMAL. fool, trick, or make fun of one.
shake a leg, hurry up.

length (lengkth *or* length), how long a thing is; what a thing measures from end to end; the longest way a thing can be measured: *the length of a room, an animal eight inches in length. n.*

lens (lenz), **1** a curved piece of glass which brings closer together or sends wider apart the rays of light passing through it. The lens of a camera forms images on film. **2** the part of the eye that focuses light rays upon the retina. *n., pl.* **lens·es.**

let's (lets), let us: *Let's go for a walk.*

let·tuce (let′is), the large, crisp, green leaves of a garden plant, used in salad. *n.*

lev·el (lev′əl), **1** having the same height everywhere; flat; even: *a level floor.* **2** an instrument for showing whether a surface is level. 1 *adj.,* 2 *n.*

li·brar·i·an (lī brer′ē ən), person in charge of a library. *n.*

li·brar·y (lī′brer′ē), **1** collection of books, magazines, films, recordings, etc. **2** room or building where such a collection is kept for public use and borrowing. *n., pl.* **li·brar·ies.**

limb (lim), a large branch: *They sawed the dead limb off the tree. n.*

line (līn), a set of points continuing without end in both directions. *n.*

li·on (lī′ən), a large, strong, flesh-eating cat, with a dull-yellowish coat, and a loud roar. It is found in Africa and southern Asia. The male has a full, flowing mane of coarse hair. *n.*

liq·uid (lik′wid), **1** substance that is not a solid or a gas; substance that flows freely like water. **2** In the form of a liquid; melted: *liquid soap, butter heated until it is liquid.* 1 *n.,* 2 *adj.*

lo·cal (lō′kəl), of a place; of a certain place or places: *the local doctor, local self-government, local news. adj.*

lo·cate (lō′kāt), establish in a place: *They located their new store on Second Avenue. v.,* **lo·cat·ed, lo·cat·ing.**

lo·ca·tion (lō kā′shən), position or place: *The camp was in a bad location as there was no water near it. n.*

lock (lok), an enclosed section of a canal or dock in which the level of the water can be changed by letting water in or out, to raise or lower ships. *n., pl.* **locks.**

lon·gi·tude (lon′jə tüd *or* lon′jə tyüd), distance east or west on the earth's surface, measured in degrees from Greenwich, England. *n.*

loose (lüs), **1** not tight: *loose clothing.* **2** not firmly set or fastened in: *a loose tooth.* 1,2 *adj.,* **loos·er, loos·est.**

lose (lüz), **1** not have any longer; have taken away from one by accident, carelessness, parting, death, etc.: *lose a finger, lose a friend, lose one's life.* **2** fail to win: *lose the prize. v.,* **lost** (lȯst), **los·ing.**

lo·tus (lō′təs), kind of water lily that grows in Egypt, India, and Asia. *n., pl.* **lo·tus·es.**

loud (loud), **1** making a great sound; not quiet or soft: *a loud voice, a loud noise.* **2** in a loud manner: *The hunter called long and loud. adj.*

love (luv), have such a warm liking or deep feeling for: *We love our parents. I love my country. v.,* **loved, lov·ing.**

lux·ur·i·ate (lug zhu̇r′ē āt or luk shu̇r′ē āt), **1** indulge in luxury. **2** take great delight: *The campers planned to luxuriate in hot baths when they came home.* **3** grow very abundantly. *v.,* **lux·ur·i·at·ed, lux·ur·i·at·ing.**

M

ma·chine (mə shēn′), arrangement of fixed and moving parts for doing work, each part having some special function: *Sewing machines and washing machines make housework easier. n.*

mag·net (mag′nit), stone or piece of metal that has the property of attracting iron or steel. A lodestone is a natural magnet. *n.*

mag·net·ic field (mag net′ik fēld′), space around a magnet or electric current in which its magnetic force is felt.

mag·net·ism (mag′nə tiz′əm), properties or qualities of a magnet; the showing of magnetic properties. *n.*

mar·ble (mär′bəl), **1** a hard rock formed from limestone by heat and pressure. It may be white or colored and can be polished to a smooth gloss. Marble is used for statues and in buildings. **2** made of marble. 1 *n.,* 2 *adj.*

March (märch), the third month of the year. It has 31 days. *n.*

mat·ter (mat′ər), importance; significance: *Let it go since it is of no matter. n.*

maul (mȯl), beat and pull about; handle roughly. *v.,* **mauled, maul·ing.**

max·im (mak′səm), a short rule of conduct; proverb: *"Look before you leap" is a maxim. n.*

may (mā), be permitted or allowed to: *May I have an apple? v., past tense* **might.**

May (mā), the fifth month of the year. It has 31 days. *n.*

mean¹ (mēn), have as a purpose; have in mind. *v.,* **meant, mean·ing.**

mean² (mēn), not noble; petty; unkind; small-minded: *It is mean to spread gossip about your friends. adj.*

meant (ment), See **mean¹.** *She explained what she meant. v.*

meet¹ (mēt), **1** come face to face (with something or someone coming from the other direction): *Our car met another car on a narrow bridge.* **2** fulfill; put an end to; satisfy: *The campers took along enough food to meet their needs for a week.* **3** a meeting; a gathering: *an athletic meet.* 1,2 *v.,* **met** (met), **meet·ing;** 3 *n.* **—meet′er,** *n.*

lotus
The **lotus** is the national flower of India.

magnet
A **magnet** attracts iron or steel.

a	hat	**ī**	ice	**u̇**	put	**ə** *stands for*	
ā	age	**o**	not	**ü**	rule	**a**	in about
ä	far, calm	**ō**	open	**ch**	child	**e**	in taken
âr	care	**ȯ**	saw	**ng**	long	**i**	in pencil
e	let	**ô**	order	**sh**	she	**o**	in lemon
ē	equal	**oi**	oil	**th**	thin	**u**	in circus
ėr	term	**ou**	out	**ŦH**	then		
i	it	**u**	cup	**zh**	measure		

meet² (mēt), OLD USE. suitable; proper; fitting: *It is meet that you should help your friends.* adj.

Mem·o·ri·al Day (mə môr'ē əl dā'), holiday for remembering and honoring members of the United States armed services who have died. In most states, it is observed on the last Monday in May.

mem·or·y (mem'ər ē), person, thing, or event that is remembered: *I was so young when we moved that our old house is only a vague memory.* n., pl. **mem·or·ies.**

memory mi·nus (mem'ər ē mī'nəs), the computer key that enables the user to subtract the display from what is in the memory.

memory plus (mem'ər ē plus'), the computer key that enables the user to add the display to what is in the memory.

memory re·call (mem'ər ē rē'kòl'), the computer key that enables the user to display what is in memory.

men·u (men'yü), list of the food served at a meal; bill of fare. n.

me·rid·i·an (mə rid'ē ən), an imaginary circle passing through any place on the earth's surface and through the North and South Poles. Meridians mark longitude. n., pl. **me·rid·i·ans.**

me·te·o·rol·o·gist (mē'tē ə rol'ə jist), a person who studies weather. n.

me·ter¹ (mē'tər), the basic unit of length in the metric system. A meter is equal to 39.37 inches. n. Also, **metre.**

me·ter² (mē'tər), **1** any kind of poetic rhythm; the arrangement of beats or accents in a line of poetry. **2** musical rhythm; the arrangement of beats in music: *Three-fourths meter is waltz time.* n.

met·ric (met'rik), of the meter or the metric system. adj.

Mich·i·gan (mish'ə gən), **Lake,** one of the five Great Lakes. It lies entirely within the United States. n.

middle ear (mid'l ir'), the three tiny bones that carry sound waves from the eardrum to the inner ear.

Middle English (mid'l ing'glish), period in the development of the English language between Old English and Modern English, lasting from 1100 to about 1500.

might (mīt), See **may.** *Mother said that we might play in the barn.* v.

might·'ve (mīt'əv), might have: *He might've been outdoors when you called.*

mis·be·have (mis'bi hāv'), behave badly. v., **mis·be·haved, mis·be·hav·ing.**

mis·for·tune (mis fôr'chən), bad luck; unlucky accident. *She had the misfortune to break her arm.* n.

mis·lead (mis lēd'), cause to go in the wrong direction; lead astray: *Our guide misled us and we got lost.* v., **mis·led, mis·lead·ing.**

mis·led (mis led'), See **mislead.** *We were misled on our hike by a careless guide.* v.

mis·place (mis plās'), put in a place and then forget where it is; mislay: *I have misplaced my pencil.* v., **mis·placed, mis·plac·ing.**

miss (mis), **1** fail to hit: *I swung at the ball and missed it.* **2** fail to catch: *miss the train.* **3** notice the absence of; feel keenly the absence of: *I missed you while you were away.* v., **missed, miss·ing.**

mis·sion (mish'ən), a sending or being sent on some special work; errand. An operation by one or more aircraft against the enemy is called a mission. n.

Mis·sis·sip·pi (mis'ə sip'ē), **1** large river in the United States. It flows south from N Minnesota to the Gulf of Mexico. **2** one of the south central states of the United States. *Abbreviation:* Miss. or MS. *Capital:* Jackson. n.

mis·spell (mis spel'), spell incorrectly. v.

mis·treat (mis trēt'), treat badly. v.

mod·el (mod'l), **1** a small copy: *a model of a ship or an engine.* **2** thing or person to be copied or imitated: *Your mother is a fine person; make her your model.* n.

model (definition 1)
painting a **model** of the
space shuttle

mois·ture (mois′chər), slight wetness; water or other liquid suspended in drops in the air or spread on a surface. *n.*

mo·lar (mō′lər), tooth with a broad surface for grinding. A person's back teeth are molars. *n.*

mo·ment (mō′mənt), a very short space of time; instant. *n.*

mon·ey (mun′ē), coins of gold, silver, or other metal, or paper notes which represent these metals, issued by a government for use in buying and selling. *n., pl.* **mon·eys** or **mon·ies.**

mon·key (mung′kē), **1** animal of the group most like human beings. **2** person, especially a child, who is full of mischief. *n., pl.* **mon·keys.**

mood (müd), state of mind or feeling: *I am in the mood to play now; I don't want to study. n.*

morn·ing (môr′ning), the early part of the day, ending at noon. *n.*

moth·er (muᴛʜ′ər), a female parent. *I'll have to ask my mother. n.*

mo·tor (mō′tər), an engine, such as a gasoline or diesel engine, that makes a machine go. *n.*

mo·tor·cy·cle (mō′tər sī′kəl), a two-wheeled motor vehicle which resembles a bicycle but is heavier and larger. *n.*

moun·tain (moun′tən), a very high hill. *n.*

mouth (mouth), the opening through which a person or animal takes in food; space containing the tongue and teeth. *n.*
down in the mouth, INFORMAL. in low spirits; discouraged.

move·ment (müv′mənt), **1** act or fact of moving: *We run by movements of the legs.* **2** the moving parts of a machine; special group of connected parts that move together. The movement of a watch consists of many little wheels. *n.*

Mr. or **Mr** (mis′tər), Mister, a title put in front of a man's name or the name of his position: *Mr. Stern, Mr. President. pl.* **Messrs.**

Mrs. or **Mrs** (mis′iz), a title put in front of a married woman's name: *Mrs. Weiss. pl.* **Mmes.**

Ms. (miz), a title put in front of a woman's name: *Ms. Karen Hansen. pl.* **Mses.**

muf·fin (muf′ən), a small, round cake made of wheat flour, corn meal, or the like, often without sugar. *n.*

mul·ti·pli·ca·tion (mul′tə plə kā′shən), operation of multiplying one number by another. *n.*

mu·sic (myü′zik), beautiful, pleasing, or interesting arrangements of sounds. *n.*

music box (myü′zik boks′), box or case containing apparatus for producing music mechanically.

music hall (myü′zik hȯl′), hall for musical performances.

music vid·e·o (myü′zik vid′ē ō), a short musical film or videotape or videodisc. *pl.* **music vid·e·os.**

mus·tard (mus′tərd), a yellow powder or paste made from the seeds of the mustard plant, used as seasoning. *n.*

must·n't (mus′nt), must not: *You mustn't wake the baby.*

my·self (mī self′), form used instead of *me* or *I* in cases like: *I can cook for myself. I hurt myself. pron.*

mys·ter·y (mis′tər ē), something that is hidden or unknown; secret. *n., pl.* **mys·ter·ies.**

monkey (definition 1)

mountain

a	hat	ī	ice	u̇	put	ə stands for
ā	age	o	not	ü	rule	a in about
ä	far, calm	ō	open	ch	child	e in taken
âr	care	ȯ	saw	ng	long	i in pencil
e	let	ô	order	sh	she	o in lemon
ē	equal	oi	oil	th	thin	u in circus
ėr	term	ou	out	ᴛʜ	then	
i	it	u	cup	zh	measure	

275

N

na·tion (nā′shən), people occupying the same country, united under the same government, and usually speaking the same language. *n.*

na·tion·al (nash′ə nəl), of a nation; belonging to a whole nation: *national laws, a national disaster. adj.*

na·tur·al gas (nach′ər əl gas′), a combustible gas formed naturally in the earth, consisting primarily of methane. It is used as a fuel.

Nav·a·jo (nav′ə hō), member of a tribe of American Indians living mainly in New Mexico, Arizona, and Utah. *n., pl.* **Nav·a·jos** or **Nav·a·joes.**

nee·dle·leaf (nē′dl lēf′), of or about a type of tree with thin, sharp needles. A pine is a needleleaf tree. *adj.*

neg·a·tive (neg′ə tiv), a photographic image in which the lights and shadows are reversed. Prints are made from it. *n.*

neigh·bor (nā′bər), someone who lives in the next house or nearby. *n.*

neph·ew (nef′yü), son of one's brother or sister; son of one's brother-in-law or sister-in-law. *n.*

nerve (nėrv), **1** mental strength; courage: *nerves of steel.* **2** INFORMAL. rude boldness; impudence. *n.*

net (net), an open fabric made of string, cord, or thread, knotted together in such a way as to leave holes regularly arranged. *n.*

news·cast·er (nüz′kas′tər or nyüz′kas′tər), person or commentator who gives the news on a newscast. *n.*

news·pa·per (nüz′pā′pər or nyüz′pā′pər), a daily or weekly publication printed on large sheets of paper folded together, telling the news, carrying advertisements, and having stories, pictures, articles, and useful information. *n.*

newspaper
We read **newspapers** for information.

nic·o·tine (nik′ə tēn′), poison contained in the leaves, roots, and seeds of tobacco. *n.* [*Nicotine* comes from Jean *Nicot*, about 1530-1600, a Frenchman who introduced tobacco to France in about 1560.]

night (nīt), **1** the time between evening and morning, especially when it is dark. **2** the darkness of night; the dark. *n.*

night crawl·er (nīt′ król′ər), a large earthworm that comes to the surface of the ground at night.

night·gown (nīt′goun′), a long, loose garment worn by a woman or child in bed. *n.*

night·mare (nīt′mâr′), a very distressing dream or experience: *The hurricane was a nightmare. n.*

night·time (nīt′tīm′), time between evening and morning. *n.*

non·sense (non′sens), worthless stuff; junk: *a drawer full of useless gadgets and other nonsense. n.*

noon (nün), 12 o'clock in the daytime; middle of the day. *n.*

nose (nōz), the part of the face or head just above the mouth. The nose has openings for breathing and smelling. *n.*
lead by the nose, have complete control over.

No·vem·ber (nō vem′bər), the 11th month of the year. It has 30 days. *n.*

num·ber (num′bər), **1** the count or sum of a group of things or persons; amount: *The number of students in our class is twenty.* **2** figure or mark that stands for a number; numeral. *n.*

number key (num′bər kē′), a key on a calculator that shows one of the numbers 0 through 9. *n., pl.* **number keys.**

number sen·tence (num′bər sen′təns), a way to write a relationship between numbers. 18 + 27 = 45 and 9 > 6 are number sentences.

o

oak (ōk), several kinds of trees or shrubs found in most parts of the world, with strong, hard, durable wood and nuts called acorns. *n.*

oc·cur (ə kėr′), take place; happen: *Storms often occur in winter. v.,* **oc·curred, oc·cur·ring.**

o·cean (ō′shən), the great body of salt water that covers almost three-fourths of the earth's surface; the sea. *n.*

oc·e·lot (os′ə lot *or* ō′sə lot), a spotted cat somewhat like a leopard, but smaller, found from Texas through Mexico and into parts of South America. *n.*

o'clock (ə klok′), of the clock; by the clock: *It is one o'clock. adv.*

Oc·to·ber (ok tō′bər), the tenth month of the year. It has 31 days. *n.*

odd (od), strange; peculiar; unusual: *What an odd house; it has no windows. adj.*

of (ov *or* uv; *unstressed* əv), **1** belonging to: *a friend of my childhood, the news of the day, the driver of the car.* **2** in regard to; concerning; about: *think well of somebody. prep.*

off (ȯf), so as to stop or lessen: *Turn the water off. adv.*

of·fer (ȯ′fər), hold out to be taken or refused; present: *offer one's hand. She offered us her help. v.*

of·fice (ȯ′fis), place in which the work of a business or profession is done; room in which to work: *The doctor's office is closed. n.*

of·ten (ȯ′fən), in many cases; many times; frequently: *Blame is often misdirected. We come here often. adv.*

oil (oil), any of several kinds of thick, fatty or greasy liquids that are lighter than water, burn easily, and are soluble in alcohol, but not in water, such as mineral oils, kerosene, vegetable and animal oils, olive oils. *n.*

oil gland (oil′ gland′), gland of the skin that secretes oil.

Old Eng·lish (ōld′ ing′glish), period in the history of the English language before 1100.

om·niv·ore (om′nə vôr′), a consumer that eats producers and consumers. *n.*

on·ly (ōn′lē), merely; just: *only on weekends. adv.*

On·tar·io (on ter′ē ō), **Lake,** one of the five Great Lakes that borders New York and Canada. The water from Niagara Falls flows from Lake Erie to Lake Ontario. It is the smallest of the five Great Lakes. *n.*

o·pen (ō′pən), **1** not shut; not closed; letting (anyone or anything) in or out: *Open windows let in the fresh air.* **2** make or become open: *He is opening the window. The door opened.* **3** spread out or unfold: *open a book, open a letter.* 1 *adj.,* 2,3 *v.,* **o·pened, o·pen·ing.**

op·e·ra·tion (op′ə rā′shən), the way a thing works: *The operation of this machine is simple. n.*

operation key (op′ə rā′shən kē′), the key which tells the calculator what to perform. The symbols +, −, ×, and ÷ appear on the operation keys. *n., pl.* **operation keys.**

op·tic (op′tik), of the eye; of the sense of sight. The **optic nerve** goes from the eye to the brain. *adj.*

or·ches·tra (or′kə strə), group of musicians playing together on various stringed, wind, and percussion instruments. *n., pl.* **or·ches·tras.**

ocelot
An **ocelot** can be up to 3 feet long without the tail.

a	hat	ī	ice	u̇	put	ə *stands for*	
ā	age	o	not	ü	rule	a	in about
ä	far, calm	ō	open	ch	child	e	in taken
âr	care	ȯ	saw	ng	long	i	in pencil
e	let	ô	order	sh	she	o	in lemon
ē	equal	oi	oil	th	thin	u	in circus
ėr	term	ou	out	ᴛH	then		
i	it	u	cup	zh	measure		

parallel (definition 1)
parallel stripes on a
piece of fabric

oth·er (uTH′ər), **1** additional or further: *I have no other place to go.* **2** other person or thing. 1 *adj.,* 2 *pron.*

our (our), of us; belonging to us: *We need our coats now. adj.*

our·selves (our selvz′), form used instead of *we* or *us* in cases like: *We cook for ourselves. pron. pl.*

out·cast (out′kast′), person or animal cast out from home and friends. *n.*

out·er ear (ou′tər ir′), the part of the ear outside of the head and the ear canal.

out·look (out′lůk′), way of thinking about things; attitude of mind; point of view: *a cheerful outlook on life. n.*

out·side (out′sīd′), **1** the side or surface that is out; outer part: *polish the outside of a car, the outside of a house.* **2** on or to the outside; outdoors: *Run outside and play.* 1 *n.,* 2 *adv.*

o·ven (uv′ən), an enclosed space, usually in a stove, for baking, roasting, and sometimes broiling food. *n.*

P

pack·age (pak′ij), bundle of things packed or wrapped together; box with things packed in it; parcel. *n.*

pad·dle (pad′l), row (a boat or canoe) with a paddle or paddles. *v.,* **pad·dled, pad·dling.**

pain·ful (pān′fəl), causing pain; unpleasant; hurting: *a painful illness, a painful duty. adj.*

pan·ic (pan′ik), a fear spreading through a multitude of people so that they lose control of themselves; unreasoning fear: *When the theater caught fire, there was a panic. n.*

Parthenon
the ancient **Parthenon**
in Greece

par·al·lel (par′ə lel), **1** straight lines or planes, lying or extending alongside of one another, always equidistant, but never meeting. **2** any of the imaginary circles around the earth parallel to the equator, marking degrees of latitude that run east and west. 1 *adj.,* 2 *n., pl.* **par·al·lels.**

par·al·lel cir·cuit (par′ə ləl sèr′kit), a circuit that connects several objects in a way that the current for each object has its own path.

par·ent (pâr′ənt *or* par′ənt), father or mother. *n., pl.* **par·ents.**

Par·the·non (pär′thə non), temple of Athena on the Acropolis in Athens, regarded as the finest example of Doric architecture. *n.*

par·tic·i·pate (pär tis′ə pāt), have a share; take part. *v.,* **par·tic·i·pat·ed, par·tic·i·pat·ing.**

pave·ment (pāv′mənt), a covering or surface for streets, sidewalks, etc., made of asphalt, concrete, gravel, stones, etc. *n.*

pay·ment (pā′mənt), amount paid: *a monthly payment of $10. n.*

peace (pēs), freedom from war: *work for world peace. n.*

peace·ful (pēs′fəl), **1** full of peace; quiet; calm: *It was peaceful in the mountains.* **2** free from trouble or disturbance. *adj.*

ped·al (ped′l), **1** lever worked by the foot; the part on which the foot is placed to move any kind of machinery. **2** move by pedals: *He pedaled his bicycle slowly up the hill.* 1 *n.,* 2 *v.,* **ped·aled, ped·al·ing** *or* **ped·alled, ped·al·ling.**

pe·des·tri·an (pə des′trē ən), person who goes on foot; walker. *n., pl.* **pe·des·tri·ans.**

peep (pēp), **1** the cry of a young bird or chicken; a sound like a chirp or squeak. **2** make such a sound; chirp. 1 *n.,* 2 *v.*

pe·o·ny (pē′ə nē), garden plant with large, showy red, pink, or white flowers. *n., pl.* **pe·o·nies.** [The *peony* was named by the Greeks for Paeon, physician of the gods (because the plant was used in medicine).]

peo·ple (pē′pəl), men, women, and children; persons. *n. pl.*

per·fect (pèr′fikt), without defect; not spoiled at any point; faultless: *a perfect spelling paper. adj.*

pe·rim·e·ter (pə rim′ə tər), the outer boundary of a figure or area: *the perimeter of a circle, the perimeter of a garden. n.*

per·pen·dic·u·lar (pėr′pən dik′ yə lər), at right angles to. Perpendicular lines intersect to form right angles. *adj.*

per·son·al (pėr′sə nəl), of a person; individual; private: *a personal letter, a personal matter. adj.*

per·son·al·i·ty (pėr′sə nal′ə tē), pleasing or attractive qualities of a person: *The boy is developing a personality. n., pl.* **per·son·al·i·ties.**

pet·al (pet′l), one of the parts of a flower that are usually colored. A daisy has many petals. *n.*

pho·to (fō′tō), picture made with a camera. A photograph is made by the action of light rays from the thing pictured passing through the lens of the camera onto the film. *n.*

pick·le (pik′əl), cucumber preserved in salt water, vinegar, or other liquid. *n.*

piece (pēs), **1** one of the parts into which a thing is divided or broken; bit. **2** portion; limited part; small quantity: *a piece of bread. n.*

pig·eon (pij′ən), any of a group of birds with thick bodies, short tails and legs, which makes a cooing sound, including doves and many varieties of domestic pigeons. *n.*

Pil·grim (pil′grəm), one of the Puritan settlers of Plymouth Colony in 1620. *n., pl.* **Pil·grims.**

pint (pīnt), unit of measure for liquids and dry things, equal to ½ quart; 2 cups; 16 fluid ounces. *n.*

pis·til (pis′tl), the part of a flower that produces seeds. It consists, when complete, of an ovary, a style, and a stigma. *n.*

pitch·er[1] (pich′ər), container for holding and pouring liquids, with a lip on one side and a handle on the other. *n.*

pitch·er[2] (pich′ər), a baseball player who pitches the ball to the batter. *n.*

piz·za (pēt′sə), a spicy Italian dish made by baking a large flat layer of bread dough covered with cheese, tomato sauce, herbs, etc. *n., pl.* **piz·zas.**

plain (plān), a flat stretch of land; prairie: *Cattle and horses wandered over the plains. n., pl.* **plains.**

pla·teau (pla tō′), plain in the mountains or at a height considerably above sea level; large, high plain. *n., pl.* **pla·teaus** (pla tōz′).

plate (plāt), a large section of rock that makes up part of the earth's crust. *n., pl.* **plates.**

play (plā), **1** something done to amuse oneself; fun; sport; recreation: *The children are happy at play.* **2** have fun; do something in sport. *The kitten plays with its tail. He played a joke on his sister.* 1 *n.,* 2 *v.*

pledge (plej), **1** a solemn promise: *they made a pledge to give money to charity.* **2** promise solemnly: *We pledge allegiance to the flag.* 1 *n.,* 2 *v.,* **pledged, pledg·ing.**

pluck·y (pluk′ē), having or showing courage: *a plucky dog. adj.,* **pluck·i·er, pluck·i·est.**

pock·et (pok′it), a small bag or pouch sewed into clothing for carrying money or other small articles. *n.*

pod (pod), a small herd of whales or seals. *n.*

po·et·ry (pō′i trē), poems: *a collection of poetry. n.*

point (point), (in mathematics) something that has position without length or width. *n.*

pitcher[1]
a **pitcher** of milk

a	hat	ī	ice	u̇	put		ə *stands for*
ā	age	o	not	ü	rule		a in about
ä	far, calm	ō	open	ch	child		e in taken
âr	care	ȯ	saw	ng	long		i in pencil
e	let	ô	order	sh	she		o in lemon
ē	equal	oi	oil	th	thin		u in circus
ėr	term	ou	out	ᵺ	then		
i	it	u	cup	zh	measure		

polar bear

po·lar bear (pō′lər bâr′) a large, white bear of the artic regions.

pole (pōl), either of two parts where opposite forces are strongest. A magnet or battery has both a positive pole and a negative pole. *n., pl.* **poles.**

pol·len (pol′ən), tiny grains that make seeds when combined with a flower's eggs. *n.*

pol·lu·tion (pə lü′shən), anything that dirties the environment, especially waste material: *pollution in the air. n.*

pond (pond), body of still water, smaller than a lake. *n.*

pop (pop), make a short, quick, explosive sound. *v.,* **popped, pop·ping.**

pore (pôr), a very small opening. Sweat comes through the pores in the skin. *n.*

por·trait (pôr′trit *or* pôr′trāt), picture of a person, especially of the face. *n.*

pot·ter·y (pot′ər ē), pots, dishes, vases, etc., made from clay and hardened by heat. *n., pl.* **pot·ter·ies.**

pottery
ancient **pottery** made
by North American Indians

pour (pôr), flow or cause to flow in a steady stream: *I poured the milk from the bottle. The rain poured down on the field. v.*

pow·er (pou′ər), **1** strength or force; might. **2** authority; influence; control; right: *Congress has power to declare war. n.*

pow·er·ful (pou′ər fəl), having great power or force; mighty; strong: *a powerful person, a powerful medicine, a powerful argument. adj.*

pred·a·tor (pred′ə tər), a consumer that hunts and eats animals. *n.*

pres·sure (presh′ər), a state of trouble or strain: *She has been working under pressure. n.*

prey (prā), animal hunted and killed for food by another animal: *Mice and birds are the prey of cats. n.*

prime me·rid·i·an (prīm′ mə rid′ē ən), meridian from which the longitude east and west is measured. It passes through Greenwich, England, and its longitude is 0 degrees.

print (print), **1** photograph produced from a negative. **2** produce a photograph by transmission of light through a negative. 1 *n.,* 2 *v.*

pri·vate (prī′vit), not for the public; for just a few special people or for one: *a private road, a private house. adj.*

prob·a·bly (prob′ə blē), more likely than not. *adv.*

pro·duc·er (prə dü′sər), a living thing that can use sunlight to make sugars. *n., pl.* **pro·duc·ers.**

prod·uct (prod′əkt), **1** that which is produced; result of work or of growth: *factory products, farm products.* **2** number resulting from multiplying two or more numbers together: *40 is the product of 8 and 5. n., pl.* **prod·ucts.**

proud (proud), feeling or thinking well of, showing satisfaction: *I am proud to call him my friend. adj.*

psy·chol·o·gist (sī kol′ə jist), an expert who is trained to help people with feelings, especially troubled feelings that last a long time. *n.*

pud·ding (pùd′ing), a soft cooked food, usually sweet: *rice pudding. n.*

pueb·lo (pweb′lō), an Indian village built of adobe and stone. *n., pl.* **pueb·los.**

pun·ish (pun′ish), cause pain, loss, or discomfort to for some fault or offense: *punish criminals for wrongdoing. v.* [*Punish* is from Old French *puniss-,* a form of *punir,* meaning "punish," which came from Latin *punire,* meaning "penalty."]

pun·ish·ment (pun′ish mənt), pain, suffering, or loss: *Her punishment for lying was not being allowed to watch TV. n.*

pup (pup), a young dog; puppy. *n.*

pu·pil¹ (pyü′pəl), person who is learning in school or being taught by someone. *n.*

pu·pil² (pyü′pəl), the opening in the center of the iris of the eye which looks like a black spot and where light can enter the eye. *n.*

pur·suit (pər süt′), a chase: *The dog is in pursuit of the cat. n.*

Q

quart (kwôrt), measure of capacity for liquids, equal to one-fourth of a gallon: *a quart of milk. n.*

queen (kwēn), woman who rules a country and its people. *n.*

ques·tion (kwes′chən), thing asked in order to get information; inquiry: *The teacher answered the children's questions. n.*

quick (kwik), fast and sudden; swift: *The cat made a quick jump. Many weeds have a quick growth. adj.*

qui·et (kwī′ət), making no sound; with little or no noise: *quiet footsteps, a quiet room. adj.*

quilt (kwilt), cover for a bed, usually made of two pieces of cloth with a soft pad between, held in place by stitching. *n.*

quit (kwit), **1** stop: *They quit work at five.* **2** leave: *quit one's job. v.,* **quit** or **quit·ted, quit·ting.**

quite (kwīt), **1** completely; entirely: *a hat quite out of fashion. I am quite alone.* **2** actually; really; positively: *quite the thing. adv.*

quo·tient (kwō′shənt), number arrived at by dividing one number by another. In 26 ÷ 2 = 13, 13 is the quotient. *n.*

R

rain gauge (rān′ gāj′), a tool that measures precipitation. *n.*

rat·tle (rat′l), toy, instrument, etc., that makes a noise when it is shaken. *n.*

ray (rā), a set of points that has one endpoint and that extends without end in one direction. *n.*

Rd., Road.

re·act (rē akt′), act in response: *Dogs react to affection. v.*

re·al·ly (rē′ə lē), actually; truly; in fact. *adv.*

rea·son (rē′zn), **1** justification; explanation: *What is your reason for being so late?* **2** think logically; think things out: *Most animals can't reason.* 1 *n.,* 2 *v.*

re·bound (rē′bound′), (in basketball) a ball that bounds back off the backboard or the rim of the basket after a shot has been made. *n.*

re·build (rē bild′), build again or anew. *v.,* **re·built** (rē bilt′), **re·build·ing.**

re·call (ri kȯl′), call back to mind; remember: *I can recall stories told to me when I was a small child. v.*

re·ceiv·er (ri sē′vər), thing that receives: *Public telephones have coin receivers for change. n.*

re·cent (rē′snt), done or made not long ago: *recent events. adj.*

re·cess (rē′ses or ri ses′), time during which work stops: *There will be a short recess before the next meeting. n.*

rec·og·nize (rek′əg nīz), **1** know again: *You have grown so much that I scarcely recognized you.* **2** identify: *recognize a person from a description. v.,* **rec·og·nized, rec·og·niz·ing.**

quilt
a sampler **quilt**

a	hat	ī	ice	u̇	put	ə stands for	
ā	age	o	not	ü	rule	a	in about
ä	far, calm	ō	open	ch	child	e	in taken
âr	care	ȯ	saw	ng	long	i	in pencil
e	let	ô	order	sh	she	o	in lemon
ē	equal	oi	oil	th	thin	u	in circus
ėr	term	ou	out	ŦH	then		
i	it	u	cup	zh	measure		

scratch (skrach), 1 rub or scrape to relieve itching: *Don't scratch your mosquito bites.* 2 a mark made by scratching: *He had a large scratch on his arm.* 1 v., 2 n., pl. scratch·es.
from scratch, with no advantages; without help; without prepackaged ingredients.

scream (skrēm), a loud, sharp, piercing cry. n.

screen (skrēn), 1 wire woven together with small openings in between. 2 a glass surface on which television pictures, computer information, radar images, etc., appear. n.

scrub (skrub), 1 rub hard; wash or clean by rubbing: *I scrubbed the floor with a brush and soap.* 2 a scrubbing: *Give your hands a good scrub.* 1 v., scrubbed, scrub·bing; 2 n.

seal (sēl), a flesh-eating sea mammal with large flippers, living usually in cold regions. n., pl. seals or seal.

sea·son (sē′zn), 1 one of the four periods of the year; spring, summer, autumn, or winter. 2 any period of time marked by something special: *a holiday season, the harvest season.* n.

see (sē), be aware of by using the eyes; look at: *See that black cloud.* v., saw (so), seen, see·ing.

seed (sēd), the part of a plant from which another plant like it can grow. A seed has an outer skin or coat which encloses the embryo that will become the new plant and a supply of food for its growth. n., pl. seeds or seed.

seen (sēn), See see. *Have you seen Father?* v.

seg·ment (seg′mənt), two points and the part of a line between them. n.

seis·mo·graph (sīz′mə graf), instrument for recording the direction, strength and length of earthquakes. n. [*Seismograph* comes from Greek *seismos,* meaning "earthquake," and the combining form *-graph.*]

seal
Seals usually live in cold areas.

seismograph
A **seismograph** records sudden movements of the earth's crust.

sep·a·rate (sep′ə rāt′), 1 keep apart; be between; divide: *The Atlantic Ocean separates America from Europe.* 2 divide into parts or groups: *separate a tangle of yarn.* v., sep·a·rat·ed, sep·a·rat·ing.

sep·a·ra·tion (sep′ə rā′shən), a being apart; being separated: *The friends were glad to meet after so long a separation.* n.

Sep·tem·ber (sep tem′bər), the ninth month of the year. It has 30 days. n.

ser·ies cir·cuit (sir′ēz sėr′kit), a circuit that connects several objects one after the other so that the current flows in a single path.

ser·i·ous (sir′ē əs), showing deep thought or purpose; thoughtful; grave: *a serious manner, a serious face.* adj.

serve (sėrv), 1 put (food or drink) on the table. 2 in tennis, a player's turn to start the play by hitting the ball. 1 v., served, serv·ing; 2 n.

set (set), 1 put in the right place, position, or condition; put in proper order; arrange: *The doctor set my broken leg. Set the clock. Set the table for dinner.* 2 number of things or persons belonging together; group; outfit: *a set of dishes.* 1 v., set, set·ting; 2 n.

sev·er·al (sev′ər əl), more than two or three but not many; some; a few: *gain several pounds (adj.). Several have given their consent (n.)*

sham·poo (sham pü′), 1 wash (the hair, the scalp, a rug, etc.) with a soapy or oily preparation. 2 a washing of the hair, the scalp, a rug, etc., with such a preparation. 3 the preparation used in this way. 1 v., sham·pooed, sham·poo·ing; 2,3 n., pl. sham·poos.

share (shâr), use together; enjoy together; have in common: *The sisters share the same room.* v., shared, shar·ing.

she (shē), anything thought of as female and spoken about or mentioned before: *She was my sister. She was a fine old ship.* pron.

sheep (shēp), mammal with a thick coat and hoofs that chews its cud, and makes a baaing sound. Sheep are related to goats and are raised for wool, meat, and skin. *n., pl.* **sheep.**

she'll (shēl), she will: *She'll help you with your problem.*

shel·ter (shel′tər), **1** something that covers or protects from weather, danger, or attack. **2** protection; refuge. *n.*

sher·iff (sher′if), the most important law-enforcing officer of a county. A sheriff appoints deputies who help to keep order in the county. *n.*

shoot (shüt), **1** send swiftly: *A bow shoots an arrow. She shot question after question at us.* **2** move suddenly and swiftly: *A car shot by us. Flames shot up from the burning house.* **3** take (a picture) with a camera; photograph. **4** send (a ball, puck, marble, etc.) toward the goal, pocket, etc. *v.,* **shot** (shot), **shoot·ing.**

short (shôrt), not long; of small extent from end to end. *adj.*

should·n't (shůd′nt), should not: *You shouldn't cross the street without looking both ways.*

show (shō), **1** make clear to; explain to: *Show us how to do the problem.* **2** a play, motion picture, etc., or a performance of one of these: *The show starts at 6:00.* **1** *v.,* **showed, shown** or **showed, show·ing;** **2** *n.*

show·er (shou′ər), bath in which water pours down on the body from an overhead nozzle. *n.*

shown (shōn), See **show.** *We were shown many tricks by the magician. v.*

shud·der (shud′ər), tremble with horror, fear, cold. *v.*

shut·ter (shut′ər), a movable cover, slide, etc., for closing an opening. The device that opens and closes in front of the lens of a camera is the shutter. *n.*

sign (sīn), **1** write: *Sign your initials here.* **2** an inscribed board, space, etc., serving for advertisement, information, regulations, etc.: *See the sign over the door. The stop sign is used by the crossing guard.* **3** motion or gesture used to mean, represent, or point out something: *talk to a deaf person by signs.* **1** *v.,* **2,3** *n.*

sig·nal (sig′nəl), **1** a sign giving notice, warning, or pointing out something. **2** make a signal or signals to: *She signaled the car to stop by raising her hand.* **1** *n.,* **2** *v.,* **sig·naled, sig·nal·ing** or **sig·nalled, sig·nal·ling.**

sil·ver (sil′vər), **1** a shiny, white, precious metal. **2** made of silver: *a silver spoon.* **1** *n.,* **2** *adj.*

sim·ple (sim′pəl), easy to do or understand: *a simple problem. adj.,* **sim·pler, sim·plest.**

si·ren (sī′rən), kind of whistle that makes a loud, piercing sound: *We heard the fire engine's siren. n.*

sis (sis), INFORMAL. sister. *n.*

sit (sit), rest on the lower part of the body with the weight off the feet: *She sat in a chair. v.,* **sat** (sat), **sit·ting.**

skate·board (skāt′bôrd′), **1** a narrow board resembling a surfboard, with roller-skate wheels attached to each end, used for gliding or moving on any hard surface. **2** to ride a skateboard: *The neighborhood children love to skateboard in the summer.* **1** *n.,* **2** *v.*

skate·board·ing (skāt′bôr′ding), the sport of riding a skateboard. *n.*

sheep
a **sheep** and its young

silver
a **silver** table setting

a	hat	ī	ice	ů	put	ə *stands for*	
ā	age	o	not	ü	rule	a	in about
ä	far, calm	ō	open	ch	child	e	in taken
âr	care	ȯ	saw	ng	long	i	in pencil
e	let	ô	order	sh	she	o	in lemon
ē	equal	oi	oil	th	thin	u	in circus
ėr	term	ou	out	ŦH	then		
i	it	u	cup	zh	measure		

ski (definition 1)

skis and ski poles

ski (skē), **1** one of a pair of long, slender pieces of hard wood, plastic, or metal, that can be fastened to the shoes or boots to enable a person to glide over snow. **2** glide over the snow on skis. 1 *n., pl.* **skis** or **ski;** 2 *v.,* **skied, ski·ing.**

skirt (skėrt), **1** a woman's or girl's garment that hangs from the waist. **2** something like a skirt: *A skirt covered the legs of the chair. n.*

skulk (skulk), a group of animals that prey on game, as the fox or weasel. *n.*

sky·scrap·er (skī/skrā/pər), a very tall building. *n.*

slam-dunk (slam/dungk/), (in basketball) a shot made by leaping so that the hands are above the rim of the basket, and throwing the ball down through the netting. *n.*

slap (slap), put, dash, or cast with force. *v.,* **slapped, slap·ping.**

slip (slip), slide suddenly without wanting to: *He slipped on the icy sidewalk. v.,* **slipped, slip·ping.**

slip·per (slip/ər), a light, low shoe that is slipped on easily: *dancing slippers, bedroom slippers. n., pl.* **slip·pers.**

slow (slō), not fast: *Traffic is very slow during rush hour. I walked slowly home. adj.* —**slow/ly,** *adv.*

small (smôl), **1** not large; little; not large as compared with other things of the same kind: *A cottage is smaller than a house.* **2** not great in amount, value: *The cent is our smallest coin. adj.,* **small·er, small·est.**

smoke (smōk), the mixture of gases and particles of carbon that can be seen rising in a cloud from anything burning. *n.*

smug·gle (smug/əl), bring, take, put, etc., secretly: *I tried to smuggle my puppy into the house. v.,* **smug·gled, smug·gling.**

snack (snak), **1** a light meal, especially one eaten between regular meals. **2** to eat a light meal. *We snacked on fruit after school.* 1 *n.,* 2 *v.*

soccer

playing the game of

soccer

snail (snāl), a small, soft-bodied animal that crawls very slowly. Most snails have spiral shells on their backs into which they can move for protection. *n.*

snap·shot (snap/shot/), photograph taken quickly with a small camera. *n.*

snore (snôr), a harsh rough sound made in sleeping. *n.*

soc·cer (sok/ər), game played with a round ball between two teams of eleven players each. The players may strike the ball with any part of the body except the hands and arms. Only the goalkeeper may touch the ball with the hands and arms. Players score by knocking the ball into a net cage at either end of the field. *n.*

soft (sôft), **1** not hard; not stiff; yielding easily to touch: *a soft pillow.* **2** not loud: *a soft voice.* 1,2 *adj.* —**soft/ness,** *n.*

soft·ball (sôft/bôl/), **1** a kind of baseball that is played on a smaller field, with a larger and softer ball, and lighter bats. Softball must be pitched underhand. **2** the ball used in this game. *n.*

soft-boiled (sôft/boild/), (of an egg) boiled only a little so that the yolk is still soft. *adj.*

soft drink (sôft/ dringk/), drink that does not contain alcohol.

soft·en (sôf/ən), make or become soft: *Hand lotion softens the skin. Soap softens in water. v.*

soft soap (sôft/ sōp/), a liquid or semiliquid soap.

some·one (sum/wun), some person; somebody: *Someone is coming. pron.*

some·thing (sum/thing), some thing; a particular thing not named or known: *I'm sure I've forgotten something. n.*

some·times (sum/tīmz), now and then; at times. *adv.*

some·where (sum/hwâr), in or to some place; in or to one place or another: *She lives somewhere in the area. adv.*

source (sôrs), person or place from which anything comes or is obtained: *The newspaper gets news from many sources. Mines are the chief source of diamonds.* *n., pl.* **sourc•es.**

south•ern (suᴛʜ′ərn), **1** toward the south: *a southern view.* **2** from the south: *a southern breeze. adj.*

speak (spēk), **1** say words; talk: *speak clearly.* **2** use (a language): *Do you speak French? v.,* **spoke** (spōk), **spo•ken** (spō′kən), **speak•ing.**

spe•cial (spesh′əl), more than ordinary; unusual; exceptional. *adj.*

speech (spēch), what is said; the words spoken: *We made the usual farewell speeches. n., pl.* **speech•es.**

spi•der (spī′dər), a small animal with eight legs, no wings, and a body divided into two parts. Spiders are arachnids that spin webs to catch insects for food. *n.*

spider web (spī′dər web′), the delicate, silken threads spun by a spider.

spore (spôr), a single cell capable of growing into a new plant or animal. Spores are produced by plants that do not have flowers, such as ferns or molds. *n., pl.* **spores.**

spot•less (spot′lis), without a spot: *a spotless white shirt. adj.*

square (skwâr), **1** a plane figure with four equal sides and four right angles. **2** having this shape: *a square box. A block of stone is usually square.* 1 *n.*, 2 *adj.,* **squar•er, squar•est.**

squash (skwäsh), press or be pressed until soft or flat; crush: *She squashed the bug. Carry the cream puffs carefully, for they squash easily. v.*

squeak (skwēk), make a short, sharp, shrill sound: *A mouse squeaks. v.*

squeal (skwēl), **1** make a long, sharp, shrill cry: *A pig squeals when it is hurt.* **2** such a cry. 1 *v.*, 2 *n.*

squeeze (skwēz), **1** press hard; compress: *Don't squeeze the kitten; you'll hurt it.* **2** force out by pressure: *squeeze juice from a lemon.* **3** crush; crowd: *Six people squeezed into the little car. v.,* **squeezed, squeez•ing. —squeez′a•ble,** *adj.*

squirm (skwėrm), turn and twist; writhe: *The restless boy squirmed in his chair. v.*

squir•rel (skwėr′əl), a small, bushy-tailed rodent that usually lives in trees. *n.*

squirt (skwėrt), force out (liquid) through a narrow opening: *squirt water through a tube, squirt water at the statue. v.*

sta•men (stā′mən), the part of a flower that contains the pollen. The stamens are surrounded by the petals. *n., pl.* **sta•mens, stam•i•na** (stam′ə nə).

stand (stand), be set upright; be placed; be located: *The box stands over there. Some food stood on the table. v.,* **stood, stand•ing.**

state (stāt), of a state: *a state road, state police, state government. adj.*

state•ment (stāt′mənt), something stated; report; account: *Her statement was correct. n.*

sta•tion (stā′shən), a regular stopping place: *She met her at the bus station. n.*

steal (stēl), **1** take (something) that does not belong to one; take dishonestly. **2** move secretly or quietly: *She stole softly out of the house.* **3** (in baseball) run to (second base, third base, or home plate) as the pitcher throws the ball to the catcher. *v.,* **stole, sto•len** (stō′lən), **steal•ing.**

spider

a crab **spider**

a	hat	**ī**	ice	**u̇**	put	**ə stands for**	
ā	age	**o**	not	**ü**	rule	**a**	in about
ä	far, calm	**ō**	open	**ch**	child	**e**	in taken
âr	care	**ȯ**	saw	**ng**	long	**i**	in pencil
e	let	**ô**	order	**sh**	she	**o**	in lemon
ē	equal	**oi**	oil	**th**	thin	**u**	in circus
ėr	term	**ou**	out	**ᴛʜ**	then		
i	it	**u**	cup	**zh**	measure		

steam (stēm), give off steam: *The cup of coffee was steaming. v.*

steel (stel), an alloy of iron and carbon. Steel has greater hardness and flexibility than cast iron and is used for tools and machinery. *n.*

stiff (stif), **1** not easily bent; fixed; rigid. **2** hard to move. *adj.*

St. Law·rence Sea·way (sānt' lôr'əns sē'wā'), waterway that links the Great Lakes to the Atlantic Ocean by means of canals and the St. Lawrence River.

stole (stōl), See **steal**. *They stole my car. v.*

stom·ach (stum'ək), the large muscular bag in the body which receives swallowed food, and digests some of it before passing it on to the intestines. *n.*

stood (stůd), See **stand**. *She stood in the corner for five minutes. I had stood in line all morning to buy tickets to the game. v.*

stop (stop), leave off (moving, acting, doing, being, etc.); come to an end; cease: *The baby stopped crying. The rain is stopping. v.*, **stopped, stop·ping.**

storm (stôrm), a strong wind often accompanied by rain, snow, hail, or thunder and lightning. In deserts there are storms of sand. *n.*

St. Pat·rick's Day (sānt' pat'riks dā'), a holiday celebrated in honor of St. Patrick, who converted Ireland to Christianity; March 17.

storm

a lightning **storm**

strange (strānj), unusual; odd; peculiar: *a strange accident, a strange experience. adj.*, **strang·er, strang·est.**

strat·e·gy (strat'ə jē), plan based on skillful planning: *We need some strategy to win this game. n., pl.* **strat·e·gies.**

straw·ber·ry (strȯ'ber'ē), the small, juicy, red fruit of a plant that grows close to the ground. Strawberries are good to eat. *n., pl.* **straw·ber·ries.**

street (strēt), place or way for automobiles, wagons, etc., to go. *n.*

strength (strengkh), **1** quality of being strong; power; force; vigor. **2** something a person is strong in or can do well. *n.*

strike (strīk), **1** set or be set on fire by hitting or rubbing: *strike a match.* **2** a stopping of work to get better pay, shorter hours, and so on. *The workers were home for six weeks during the strike last year.* **3** baseball pitched through the strike zone and not swung at, any pitch that is swung at and missed, or any pitch that is hit foul. After three strikes, a batter is out. **1** *v.*, **struck** (struk), **struck** or **strick·en** (strik'ən), **strik·ing;** 2,3 *n.*

stroke (strōk), a single complete movement to be made again and again: *He rowed with a strong stroke of the oars. She swims a fast stroke. n.*

stud·y (stud'ē), try to learn: *She studied her spelling lesson for half an hour. I am studying to be a doctor. v.*, **stud·ied, stud·y·ing.**

stuff (stuf), belongings; goods: *What will we do with all this stuff? n.*

suc·cess·ful (sək ses'fəl), having success; ending in success; prosperous; fortunate. *adj.*

sud·den (sud'n), happening without warning or notice; not expected: *a sudden stop, a sudden rainstorm, a sudden rise to power. adj.*

sud·den·ly (sud'n lē), in a sudden manner. *adv.*

suf·fer (suf'ər), **1** have or feel (pain, grief, etc.): *I suffered sunburn from being at the beach all day.* **2** bear with patiently; endure: *I will not suffer such insults. v.*

suf·fix (suf'iks), syllable or syllables put at the end of a word to change its meaning or to make another word, as -ly in *badly*, -ness in *goodness*, and -ful in *spoonful*. *n., pl.* **suf·fix·es.**

sug·ar (shůg'ər), a sweet substance obtained chiefly from sugar cane or sugar beets and used extensively in food products; sucrose. *n.*

suit (süt), set of clothes to be worn together. A man's suit consists of a coat, pants, and sometimes a vest. A woman's suit consists of a coat and either a skirt or pants. *n.*

Sun., Sunday.

su·pe·ri·or (sə pir′ē ər), above the average; very good; excellent: *superior work in school. adj.*

Su·pe·ri·or (sə pir′ē ər), **Lake,** the largest of the five Great Lakes. These lakes form the largest group of freshwater lakes in the world. *n.*

sup·per (sup′ər), the evening meal; meal eaten early in the evening. *n.*

sup·ply (sə plī′), **1** provide (what is lacking); furnish: *Many cities supply books for children in school.* **2 supplies,** *pl.* the food, equipment, etc., necessary for an army drive, or the like. 1 *v.,* **sup·plied, sup·ply·ing;** 2 *n., pl.* **sup·plies.**

sup·port (sə pôrt′), **1** give strength or courage to; keep up; help. **2** be in favor of; back; second: *She supports the amendment.* **3** help or assistance: *They need our financial support.* 1,2 *v.,* 3 *n.*

sup·pose (sə pōz′), **1** consider as possible; take for granted; assume. **2** believe, think, or imagine: *I suppose he will come at noon. v.,* **sup·posed, sup·pos·ing.**

sur·prise (sər prīz′), cause to feel surprised; astonish: *The victory surprised us. v.,* **sur·prised, sur·pris·ing.**

sus·pense·ful (sə spens′fəl), characterized by or full of suspense. *adj.*

swarm (swôrm), group of bees settled together in a hive. *n.*

sweat gland (swet′ gland′), gland of the skin that secretes sweat. A sweat gland is connected with the surface of the skin by a tube or duct that ends in a pore.

swim (swim), move along on or in the water by using arms, legs, fins, etc.: *Fish swim. Most boys and girls like swimming in the lake. v.,* **swam** (swam), **swum, swim·ming.**

sword (sôrd), weapon, usually metal, with a long, sharp blade fixed in a handle or hilt. *n.*

swum (swum) See **swim.** *We have swum in that lake many times. v.*

swim
swimming the
backstroke

T

Taj Ma·hal (täj′ mə häl′), a famous white marble mausoleum in northern India, built in the 1600s.

take (tāk), **1** lay hold of; grasp: *I took her hand when we crossed the street.* **2** indulge in: *take a nap, take a vacation. v.,* **took, tak·en** (tā′kən), **tak·ing.**

tax (taks), money paid by people for the support of the government and services; money regularly collected from citizens by the government. *n., pl.* **tax·es.**

teach·er (tē′chər), person who teaches, especially one who teaches in a school: *We entered the teachers' lounge. n.*

team·mate (tēm′māt′), a fellow member of a team. *n.*

tear (tir), drop of salty liquid coming from the eye. *n., pl.* **tears.**

tem·per·a·ture (tem′pər ə chər), **1** degree of heat or cold. The temperature of freezing water is 32 degrees Fahrenheit (0 degrees Celsius). **2** a body temperature higher than normal; fever: *A sick person may have a temperature. n.*

a	hat	**ī**	ice	**u̇**	put	**ə** stands for	
ā	age	**o**	not	**ü**	rule	**a**	in about
ä	far, calm	**ō**	open	**ch**	child	**e**	in taken
âr	care	**ȯ**	saw	**ng**	long	**i**	in pencil
e	let	**ô**	order	**sh**	she	**o**	in lemon
ē	equal	**oi**	oil	**th**	thin	**u**	in circus
ėr	term	**ou**	out	**ᵺ**	then		
i	it	**u**	cup	**zh**	measure		

thrill

The roller coaster gave us

a **thrill**.

tiger

The **tiger** is about 9 feet long with the tail.

tem·ple (tem′pəl), building used for the service or worship of a god or gods. *n.*

ten·sion (ten′shən), **1** a stretching. **2** mental strain: *Tension may be brought on by overwork. n.*

Tex·as (tek′səs), one of the southwestern states of the United States. *Abbreviation:* Tex. or TX *Capital:* Austin. *n.*

than (ᴛʜan; *unstressed* ᴛʜən), **1** in comparison with. **2** compared to that which: *You know better than I do.* 1,2 *conj.,* 1 *prep.*

that's (ᴛʜats), that is: *That's a beautiful picture.*

their (ᴛʜâr), of them; belonging to them: *I like their house. adj.*

them (ᴛʜem; *unstressed* ᴛʜəm), the persons, animals, things, or ideas spoken about: *The books are new; take care of them. pron.*

then (ᴛʜen), **1** being at that time; existing then: *the then President.* **2** soon afterwards. 1 *adj.,* 2 *adv.*

there (ᴛʜâr), in or at that place: *Finish reading the page and stop there. adv.*

they (ᴛʜā), the persons, animals, things, or ideas spoken about: *I had three books yesterday. Do you know where they are? They are on the table. pron. pl.*

they'd (ᴛʜād), **1** they had: *They'd arrived late.* **2** they would: *They'd come if they could.*

they'll (ᴛʜāl), they will: *They'll be a few minutes late.*

they're (ᴛʜâr), they are: *They're going to be leaving soon.*

thirst·y (thėr′stē), **1** feeling thirst; having thirst: *The dog is thirsty; please give it some water.* **2** having a strong desire or craving; eager. *adj.,* **thirst·i·er, thirst·i·est.**

thought·ful (thȯt′fəl), full of thought; thinking: *He was thoughtful for a while and then replied, "No." adj.*

thou·sand (thou′znd), ten hundred; 1000. *n., adj.*

threat (thret), sign or cause of possible evil or harm. *n.*

thrill (thril), a shivering, exciting feeling. *n.*

throat (thrōt), the passage from the mouth to the stomach or the lungs. *n.*

throne (thrōn), chair on which a king, queen, bishop, or other person of high rank sits during official ceremonies. *n.*

through (thrü), **1** from end to end of; from side to side of; between the parts of; from beginning to end of: *march through a town, cut a tunnel through a mountain.* **2** here and there in; over; around: *stroll through the streets of a city. prep.*

throw (thrō), **1** send through the air; toss; hurl. **2** bring to the ground: *His horse threw him.* **3** put by force: *throw someone into jail. v.,* **threw** (thrü), **thrown, throw·ing.**

thrown (thrōn), See **throw.** *She has thrown her old toys away. v.*

thumb (thum), the short, thick finger of the hand. It can be moved against any of the other four fingers to grasp things. *n.*

ti·ger (tī′gər), a large, fierce, flesh-eating mammal of Asia, that has dull-yellow fur striped with black. It is related to the cat and the lion. *n., pl.* **ti·gers.**

ti·tle (tī′tl), **1** the name of a book, poem, picture, song, etc. **2** name showing rank, occupation, or condition in life. King, duke, lord, majesty, highness, captain, doctor, and Miss are titles. *n.*

to (tü; *unstressed* tu *or* tə), **1** in the direction of; toward a destination: *She came to school.* **2** *To* is used with verbs. *I like to play the piano.* **3** on against: *Nail the shelf to the wall.* **4** *To* is used to show action toward. *Give the book to me. prep.*

toe (tō), one of the five divisions that end the foot. *n., pl.* **toes.**

tomb (tüm), grave, vault, mausoleum, etc., for a dead body, often above ground. *n.*

to·mor·row (tə mor′ō), **1** the day after today. **2** on the day after today. 1 *n.*, 2 *adv.*

tongue (tung), the movable fleshy organ in the mouth. The tongue is used in tasting and by people, for talking. *n.*

too (tü), **1** in addition; also; besides. **2** beyond what is desirable, proper, or right; more than enough. *adv.*

took (tùk), See **take.** *She took the car an hour ago. v.*

toot (tüt), sound of a horn or whistle. *n.*

tot (tot), a little child. *n.*

touch·down (tuch′doun′), score of six points made in football by putting the ball on the ground behind the opponent's goal line. *n.*

tough (tuf), **1** hard to cut, tear, or chew. **2** strong; hard: *a tough team. adj.*

track (trak), **1** a double, parallel line of metal rails for cars to run on: *railroad tracks.* **2** a course for running or racing. *n.*

trash (trash), **1** broken or torn bits, such as leaves, twigs, husks, etc.: *Rake up the trash in the yard.* **2** worthless stuff; rubbish: *That magazine is trash. n.*

tread (tred), **1** set the foot down; walk; step: *Don't tread on the flower beds. They trod through the meadow.* **2** move the legs and feet as if walking: *Everyone in swimming class treads water for five minutes.* **3** act or sound of treading: *We heard the tread of marching feet.* 1,2 *v.*, **treads, trod** (trod), **trod·den** (trod′n) or **trod, tread·ing;** 3 *n.*

treat (trēt), **1** entertain with food, drink, or amusement: *treat some friends to ice cream.* **2** anything that gives pleasure. 1 *v.*, 2 *n.*

treat·ment (trēt′mənt), way of treating: *This cat has suffered from bad treatment. n.*

tre·men·dous (tri men′dəs), INFORMAL. very great; enormous: *That is a tremendous house for a family of three. adj.*

tri·an·gle (trī′ang′gəl), a plane figure having three sides and three angles. *n.*

trou·ble (trub′əl), **1** cause trouble to; disturb: *The lack of business troubled the grocer.* **2** extra work; bother; effort: *Take the trouble to work.* 1 *v.*, **trou·bled, trou·bling;** 2 *n.*

truth·ful (trüth′fəl), telling the truth: *He is a truthful boy and will tell exactly what happened. adj.* —**truth′ful·ly,** *adv.*

tun·dra (tun′drə), a vast, level, treeless plain in the arctic regions. The ground beneath its surface is frozen even in summer. Much of Alaska and northern Canada is tundra. *n.*

two (tü), one more than one; 2. *n., pl.* **twos;** *adj.*

track (definition 2) running on a **track**

U

ug·ly (ug′lē), very unpleasant to look at. *adj.*, **ug·li·er, ug·li·est.**

un·con·test·ed (un′kən tes′tid), undisputed; unopposed: *The referee's decision was uncontested. adj.*

un·for·tu·nate (un fôr′chə nit), not lucky; having bad luck. *adj.* —**un·for′tu·nate·ly,** *adv.*

un·friend·ly (un frend′lē), not friendly; hostile. *adj.*

un·heard (un hėrd′), not listened to; not heard: *unheard melodies. adj.*

a	hat	ī	ice	u̇	put	ə stands for	
ā	age	o	not	ü	rule	a	in about
ä	far, calm	ō	open	ch	child	e	in taken
âr	care	ȯ	saw	ng	long	i	in pencil
e	let	ô	order	sh	she	o	in lemon
ē	equal	oi	oil	th	thin	u	in circus
ėr	term	ou	out	ŦH	then		
i	it	u	cup	zh	measure		

u·ni·verse (yü′nə vėrs′), the whole of existing things; everything there is, including all space and matter; the cosmos: *Our world is but a small part of the universe. n.*

un·known (un nōn′), not known; not familiar; strange. *adj.*

un·til (un til′), up to the time when. *conj.*

un·u·su·al (un yü′zhü əl), not usual; not ordinary; not in common use; uncommon; rare. *adj.*

up·on (ə pon′), on. *prep.*

up·set (up′set′), an unexpected defeat: *The hockey team suffered an upset. n.*

up·stairs (up′stârz′), on or to an upper floor: *She lives upstairs (adv.). He is waiting in an upstairs hall (adj.).*

use·less (yüs′lis), of no use; worthless: *A television set would be useless in a house without electricity. adj.*

u·su·al (yü′zhü əl), commonly seen, found, or happening; ordinary; customary. *adj.*

u·su·al·ly (yü′zhü ə lē), according to what is usual; commonly; ordinarily; customarily; often: *We usually eat dinner at 6. adv.*

walrus
The **walrus** has ivory tusks.

V

va·ca·tion (vā kā′shən), **1** freedom from school, business, or other duties: *There is a vacation from school every summer.* **2** take a vacation. 1 *n.,* 2 *v.*

Val·en·tine's Day (val′ən tīnz dā′), a holiday in which cards or small gifts are given to friends and loved ones; February 14.

val·ley (val′ē), low land between hills or mountains. *n., pl.* **val·leys.**

van·ish (van′ish), disappear, especially suddenly: *The sun vanished behind a cloud. v.*

ver·i·fy (ver′ə fī), test the correctness of; check for accuracy: *You can verify the spelling of a word by looking in a dictionary. v.,* **ver·i·fied, ver·i·fy·ing.**

ver·tex (vėr′teks), the point where two sides of an angle meet. *n., pl.* **ver·tex·es, ver·ti·ces** (vėr′tə sēz).

vil·lage (vil′ij), group of houses, usually smaller than a town. *n.*

vol·ca·no (vol kā′nō), an opening in the earth's crust through which steam, ashes, and lava are forced out in periods of activity. *n., pl.* **vol·ca·noes** or **vol·ca·nos.**

vol·ume (vol′yəm), space occupied: *The storeroom has a volume of 800 cubic feet. n.*

W

waist (wāst), the part of the human body between the ribs and the hips. *n.*

wal·rus (wȯl′rəs or wol′rəs), a large sea mammal of the arctic regions, resembling a seal but having long tusks. It is hunted for its hide, tusks, and blubber oil. *n., pl.* **wal·rus·es** or **wal·rus.**

want (wänt), wish for; wish: *We want a new car. I want to become an engineer. v.*

wash (wäsh), clean with water or other liquid: *wash one's face, wash clothes, wash dishes. v.,* **washed, wash·ing.**

wash·a·ble (wäsh′ə bəl), able to be washed without damage: *washable silk. adj.*

wash·cloth (wäsh′klȯth′), a small cloth for washing oneself. *n.*

was·n't (wuz′nt or wäz′nt), was not.

waste (wāst), **1** make poor use of; spend uselessly; fail to get full value or benefit from: *Though I had much work to do, I wasted my time doing nothing.* **2** poor use; useless spending; failure to get the most out of something: *Buying that suit was a waste of money.* 1 *v.* **wast·ed, wast·ing;** 2 *n.*

watch (wäch), **1** look attentively or carefully. **2** device for telling time, small enough to be carried in a pocket or worn on the wrist. 1 *v.,* 2 *n., pl.* **watch·es.**

wa·ter foun·tain (wȯ′tər foun′tən),
1 water flowing or rising into the air
in a spray. 2 place to get a drink.

wa·ter·way (wȯ′tər wā′), river,
canal, or other body of water
that ships can go on. n.

weak·ness (wēk′nis), a weak point;
slight fault: *Putting things off is her
weakness.* n., pl. **weak·ness·es.**

weave (wēv), make out of thread,
strips, or strands of the same
material. v., **wove** (wōv), **wo·ven**
(wō′vən) or **wove, weav·ing.**

we'd (wēd), 1 we had: *We'd left
the party early.* 2 we would:
We'd love to see you again.

Wed., Wednesday.

week·end (wēk′end′), Saturday and
Sunday as a time for recreation,
visiting, etc. n.

week·ly (wēk′lē), of a week; for a
week; lasting a week: *a weekly
wage of $150.* adj.

weight (wāt), how heavy a thing is:
the amount a thing weighs. n.

weight·less (wāt′lis), being free from
the pull of gravity. adj.

weird (wird), 1 unearthly or
mysterious; wild; strange: *They
were awakened by a weird shriek.
It was the weirdest noise I had
ever heard.* 2 odd; fantastic; queer:
*The robin made a weirder sound
than the sparrow.* adj., **weird·er,
weird·est.**

wel·come (wel′kəm), 1 greet kindly;
give a friendly reception to: *We
always welcome guests at our
house.* 2 a kind or friendly
reception: *You will always
have a welcome here.* 1 v.,
wel·comed, wel·com·ing; 2 n.

we'll (wēl), we will: *We'll be arriving
at about 6:00.*

went (went), See **go.** *I went home
promptly after school.* v.

we're (wir), we are: *We're all looking
forward to your visit.*

were (wėr), form of the verb **be** used
with *you, we, they* or any plural
noun to indicate the past tense.
The officer's orders were obeyed. v.

we've (wēv), we have: *We've had a
wonderful time.*

whale (hwāl), mammal shaped like a
huge fish and living in the sea. Oil
from whales used to be burned in
lamps. n., pl. **whales** or **whale.**

what·ev·er (hwot ev′ər or hwut
ev′ər), anything that: *Do whatever
you like.* pron.

what's (hwots or hwuts), 1 what is:
What's the latest news? 2 what
has: *What's been going on here
lately?*

wheat (hwēt), the grain of a common
cereal grass, used to make flour. n.

when (hwen), 1 at what time: *When
does school close?* 2 at the time
that: *Stand up when your name
is called.* 1 adv., 2 conj.

when·ev·er (hwen ev′ər), when; at
whatever time; at any time that:
*Come whenever you wish (conj.).
I'll come whenever possible (adv.).*
conj., adv.

where (hwâr), in what place; at what
place: *Where do you live? Where
is he?* adv.

wher·ev·er (hwâr ev′ər), where;
to whatever place; in whatever
place: *Sit wherever you like (conj.)
Wherever are you going? (adv.).*
conj., adv.

whirl (hwėrl), 1 turn or swing round
and round; spin: *The leaves
whirled in the wind.* 2 move
round and round: *whirl a lasso.
We whirled about the room.* v.

weave
weaving on a large loom

a	hat	ī	ice	u̇	put	ə stands for
ā	age	o	not	ü	rule	a in about
ä	far, calm	ō	open	ch	child	e in taken
âr	care	ȯ	saw	ng	long	i in pencil
e	let	ô	order	sh	she	o in lemon
ē	equal	oi	oil	th	thin	u in circus
ėr	term	ou	out	ŦH	then	
i	it	u	cup	zh	measure	

whole (hōl), **1** having all its proper parts; complete: *whole egg, whole milk.* **2** full; entire: *He ate the whole melon. adj.*

whole milk (hōl′ milk′), milk from which none of the natural elements have been removed.

whole note (hōl′ nōt′), (in music) note to be played four times as long as one quarter note.

whole-wheat (hōl′hwēt′), made from whole-wheat flour: *whole-wheat bread. adj.*

who'll (hül), who will: *Who'll help me wash the dishes?*

who's (hüz), **1** who is: *Who's going with me?* **2** who has: *Who's seen the new wildlife documentary?*

whose (hüz), of whom; of which: *The girl whose work got the prize is very talented. Whose book is this? pron.*

width (width), how wide a thing is; distance across; breadth: *The room is 12 feet in width. n.*

wild (wīld), not in proper control or order: *wild hair. adj.*

will (wil), am going to; is going to; are going to: *We will go to the beach on Saturday. v., past tense* **would.**

win (win), be successful over others; get victory or success in: *We all hope our team will win. v.,* **won** (wun), **win·ning.**

win·dow (win′dō), an opening to let in light or air set into an outer wall or roof of a building or into a vehicle. *n.*

wind sock (wind′ sok′), device somewhat like a large sock, mounted on a pole and open at one end to catch the wind and show its direction.

wind vane (wind′ vān′), a tool that shows wind direction.

wish·y-wash·y (wish′ē wäsh′ē), lacking strength of character; indecisive: *a wishy-washy person. adj.*

wisp (wisp), a flock of birds, especially of marsh birds called snipe. *n.*

with (wiŦH or with), *With* shows that persons or things are taken together in some way. **1** in the company of: *Come with me.* **2** by means of: *The man cut the meat with a knife. prep.*

with·draw (wiŦH drȯ′ or with drȯ′), draw back; draw away. *v.,* **with·drew, with·drawn, with·draw·ing.**

with·hold (with hōld′ or wiŦH hōld′), refrain from giving or granting. *v.,* **with·held, with·hold·ing.**

with·stand (with stand′ or wiŦH stand′), stand against; hold out against; resist; oppose, especially successfully. *v.,* **with·stood, with·stand·ing.**

wood (wùd), trees or parts of trees cut up for use in building houses, making boats and furniture, etc. *n.*

wor·ry (wėr′ē), **1** feel anxious; be uneasy: *Don't worry about little things. They will worry if we are late.* **2** make anxious; trouble: *The problem worried me. v.,* **wor·ried, wor·ry·ing.**

worth·less (wėrth′lis), without worth; good-for-nothing; useless: *Throw those worthless, broken toys away. adj.*

would (wùd), See **will.** *Would you help us, please? v.*

would·n't (wùd′nt), would not.

would've (wùd′əv), would have.

wow (wou), exclamation of surprise, joy, etc. *interj.*

wreath (rēth), a ring of flowers or leaves twisted together. *n., pl.* **wreaths** (rēŦHz).

wreck (rek), **1** what is left of anything that has been destroyed or much injured. **2** cause the wreck of; destroy; ruin: *Raccoons wrecked our campsite looking for food.* **1** *n.,* **2** *v.*

wren (ren), a small songbird with a slender bill and a short tail. Wrens often build their nests near houses. *n.*

wrench (rench), tool for turning nuts, bolts, etc. *n., pl.* **wrench·es.**

wrench

A **wrench** holds and turns bolts and nuts.

wres·tler (res′lər), person who wrestles, especially as a sport. *n.*

wrist (rist), the joint connecting hand and arm. *n.*

write (rīt), make letters or words with pen, pencil, or chalk: *You can read and write. v.,* **wrote** (rōt), **writ·ten, writ·ing.**

writ·ing (rī′ting), literary work; a book or other literary production: *the writings of Benjamin Franklin. n.*

writ·ten (rit′n). See **write.** *He has written a letter. (v.) a written note. (adj.). v., adj.*

Y

yes·ter·day (yes′tər dē), the day before today. *n.*

you'd (yüd; *unstressed* yəd), **1** you had: *You'd already left.* **2** you would: *You'd love this book.*

young (yung), without much experience or practice. *adj.*

your (yu̇r; *unstressed* yər), belonging to you: *Wash your hands. adj.*

you're (yu̇r; *unstressed* yər), you are: *Tell me where you're going.*

Z

zin·ni·a (zin′ē ə), a garden plant grown for its showy flowers of many colors. *n.* [The *zinnia* was named in honor of Johann G. *Zinn,* 1727-1759, a German botanist.]

wrestler
wrestlers during a match

a	hat	ī	ice	u̇	put		ə *stands for*	
ā	age	o	not	ü	rule		a	in about
ä	far, calm	ō	open	ch	child		e	in taken
âr	care	ȯ	saw	ng	long		i	in pencil
e	let	ô	order	sh	she		o	in lemon
ē	equal	oi	oil	th	thin		u	in circus
ėr	term	ou	out	ŦH	then			
i	it	u	cup	zh	measure			

Writer's Thesaurus

Many of your spelling words have synonyms, which are words with same or similar meanings. This thesaurus lists those spelling words alphabetically, defines them, and provides synonyms. For many words, you can also look up antonyms, which are words with opposite meanings. This book can even introduce you to new words.

Understand a Thesaurus Entry

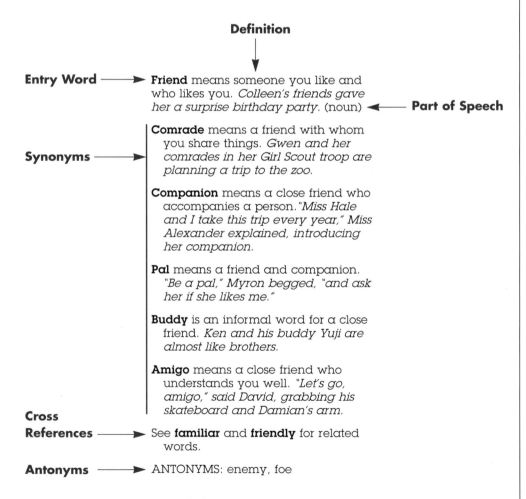

Definition

Entry Word → **Friend** means someone you like and who likes you. *Colleen's friends gave her a surprise birthday party.* (noun) ◄— **Part of Speech**

Synonyms →

Comrade means a friend with whom you share things. *Gwen and her comrades in her Girl Scout troop are planning a trip to the zoo.*

Companion means a close friend who accompanies a person. "*Miss Hale and I take this trip every year,*" *Miss Alexander explained, introducing her companion.*

Pal means a friend and companion. "*Be a pal,*" *Myron begged,* "*and ask her if she likes me.*"

Buddy is an informal word for a close friend. *Ken and his buddy Yuji are almost like brothers.*

Amigo means a close friend who understands you well. "*Let's go, amigo,*" *said David, grabbing his skateboard and Damian's arm.*

Cross References → See **familiar** and **friendly** for related words.

Antonyms → ANTONYMS: enemy, foe

A a

Ability means the power to do something well. *Renee's ability to make her own clothes has saved her a lot of money.* (noun)

Talent means an inborn ability. *Julio's drumming shows real musical talent.*

Capacity means an inborn ability. *Bob has a great capacity for foreign languages and speaks three.*

Skill means an ability gotten by means of training and practice. *Michiko's skill in cooking has improved.*

Announce means to make something known to the public. *The manager announced that the team had traded two pitchers.* (verb)

Broadcast means to make something widely known by radio or television. *Warnings of the approaching hurricane were broadcast to residents of the coast.*

Advertise means to make something known to the public by paying for it. *The sale was advertised in the local newspaper.*

Publicize means to make something known to as many people as possible. *The kids publicized their car wash by posting signs.*

Ask means to try to get information by using words. *Ask Marcy where she got that great jacket.* (verb)

Inquire means to ask in order to get detailed information. *Yukio inquired about the hours that the video store is open.*

Quiz means to ask questions about what has been learned. *Our science teacher always quizzes us on last night's homework.*

Question means to ask over and over again, in a systematic way. *The police questioned several suspects about the bank robbery.*

ANTONYMS: answer, reply

Attack means to begin fighting someone or something with actions or words. *A mother bear may attack anyone who gets close to her cubs. A group of parents has attacked the plan to close the schools early.* (verb)

Assault means to attack suddenly, usually with weapons. *The enemy assaulted our fort with bombs and cannons.*

Charge can mean to attack by a sudden rush. *An elephant opens its ears wide when it charges.*

ANTONYM: defend

B b

Beat means to hit over and over. *José and his friends spend Saturday mornings beating conga drums at the Caribbean Cultural Center.* (verb)

Winds howled, and waves **pounded** the little ship.

Hammer can mean to beat. *"Why can't I remember?" said Shirley, hammering her head with her fists.*

Pound means to hit hard, over and over. *Winds howled, and waves pounded the little ship.*

Bang can mean to beat noisily. *Liza's little sister loves to bang on pots and pans.*

Beautiful means very pleasing to the senses or the mind. *These beautiful rugs were made by hand in Turkey 100 years ago, but they still look almost like new.* (adjective)

Pretty means pleasing to see or hear. It is often used to describe girls and women. *Mariko looks really pretty in that hat.*

Handsome means pleasing to see. It is often used instead of beautiful or pretty to describe a man or boy. *Candace thinks Mr. Walking Bear, the science teacher, is awfully handsome.*

Lovely means especially beautiful and fine. *The rose garden in the park is so lovely, I could stay there for hours.*

ANTONYMS: ugly, unattractive

Beginning means the time when something first happens or first exists. *The Declaration of Independence marked the beginning of the United States.* (noun)

Start can mean a beginning. *Jason led the sack race from start to finish.*

Creation means the act of making something that did not exist before. *Since the creation of the Cafeteria Committee, we've had better desserts.*

Opening can mean a beginning, especially of a story, music, or other works of art. *The opening of the musical, with its great song and fabulous dancers, really grabbed Mike's attention.*

Introduction can mean a beginning in common use. *Since the introduction of the microwave, cooking habits have changed greatly.*

ANTONYMS: conclusion, end, finish

C c

Care means an unhappy, nervous feeling, with fear of pain or loss. *After weeks of struggle and care, the refugees have escaped from the fighting.* (noun)

Concern can mean an uneasy feeling because something or someone important to you is in trouble. *Marcia's parents feel a lot of concern because she wants to quit school.*

Worry means repeated, nervous thought about possible pain or loss. *Our worry about Billy Don's safety turned to anger when he strolled in two hours late.*

Anxiety means strong worry and fear. *Every time Coach Petrangelis tells us how important this next game is, my anxiety gets worse.*

Tension can mean worry and emotional upset, especially lasting a long time and using up much strength. *After the tension of waiting for the audition, White Bird felt that actually performing was almost easy.*

SEE **worried** for related words.

Careful means paying close attention to what you say and do. *I feel safe in the car with Mrs. Gomez, who is a very careful driver.* (adjective)

Cautious means careful to avoid danger. *Pia has been very cautious about riding her bike in the street after seeing the bike safety movie.*

Wary means very careful and expecting danger. *Mice have to be wary of cats and owls.*

Guarded can mean cautious. It is used especially to describe someone's way of talking. *The scientists are very guarded about their invention, and they say it needs more tests.*

ANTONYMS: careless, negligent, thoughtless

Careless means not paying attention to what you say or do. *Tom was careless, and now his shoes are all wet.* (adjective)

Thoughtless means not thinking before doing or saying something. *Those thoughtless girls talk loudly while everyone else is trying to study.*

Inconsiderate means thoughtless of other people's feelings. *Taking a parking space reserved for the disabled isn't just inconsiderate, it's illegal.*

Reckless means not thinking about possible danger. *Reckless driving frequently causes accidents.*

Rash means dangerously careless, often because of haste. *Maryanne now regrets her rash decision to quit school.*

ANTONYMS: careful, cautious

Change means to make or become different. *Jermayne changes her nail polish every couple of days. Inside its case, the pupa changes to a butterfly.* (verb)

Alter means to change slightly. It suggests limited change of a particular sort. *The pilot altered her flight plan to avoid a bad thunderstorm.*

Vary means to change in a number of ways. It suggests change for the sake of difference, or change according to circumstances. *The form of government varies from country to country.*

Turn can mean to change. It often describes change in color or form. *The sun turned Alan's face red. Water turns to steam when it boils.*

IDIOMS

Change is a key word in several idioms. Here are some of them:

Change hands means to go from one owner to another. *The gas station changed hands twice in one year before Mr. Ortega bought it.*

Change off means to take turns. *Mariolet and I change off doing the dishes and setting the table.*

Change your tune means to say something very different from before. *Cassie thinks she's a better cook than I am, but she'll change her tune when she tastes my barbecue.*

Climb means to move upward, most often by using feet or hands or both. *The squirrels climb the pole to get the birdseed.* (verb)

Ascend means to move upward toward the highest point. *The Japanese mountaineers will try to ascend one of the highest peaks in the Andes.*

Mount means to go up or climb up. *Mrs. Vargas slowly mounted the stairs to her apartment.*

Scramble means to climb where climbing is especially hard and awkward. It may suggest climbing on all fours. *An otter will scramble up a steep, muddy riverbank and slide down again, over and over, just for fun.*

ANTONYM: descend

Clothes means covering for a person's body. *Miguel has grown so much he needs new clothes.* (noun)

Clothing means clothes. It is a slightly more formal word. *New-to-You Fashion Shop sells both women's and men's clothing.*

poncho

kimono

caftan

Wardrobe means all the clothes a person has. *Most of Ray's wardrobe came from his older brothers.*

Outfit can mean clothes that go together. *Mom has a plaid skirt and a red blouse that she wears as an outfit with her velvet blazer.*

Uniform means the clothes worn by some special group while at work. *When Aunt Phyllis goes to her Army Reserve training, she looks strong and proud in her uniform.*

Common means happening often or often met with. *"It's just a common cold," Dr. Wu told Jerome.* (adjective)

Ordinary means like most others. *Since the note was written on ordinary paper, the police concentrated on tracing its rare purple ink.*

Average can mean like most others. It is often used with numbers. *On an average day, the store sells two dozen sponges.*

Normal means like most others. It suggests that this is a good way to be. *It is normal for people to want to be liked and respected.*

Popular can mean widespread and done, had, or known by many people. *Grandpa and Grandma like to do popular dances from years ago.*

SEE **usual** for related words.

Confused means unable to think clearly or act correctly. *Alan's directions got us so confused that we arrived more than an hour late.* (adjective)

Bewildered means confused, especially by many parts or items. *On his first day at school, Luis was bewildered by all the long halls, doors, and hurrying students.*

Puzzled means unsure or unable to understand. *The ranger was puzzled by the strange tracks he found.*

Perplexed is a formal word that means very puzzled. *Perplexed by the new disease attacking the sheep, the vet sent for experts from the university.*

Mixed up means confused. *Our waiter got mixed up and brought baked potatoes instead of the rice we had ordered.*

■ WRITER'S THESAURUS

WATCH IT !

There are many words that we use to describe people and things that are strange, abnormal, senseless, or just plain silly. You and your friends might call each other "crazy" or names like that and then laugh together about them. But it is not polite to use *crazy, mad,* or *lunatic* in describing sick people. *Insane* is used for legal purposes. Otherwise the phrase to use is "mentally ill."

Crazy means senseless and foolish. *Whose crazy idea was it to walk all the way home?* (adjective)

Lunatic means crazy. *It's lunatic to take foolish risks.*

Mad means very crazy and possibly dangerous. *Mr. Brady may look like a mad scientist, but he's actually a lot of fun to talk to.*

Insane means mentally ill and not legally responsible. *The murderer was insane, and he was sent to a mental hospital.*

ANTONYM: sane

Crowd means a large group of people together. *Huge crowds arrived on the day of the big game.* (noun)

Mob means a crowd, especially a noisy and violent one. *The mob made so much noise that the governor returned to her helicopter.*

Flock can mean a crowd. *A flock of preschoolers ran out the door.*

Swarm can mean a crowd moving together. *Every weekday morning and evening, swarms of commuters pour through the train station.*

D d

Danger means a chance of harm or injury. *The approaching tornado brought danger to everything in its path.* (noun)

The house was in great **peril** as the tornado approached.

Risk means a chance of harm or loss. *Lynn wonders if the view would be worth the risk of the climb.*

Hazard means a likely cause of injury or misfortune. *The hazards of mining include cave-ins, explosions, and flooding.*

Threat can mean a possible cause of injury or misfortune. *The weather forecaster warned of the threat of a statewide blizzard.*

ANTONYM: safety

Deal means an arrangement for trade or exchange. This meaning is informal. *Lucy thought that trading three cat's-eye marbles for a circus ticket was a pretty good deal.* (noun)

Bargain means a deal. *William Penn made a fair bargain with the Indians.*

Agreement means an arrangement to act in certain ways. *I thought we had an agreement: you'd vacuum and do the bathroom, and I'd do the laundry and wash the kitchen floor.*

Contract means a legal agreement. *The third baseman has signed a contract for a total of $6,000,000.*

Decide means to make up your mind. *It was such a hot day that we decided to go to the city swimming pool.* (verb)

Determine means to decide firmly, often from several choices. *Jolene is still trying to determine which hairdo looks best on her.*

Conclude can mean to decide after thinking it over. *The police concluded that the driver who caused the accident had been reckless.*

Rule can mean to decide publicly and with authority. *The referee ruled that the ball was out of bounds.*

Different means not alike. *Edgar and Edwin try hard to be different, because they don't want to be known as "the twins."* (adjective)

Various means different. It is used when there are many different things. *The recreation center offers various classes and activities.*

Miscellaneous means of many sorts, not all the same. It may suggest no effort to choose. *My sister collects only clear marbles, but she keeps some miscellaneous ones to trade.*

Mixed means of many kinds combined together. *Connie thinks "Mixed Nuts" would be a good name for our comedy act.*

ANTONYMS: alike, same, similar

Disappear means to go from sight. *Arlene turned off the TV, and the picture disappeared.* (verb)

Vanish means to disappear, usually suddenly and often mysteriously. *The magician will now make her assistant vanish from the stage.*

Evaporate can mean to disappear the way water does when it turns to vapor. *The bad feelings between Lana and Crystal evaporated when Lana broke her arm.*

Fade can mean to disappear slowly. *As the sun rises, stars fade away.*

ANTONYM: appear

Dishonest means willing to lie, cheat, or steal. *A dishonest accountant stole $4,000 from the business.* (adjective)

Crooked can mean dishonest. It expresses contempt. *That man was so crooked his own dog didn't trust him.*

Lying means not telling the truth. *The lying witness tried to mislead the jury.*

Untruthful can mean not telling the truth. *Since she is known to have been untruthful many times in the past, people tend not to believe her.*

ANTONYMS: honest, truthful

Dislike means a feeling of not liking someone or something. *Teresa has a real dislike for long bus rides.* (noun)

Distaste means a strong dislike. *Tanya's distaste for cold weather is even stronger now than when she first came to Chicago.*

Disgust means an extreme dislike of something physically unpleasant. *The smell of the garbage truck filled us with disgust.*

Disapproval means dislike of something because it is bad. *The students showed their disapproval of the movie by protesting outside the theater.*

ANTONYM: fondness

E e

Edge means the line or place where something ends. *Zena planted marigolds around the edges of the class garden.* (noun)

Margin means an area next to an edge. *In the margin of my paper, my teacher wrote a few comments about my work.*

Rim means the edge of something round. *The rims of these plates are decorated with flowers.*

Border means an edge or the area along the edge. *The white linen tablecloth had pink daisies embroidered all around the border.*

Boundary means an edge of a place or the area along the edge. *When the two countries merged, the boundary lines between them were left off the new maps.*

Excellent means having very high quality. *When it was Barry's turn to cook dinner, he made excellent tacos.* (adjective)

First-class means excellent. *"Why, Daniel, this drawing is wonderful!" the art teacher cried. "You're becoming a first-class artist!"*

Superior means having very high quality, especially compared to others. *"Now that you have seen the others," Mr. Bartholomew murmured, "I will show you a truly superior diamond."*

Outstanding means so excellent as to stand out from others. *You have to be an outstanding athlete to be considered for the Olympic team.*

ANTONYMS: bad, poor, terrible

Explain means to make something easier to understand by talking or writing about it. *This book explains the background of the war in Vietnam.* (verb)

Interpret means to explain the meaning of something. *Rob interprets the movie as a comedy, but Tara thinks it was serious.*

Clarify means to make something clearer and easier to understand. *Celia could not understand the diagram and asked her teacher to clarify it.*

Spell out means to give a careful, detailed, and easy to understand explanation. *Roger had trouble setting the VCR until Marissa spelled out the process for him, one step at a time.*

ANTONYMS: confuse, misinterpret

Extra means more than usual or more than necessary. *Every student should bring an extra pencil to the exam. Rodney always carries extra batteries for his tape player.* (adjective)

Spare can mean extra. It suggests that something will probably not be needed. *Ms. Healy checks her spare tire every few weeks.*

Surplus means extra. It suggests that there is a lot more of something than necessary. *The bakery sends its surplus bread to the church's shelter for the homeless.*

Additional means added to something else. *"Will you stop now," asked the TV host, "or risk all your prizes for an additional five thousand dollars?"*

F f

Friend means someone you like and who likes you. *Colleen's friends gave her a surprise birthday party.* (noun)

Comrade means a friend with whom you share things. *Gwen and her comrades in her Girl Scout troop are planning a trip to the zoo.*

Companion means a close friend who accompanies a person. *"Miss Hale and I take this trip every year," Miss Alexander explained, introducing her companion.*

Pal means a friend and companion. *"Be a pal," Myron begged, "and ask her if she likes me."*

Buddy is an informal word that means a close friend. *Ken and his buddy Yuji are almost like brothers.*

Amigo means a close friend who understands you well. *"Let's go, amigo," said David, grabbing his skateboard and Damian's arm.*

ANTONYMS: enemy, foe

H h

Hide means to put out of sight. *We quickly hid the birthday present we were making for Mom when we heard her at the front door.* (verb)

Conceal means to hide something on purpose so that it won't be found. *Ugo conceals his comic books, but I always find them.*

Camouflage means to hide something by giving it a false appearance. *This caterpillar's dull colors let it camouflage itself as a twig.*

Stash is an informal word that means to hide something for safekeeping or future use. *Everything the gang stole was stashed in a hiding place under the floor.*

Bury can mean to hide something by covering it. *When Tana saw the teacher coming, she quickly buried Michelle's note under her books.*

ANTONYMS: expose, reveal, show

Hopeless means without any feeling that something good will happen. *Mr. Cho stared at his flooded home and felt more hopeless than ever before in his life.* (adjective)

Desperate means hopeless and reckless. *The mountain climbers made a desperate effort to get back to camp through the raging storm.*

Pessimistic means ready to believe that bad things will happen. *Patrick is too pessimistic even to try out for the swim team.*

ANTONYMS: confident, hopeful

Huge means very big. *A huge oak tree in the park blew down in the storm last night.* (adjective)

Enormous means much larger than normal. *We're celebrating the hundredth anniversary of the founding of the town with an enormous parade and picnic.*

Giant means much larger than other things of the same kind. *That's the Happy Cow Dairy with the giant milk carton on the roof.*

Gigantic means giant. *At the county fair, Richie saw a gigantic pumpkin weighing 150 pounds.*

Colossal means tremendously large. *The colossal head of Washington on Mount Rushmore is as high as a five-story building.*

Mammoth means colossal. *Mammoth Cave has miles of passages and is hundreds of feet deep.*

ANTONYMS: little, small, tiny

I i

Interesting means making you feel like paying attention and knowing more. *To a chameleon, any insect is interesting.* (adjective)

To a chameleon, any insect is **interesting.**

Fascinating means so interesting that it's hard to stop. *Damien finds computer programming so fascinating that he'll sit at his keyboard for hours.*

Spellbinding means so interesting that it is impossible to stop paying attention. *Both pitchers have no-hitters going into the eighth inning of this spellbinding game.*

ANTONYMS: dull, boring, uninteresting

K k

Know means to have knowledge of something or someone. *Marina knows a beautiful spot in the state park.* (verb)

Realize means to understand that something is true. *Watching Mr. Brigano work in his garden, we never realized he was almost 90.*

Recognize can mean to realize. *Matt recognizes now that he was wrong to make fun of his sister's singing.*

Understand means to get the meaning of something. *After years of work, scientists understand something about the writing carved on this stone by an ancient people.*

L l

Loud means having or making a big sound. *The thunder was so loud, it seemed the storm was right over our house.* (adjective)

Noisy means with a lot of loud, harsh sounds. *Elora ran past the noisy street repairs as fast as she could.*

Roaring means making a loud, deep sound. *This is no place for kids to play, with broken glass and roaring traffic.*

Thunderous can mean very loud, like thunder. *"Just listen to that thunderous applause from these hockey fans!" said the announcer.*

Blaring means making a very loud, harsh sound. *The blaring stereo in the upstairs apartment kept Pavel's family awake.*

ANTONYMS: quiet, silent, still

M m

Misfortune means bad luck or an unfortunate happening. *Josleen had the misfortune to race against the city's best sprinter in the first round of the girls' 100-meter dash.* (noun)

Accident means an unfortunate happening, usually a sudden one. *Traffic is backed up because of the auto accident.*

Misadventure means an accident, usually not a serious one. *James and his friends were covered with mud after their misadventure while feeding the pigs.*

Mishap means a misadventure. *"Keep practicing the dance," the director said, "and it will go without any mishap."*

O o

Often means many times. *Casimir often earns a few dollars helping people carry groceries.* (adverb)

Frequently means often and at short intervals. *Rain falls frequently in the tropical forest.*

Repeatedly means many times and the same each time. *Juana must go repeatedly to the stream for her family's water.*

Regularly means often and at the same interval. *"Buses should arrive at this corner regularly," said Mr. Crankshaw, "but I haven't seen one yet."*

ANTONYMS: infrequently, rarely, seldom

IDIOMS

There are many idioms that mean to know something fully and thoroughly. You can **know** something

by heart
like the back of your hand
inside out
backwards and forwards
like a book

There are also many ways to say that someone understands the situation. You can be **in the know,** and you can **know**

the dope   the score
the ropes   what's up
the scoop   what's what

Do you have other ways of saying this?

P p

Perfect means having no faults or being the best. *The swimmer made a perfect dive. Vladimir found the perfect gift for his grandmother.* (adjective)

Ideal means perfect, or as wonderful as you could imagine. *When Saturday came, it turned out to be an ideal day for the carnival.*

Flawless means not having any defects. *On the slender fingers of her right hand, the princess wore two flawless diamonds.*

Pure can mean perfect. It suggests that something contains no bad parts. *Ronald prides himself on his homemade candy, made with pure chocolate and fluffy coconut.*

Foolproof means made so that nothing can go wrong. *The prisoners thought that their escape plan was foolproof—until they found the guards waiting in the tunnel.*

SEE **excellent** for related words.

ANTONYM: imperfect

Piece means a small part of something larger, or one thing among others like it. *Della swept the pieces of the broken glass into a pile. The platter was the largest piece of china on the Serra's dinner table.* (noun)

Bit means a small piece of something larger. *Caroline tore the letter into bits.*

Scrap means a little piece, especially a piece left over. *Andrea cut the picture to fit into the frame and then threw away the paper scraps.*

Lump means a small, solid piece of material. *Darryl gave the carnival pony a lump of sugar.*

Slice means a thin, flat, broad piece cut from something. *Franklin wants a sandwich with one slice of cheese and three slices of ham.*

Power means the ability to do something or to make something happen. *Senatur Hughes has the power to get that law changed.* (noun)

Energy can mean power. It often suggests power stored up, ready to be used. *The creative energy of the students really comes out in the school's Festival of Brazil.*

Force means active power. It suggests effort and work. *The force of the blast destroyed the building and took out the side of the mountain.*

Strength means the amount of power that someone or something has. *Most ants have enough strength to lift ten times their own weight.*

Might means great power or strength. *Janek took a deep breath and flung himself at the locked door with all his might.*

ANTONYM: weakness

Proud means pleased with yourself and with what you have done. *Congresswoman Martinez told her election workers that they should all be proud of themselves.* (adjective)

Conceited means having too high an opinion of yourself or your good qualities. *The conceited actor stopped bragging after he forgot his lines.*

Boastful means fond of talking about yourself and how good you are. *The boastful man went on and on about what a great fisherman he was.*

Stuck-up is an informal word that means conceited. *Patricia is so stuck-up that she has no friends at all.*

ANTONYMS: humble, modest

Punish means to cause pain or loss to a person who has done something wrong. *The soldiers were punished for sleeping on duty.* (verb)

Discipline can mean to punish, especially to control people. *Mr. Berman disciplines his students fairly.*

Correct can mean to punish, in order to make someone better. *Mom says she must correct our new puppy so he'll stop chewing furniture and shoes.*

Fine means to make a person pay money for doing something wrong. *Our library fines people five cents a day for late books.*

Ground can mean to punish a young person by not letting him or her go out for fun. This meaning is informal. *When he came home two hours late, Chung-Ho knew his parents would ground him.*

Most ants have enough **strength** to lift ten times their own weight.

Q q

Quick means moving, happening, or done in a short time. *Graciella made a quick grab and got her purse back from the thief.* (adjective)

Fast means moving with much speed. *Young Raven hurled his fish spear, but the salmon was too fast.*

Swift means very fast. *This train is so swift that we'll be in Los Angeles tomorrow.*

Speedy means very quick. It is often used to describe things that you want to happen or be finished. *The bank robbers could not make a speedy getaway because of the parade.*

Hasty means quick and with not enough time or thought. *Courtney's hasty reply started a quarrel.*

SEE **suddenly** for related words.

ANTONYM: slow

Quiet means to make someone or something less noisy and more peaceful. *Desi quieted his younger brothers when they were frightened by the thunderstorm.* (verb)

Calm means to make someone less excited or nervous. *Following the bomb scare, the police officer calmed the crowd.*

Soothe means to make quiet and comfortable. *Mrs. Benson soothed the crying child.*

Hush means to make someone or something less noisy or silent. *As the mailman approached, the owner hushed his barking dog.*

ANTONYMS: disturb, excite, stir up

R r

Reason means an explanation of why something happened. *Doug says his reason for quitting the job is that he didn't respect the boss.* (noun)

Cause can mean a reason. *The "A" on Jaleel's history final was cause for celebration!*

Motive means a thought or feeling that makes someone do something. *The high cost of city living was Mr. Poole's motive for moving to a small town.*

Rough means having a surface that is not smooth. *Frank snagged his sweater on the rough wall of the basement.* (adjective)

Uneven means not smooth or level. *Our car bounced along the uneven gravel road.*

Bumpy means having a lot of bumps. *The sidewalk was too bumpy for good skateboarding.*

Rugged means having a rough, uneven surface. *The slope looked easy, but the ground became rugged toward the top.*

Coarse can mean rough and heavy. *Silas used coarse sandpaper to smooth the sides of the bookshelf.*

ANTONYMS: even, level, smooth

S s

Separate means to keep things apart or take something apart. *The highway separates these apartment buildings from the neighboring houses. Separate the dark from the light clothes before you wash them.* (verb)

Divide means to separate. It is often used about equal parts or sharing. *Ms. Polanak divided the class into teams for a softball game.*

Split can mean to divide something as if by cutting. *Tom and Dave split the money they got for the empty cans.*

Segregate can mean to separate people of different races. *The people of South Africa were the last in the world to remain officially segregated.*

ANTONYMS: unite, join

Serious means showing deep thought and purpose. *"I am the man of the family now," said Tom in a serious voice.* (adjective)

Earnest means serious and full of strong feeling. *The governor made an earnest appeal for help from the federal government after his state was struck by a hurricane.*

Solemn means serious, formal, and impressive. *The President takes a solemn oath to uphold the Constitution.*

ANTONYMS: lighthearted, cheerful, carefree

Shelter means something that covers or protects from the weather or from danger. *During the rain, the church picnic continued under the shelter of the tents.* (noun)

Cover can mean shelter. *The baby crane took cover between the long legs of its mother.*

Refuge means a shelter or place of safety. It suggests escape from trouble. *The first National Wildlife Refuge was created by Theodore Roosevelt to protect pelicans.*

Sanctuary can mean a refuge or place of protection, especially one where animals are protected from hunters or other dangers. *Behind the zoo is a bird sanctuary, closed to people.*

Preserve can mean a place where animals and plants are protected. *This whole area within the bend of the river is a wildlife preserve.*

Short means taking only a small amount of time. *"This was supposed to be a short assignment, but it's taking forever," Regina sighed.* (adjective)

Brief means taking a small amount of time. *Ken gave a brief talk about collecting beetles.*

Thumbnail means very short. *Dario gave a thumbnail description of the baseball game: "They got the runs; we didn't."*

Summary means brief and limited to main ideas. *Mr. Perrera has his classes hand in summary outlines of each week's reading.*

ANTONYMS: lengthy, long, wordy

Sign means an indication of something that will happen. *The first red and yellow leaves are a sign that summer is over.* (noun)

Symptom means a sign, especially of illness or suffering. *Symptoms of the flue include a fever and nausea.*

Omen means a sign or something believed to be a sign. *Daniel thinks it's an omen of good luck if he sees an all-white pigeon.*

Warning means something that tells of possible trouble or danger to come. *"Let that be a warning to you," Alejandro told the sobbing bully.*

Soft means easy to bend or push into; not hard or stiff. *After two weeks of sleeping on a hard camp cot, Phil is glad to get back to his own soft bed.* (adjective)

Floppy means easy to bend and hanging or swaying in a loose way. *After a long week in her squad car, Mom spends Saturday morning in her floppy old bathrobe, reading and relaxing.*

Fluffy means as soft as fluff. *The young swan has short fluffy feathers.*

The young swan has short **fluffy** feathers.

Limp means so easy to bend that it cannot stay straight. *The noodles were limp when Tessa lifted them from the boiling water.*

ANTONYMS: firm, hard, rigid, stiff

Steal means to take something that belongs to someone else. *It suggests secret, usually nonviolent taking. "I saw the robbers steal the money," the witness stated.* (verb)

Rob means to take money or property from a person or place. *The convenience store over on 27th Street was robbed twice last weekend.*

Shoplift means to steal things from a store while pretending to be a customer. *Since the Trans installed a lot of mirrors and cameras, nobody shoplifts from that store.*

Hold up means to stop by force and take money or property. *Bandits held up the stagecoach outside Bitterroot Springs.*

Stick up is a slang expression that means to rob. *She stuck up a couple of banks, so she's in jail for fifteen to twenty years.*

Stiff means not easy to bend or move. *Grandpa prefers a hairbrush with stiff bristles.* (adjective)

Rigid means very stiff. *The wet clothes became rigid overnight in the frosty air.*

Firm means hard. *The butter is still cold and too firm to spread.*

Tense means stretched tight. *Every muscle was tense as the runners waited for the race to start.*

Suddenly means quickly and without being expected. *Suddenly the sky became dark, and a fierce storm began.* (adverb)

Unexpectedly means without any sign that something is going to happen. *The phone rang unexpectedly in the middle of the night.*

Immediately means instantly. *When he missed the bus, Gavin immediately called his mother to let her know he would be late.*

All of a sudden and **all at once** mean suddenly. *All of a sudden, Korinne realized that she was falling. All at once, Tony jumped up and caught her arm.*

SEE **quick** for related words.

ANTONYM: gradually

Surprised means filled with wonder because of something unexpected. *"Marceea, I'm surprised to find you here!" exclaimed Grandpa.* (adjective)

Amazed means greatly surprised. *His parents were amazed when Eldred began composing music at such an early age.*

Startled can mean caused to jump in surprise and fright. *Kazuo is such a light sleeper that once he woke up, startled by a noisy goldfish.*

Shocked means surprised and very upset. *Jamaine was shocked to find her ordinarily quiet dog barking and snapping at the mail carrier.*

T t

Thoughtful means careful of other people's feelings. *"How thoughtful!" said Angelique. "You brought my favorite flowers!"* (adjective)

Considerate means thoughtful. It suggests thinking of people's feelings without having to be told. *They were considerate of the downstairs neighbors by walking quietly in the hallway.*

Sympathetic means thoughtful, kind, and able to understand how someone else feels. *When he saw my braces, Emilio showed his own in a sympathetic smile.*

Caring means attentive. It suggests that someone else's feelings are important to you. *Everyone in class made a fuss when Jacob first broke his leg, but only Amanda was caring enough to visit him often.*

ANTONYMS: inconsiderate, thoughtless

U u

Ugly means unpleasant to look at. *Vandals have covered the wall with ugly spray paint marks.* (adjective)

Homely means not good-looking. It is also not as strong a word as ugly. *Amid the crowds in the railway station, Lise was delighted to see the smiling, homely face of her beloved Uncle Frank.*

Hideous means very ugly and horrible to look at. *Butch loves movies with hideous monsters, but I think they're mostly boring and stupid.*

Monstrous can mean hideous. *The monstrous faces stared at Mr. Williamson and chanted, "Trick or treat!"*

ANTONYMS: beautiful, good-looking

Useless means not worth using or doing, or not able to be used. *It's useless arguing with Bill, because he never admits it when he's wrong.* (adjective)

Worthless means having no use or value. *If the broken leg on that table can't be fixed, the table is really worthless.*

Needless means useless and without purpose. It suggests a waste of time. *Take a safer route to avoid any needless risk.*

Inefficient means not worth using or doing because work is wasted. *Copying whole pages of the textbook is an inefficient way to study the lesson.*

ANTONYM: useful

WORD STORY

Ugly comes from an old Scandinavian word meaning "fear." *Hideous* comes from an old French word meaning "fear." One reason we have synonyms is that sometimes the same idea came into English from different languages.

Usual means most commonly seen, found, or happening. *In Chicago some snow is usual in winter. We'll meet for lunch at the usual time.* (adjective)

Traditional means customary because it has been handed down from generation to generation. *Thanksgiving is a traditional American holiday.*

Regular means usual and according to custom or rule. *Sarah was late and missed her regular bus.*

Ordinary means usual and regular. *Visiting and helping out friends who are sick is an ordinary part of my grandmother's life.*

SEE **common** for related words.

ANTONYMS: peculiar, rare, unusual

W w

Want means to feel an urge to have or do something. *Peter wants a pair of in-line skates for his birthday.* (verb)

Wish means to want or hope for something. *"If you wish to become a ballerina," Madame Claire told Ramona, "you must work as hard as you can."*

Desire is a formal word that means to wish seriously and very much. *Many people desire to conserve the environment but wonder what they personally can do.*

Long means to desire. It suggests thinking about something over and over. *The Navajo children longed to hear more stories about their ancestors.*

Watch means to keep your eyes on something carefully for a period of time. *The burglars tied up the guard, so all he could do was watch as they emptied the warehouse.* (verb)

Look means to turn your eyes to something. *"Look at the sea lions!" Darseea called to her mother.*

Eye means to look. *Mustafa eyed each camel carefully as it approached the starting line.*

Gaze means to watch steadily. *It suggests a strong attraction to what is watched. Mr. Thurman gazed fondly at his newest grandchild.*

Stare means to watch steadily and directly, usually without blinking. *The first time Rachel got a pimple, she felt that everyone in school was staring at her.*

Weird means very strange and mysterious. *From deep in the forest, She Walks Away heard a weird croaking rumble.* (adjective)

Spooky is an informal word that means strange enough to make you nervous. *It's spooky how quiet the street gets at night when traffic stops.*

Creepy can mean weird and frightening. *The heroine of the movie has to save her friend from some creepy villains.*

The heroine of the movie has to save her friend from some **creepy** villians.

Ghostly means like a ghost. *Sometimes, when Obadele walks homeward across the fields at evening, mist rises in ghostly shapes around him.*

ANTONYMS: natural, normal

Welcome means to be glad to let someone or something in. *The Drama Club welcomes new members.*

Accept can mean to let in with approval. *Raquel's sister has been accepted by a medical school.*

Admit can mean allow to enter. *One hundred lucky contest winners will be admitted early and introduced to the band.*

Take in means to admit, especially as part of business. *The animal shelter takes in stray dogs and cats.*

Whole means with all its parts and with nothing left out. *Adam watched the whole movie, but Bert left when it got scary.* (adjective)

Complete means whole. *Consuela gave complete instructions for making a piñata.*

Entire means whole. *Did Lucy and Calvin eat the entire batch of cookies?*

Total means all added together. *The total bill was $81.16.*

ANTONYM: partial

Wild means extremely excited and out of control. *When Rita kicked the goal that won the championship, the fans went wild.* (adjective)

Frantic means wild with rage, fear, pain, or grief. *From the burning building came frantic cries for help.*

Disorderly can mean wild and causing trouble, especially in public. *Ushers asked the disorderly group to be quiet or leave the concert.*

Unruly means hard to control. *Lamar's puppy has so much energy that she is sometimes unruly.*

ANTONYM: calm

Worried means uncertain what will happen and afraid of what may happen. It suggests thinking about something over and over. *Willie Don is worried because his dog won't eat and might be sick.* (adjective)

Uneasy means having a strong feeling that trouble is coming. It suggests not knowing for sure what the trouble will be. *Changes in the Earth's atmosphere make scientists uneasy about possible climate changes.*

Nervous can mean afraid that things will not go well. It suggests restlessness. *Before the race, Emma was nervous and wheeled her chair around the block to calm herself down.*

Anxious means convinced that something bad will happen, and busy thinking about it. It suggests painful excitement. *After an anxious search, Nancy found her contact lens under the seat of the car.*

SEE **care** for related words.

ANTONYMS: calm, relaxed

Y y

Young means in the early part of life. *Some young birds can walk and swim soon after they hatch from eggs.* (adjective)

Youthful means young or like young people. It suggests hope, energy, and imagination. *Grandma Salazar dances with a youthful enthusiasm that makes her seem half her age.*

Immature means not completely grown. It is often used to suggest that feelings or behavior are not grown-up enough. *Justin apologized to the substitute teacher for his immature behavior.*

Teenage means in the years of life from thirteen to nineteen. *With two teenage sons, a job, and night school, Mrs. Chee is always busy.*

ANTONYMS: adult, elderly, mature, old

IDIOMS

There are many idioms meaning *worried* and *nervous*. They describe a restless, uncertain feeling by comparing it to being on top of something that keeps you from being comfortable.

on edge: *It's been two months since Dad had any work, and he's on edge most of the time now.*

on pins and needles: *Afraid of missing the fireworks, the children were on pins and needles until they reached the park.*

like peas on a hot griddle: *When the cat appeared at the window, the birds at the feeder were like peas on a hot griddle.*

The Word List in English and Spanish

A

ability (13)   habilidad
able (13)   capaz, poder
accomplishments (CC)   logros
action (27)   acción
adobe (CC)   adobe
again (19)   otra vez
air mass (CC)   masa de aire
alley (9)   callejón
almost (16)   casi
a lot (16)   mucho, mucha
alphabet (3)   alfabeto
always (16)   siempre
angel (32)   ángel
angle (32, CC)   ángulo
animals (31)   animales
another (32)   otro, otra
anyway (26)   de todos modos
anywhere (7)   dondequiera
appearance (CC)   apariencia
appreciate (CC)   apreciar
April (11)   abril
are (35)   eres, son, somos; estás, están, estamos
area (CC)   área
arrive (11)   llegar
articles (CC)   artículos
artist (CC)   artista
ashes (15)   cenizas
asked (19)   preguntar; pedir (pasado)
assign (2)   asignar
assignments (CC)   tareas
Atlantic Ocean (CC)   Océano Atlántico
attack (3)   atacar
August (31)   agosto
aunt's (34)   de la tía
aunts' (34)   de las tías
Ave. (33)   avenida
awhile (7)   un rato

B

babies' (34)   de los bebés
baby's (34)   del bebé
backboard (CC)   tablero
backpack (10)   mochila
backstroke (CC)   brazada de espalda
bacon (11)   tocino
band (10)   banda
barometer (CC)   barómetro
barrel (32)   barril
baseball (26)   béisbol
basketball (26)   baloncesto; balón
beaches (15)   playas
beat (9, 23)   batir; tocar; vencer
beautiful (27)   bello, bella
because (3)   porque
beet (23)   betabel; remolacha
beginning (25)   comenzando
behind (11)   detrás
believe (19)   creer
bicuspid (CC)   primer molar
bicycle (CC)   bicicleta
blanket (10)   manta
block (10)   cuadra
blubber (CC)   grasa
borrow (8)   tomar prestado
bottle (8)   botella
boy's (34)   del muchacho
boys' (34)   de los muchachos
brainstorm (CC)   torrente de ideas
brake (3, 23)   freno; frenar
break (23)   quebrar; faltar
breathe (CC)   respirar
breathless (28)   sin aliento
bridge (14)   puente
brightness (28)   claridad
broadleaf (CC)   hoja ancha
broke (11)   quebrar (pasado)
broken (32)   quebrado, quebrada
brook (21)   arroyo
brother's (34)   del hermano
brothers' (34)   de los hermanos

brought (19)	traer *(pasado)*
bruise (22)	magulladura
bubble (8)	burbuja
buffalo (31)	búfalo
build (19)	construir
bunches (15)	montones; racimos
bush (21)	arbusto
business (28)	asunto, negocio
butcher (21)	carnicero
butterfly (CC)	mariposa
button (32)	botón; abrochar
byline (CC)	renglón con nombre de autor

C

cable (11)	cable
cactus (CC)	cacto
cafeteria (CC)	cafetería
camera (25, CC)	cámara
Canada (31)	Canadá
canal (CC)	canal
canoe (31)	canoa
capacity (CC)	capacidad
care (3)	preocuparse por; preocupación; cuidar
carefully (27)	cuidadosamente
careless (28)	descuidado, descuidada
caribou (CC)	caribú
carnivore (CC)	carnívoro, carnívora
cash (10)	efectivo
catcher (7)	receptor
cathedral (CC)	catedral
caught (25)	agarrar *(pasado)*
celebrated (CC)	célebre
Celsius (CC)	celsius
cement (31)	cemento
ceremony (CC)	ceremonia
certain (20)	seguro, segura
chalkboard (26)	pizarra
change (14)	cambiar
chapter (7)	capítulo
charge (14)	cargar
Chartres (CC)	Chartres
chased (4)	perseguir *(pasado)*
chasing (4)	persiguiendo
cheerful (27)	alegre
childhood (CC)	niñez
children (CC)	niños
Chinese New Year (33)	Año Nuevo Chino

chocolate (7)	chocolate
chop (10)	cortar
chores (CC)	quehaceres
Christmas (33)	Navidad
church (7, CC)	iglesia
circuses (15)	circos
classes (15)	clases
classmate (26)	compañero, compañera
classroom (26)	salón de clases
clear key (CC)	tecla de borrar
climb (2)	escalar
close (23)	cerrar
closer (5)	más cerca
closest (5)	el más cerca, la más cerca
closet (10)	armario
clothes (23)	ropa
cloud (21)	nube
coal (CC)	carbón
collections (CC)	colecciones
color (32)	color
comb (2)	peinarse; peine
coming (16)	viniendo
common (32)	común
compass (CC)	brújula
compassionate (CC)	compasivo, compasiva
compose (13)	componer
composition (13)	composición
concert (CC)	concierto
conduct (CC)	conducir
confidence (CC)	confianza
confuse (22)	confundir
conifers (CC)	coníferas
Constitution (CC)	constitución
consumers (CC)	consumidores
contest (9)	concurso
cool (22)	fresco, fresca
coordinates (CC)	coordenadas
corn (CC)	maíz
correction (27)	corrección
could've (17)	pudiera haber
counselor (CC)	consejero, consejera
couple (10)	par
course (20)	curso
court (20)	corte
cousin (10)	primo, prima
cover (3)	tapar; cubierta
crazy (16)	loco, loca

credit | equal

credit (9)	crédito
crosswalks (CC)	cruce de peatones
crowd (21)	multitud
cruise (22)	crucero
crumb (13)	migaja
crumble (13)	desmigajar
curfew (22)	toque de queda
current (8, CC)	actual; corriente
curtains (CC)	cortinas
cushion (21)	cojín
cuspid (CC)	colmillo

D

Dad's (34)	de papá
daily (27)	diario
danced (4)	bailar *(pasado)*
dancing (4)	bailando
danger (11)	peligro
darkness (28)	oscuridad
deadline (CC)	plazo
deal (13)	repartir; tratar con; trato
dealt (13)	repartir; tratar con *(pasado)*
debris (CC)	escombros, desechos
Dec. (33)	dic.
December (25)	diciembre
decide (11)	decidir
decision (CC)	decisión
decomposer (CC)	descomponedor
deeper (5)	más profundo, más profunda
deepest (5)	el más profundo, la más profunda
degrees (CC)	grados
delays (15)	demoras
democratic (CC)	democrático, democrática
demonstrations (CC)	demostraciones
dermis (CC)	dermis
desert (CC)	desierto
design (2)	diseño; diseñar
details (CC)	detalles
determination (CC)	determinación
devastate (CC)	devastar
develops (CC)	desarrolla
didn't (16)	no *(pasado)*
different (8)	diferente
dirty (20)	sucio, sucia
disagree (29, CC)	estar en desacuerdo
disappear (29)	desaparecer

disappointment (CC)	desilusión
dishonest (29)	deshonesto, deshonesta
dislike (29)	tener aversión a
display (CC)	representación visual
distance (CC)	distancia
distrust (29)	desconfianza
dive (CC)	clavado
divide (CC)	dividir
dividend (CC)	dividendo
divisible (CC)	divisible
division (CC)	división
divisor (CC)	divisor
doctor (32)	doctor, doctora
doesn't (17)	no
dog paddle (CC)	chapotear
dolphin (3)	delfín
donkey (9)	burro
doorbell (26)	timbre
downstairs (26)	piso de abajo
Dr. (33)	Dr.
dribble (CC)	driblear
dried (4)	secar *(pasado)*
driveway (26)	camino de entrada
drove (11)	conducir *(pasado)*
drying (4)	secando
dune (CC)	duna
during (16)	durante

E

ear canal (CC)	canal auditivo
eardrum (CC)	tímpano
earrings (26)	aretes
earthquake (CC)	terremoto
edge (14)	borde
editors (CC)	editores
elected (CC)	elegido, elegida
electricity (CC)	electricidad
elephant (3)	elefante
eleven (16)	once
emergency (CC)	emergencia
enamel (CC)	enamel
endpoint (CC)	punto final
enemies (15)	enemigos, enemigas
energy (CC)	energía
engine (9)	motor
enough (3)	suficiente
epidermis (CC)	epidermis
equal (14)	igual

equals key (CC)	tecla de resultado
equator (CC)	ecuador
error (CC)	error
especially (31)	especialmente
evening (25)	tarde
evergreens (CC)	árboles de hojas perennes
everybody (25)	todos
everyone (25)	todos
excellent (14)	excelente
except (14)	menos
excited (14)	emocionado, emocionada
excuse (22)	excusa
exhibit (CC)	exhibición
expect (14)	esperar
experiment (CC)	experimento
expert (CC)	experto, experta
explain (14)	explicar
extra (14)	extra
extraordinary (CC)	extraordinario, extraordinaria
eyelashes (15)	pestañas

F

Fahrenheit (CC)	Fahrenheit
fairness (28)	imparcialidad
families' (34)	de las familias
family (CC)	familia
family of facts (CC)	familia de operaciones básicas
family's (34)	de la familia
father (16)	padre
fatter (5)	más gordo, más gorda
fattest (5)	el más gordo, la más gorda
faults (CC)	fallas
favorite (31)	preferido, preferida
Feb. (33)	feb.
February (25)	febrero
federal (CC)	federal
feelings (16)	sentimientos
fence (9)	cerca
ferns (CC)	helechos
fertilize (CC)	fertilizar
few (22)	pocos
field (19)	campo
field goal (CC)	gol de patada
film (CC)	película

finally (25)	finalmente
finger (10)	dedo
first (20)	primero, primera
first aid (CC)	primeros auxilios
flashlight (7)	linterna
floats (CC)	flota
Florida (20)	Florida
flowers (15)	flores
focus (CC)	enfocar
food chain (CC)	cadena alimentaria
food web (CC)	red alimentaria
football (21)	fútbol americano; balón
forecast (CC)	pronóstico
forest (20, CC)	bosque
forgot (10)	olvidar (pasado)
form (20)	formulario; formar
foul (CC)	falta
fourteen (20)	catorce
fourth (20)	cuarto
free throw (CC)	tiro libre
freestyle (CC)	estilo libre
friend (19)	amigo, amiga
friend's (34)	del amigo, de la amiga
friends (15)	amigos, amigas
front (CC)	frente
fruit (22, CC)	fruta
fudge (14)	dulce de chocolate
fuel (22)	combustible
fuels (CC)	combustibles
funnier (5)	más gracioso, más graciosa
funniest (5)	el más gracioso, la más graciosa
fur (CC)	piel
furniture (CC)	muebles

G

gallon (32)	galón
gasoline (CC)	gasolina
giant (31)	gigante
giraffe (3)	jirafa
girlfriend (20)	novia, amiga
girl's (34)	de la muchacha
girls' (34)	de las muchachas
glasses (15)	anteojos
goodness (28)	bondad
grandma's (34)	de la abuela
grandpa's (34)	del abuelo
grasshopper (8)	saltamontes

greatness | Kwanza

greatness (28)	grandeza
grouping (CC)	agrupación

H

hamster (16)	hámster
hand signal (CC)	señal de mano
Hanukkah (33)	Hanukkah
happened (4)	pasar (pasado)
happening (4)	pasando
happier (5)	más feliz
happiest (5)	el más feliz, la más feliz
headline (CC)	sumario de noticias
heal (13)	sanar
health (13)	salud
heard (19)	oír (pasado)
heart (19)	corazón
he'd (17)	él + (condicional)
height (19, CC)	altura
he'll (17)	él + (futuro)
helmet (CC)	casco
helpless (28)	desamparado, desamparada
hemispheres (CC)	hemisferios
herbivore (CC)	herbívoro
herself (20)	ella misma
hide (11)	esconderse
highway (26)	carretera
hobbies (15)	pasatiempos
hobby (8)	pasatiempo
hockey (9)	hockey
hogans (CC)	hogans
holidays (15)	días de fiesta
home (CC)	hogar
honey (9)	miel
honor (CC)	honor
hopefully (27)	esperanzadamente
hopeless (28)	desesperado, desesperada
hospital (19)	hospital
hotel (16)	hotel
hotter (5)	más caliente
hottest (5)	el más caliente, la más caliente
house (21)	casa
however (21)	como quiera que; sin embargo
huge (22)	enorme
humidity (CC)	humedad
humor (CC)	humor

hydroelectric (CC)	hidroeléctrico, hidroeléctrica

I

I'd (17)	yo + (condicional)
I'll (17)	yo + (futuro)
I'm (17)	soy, estoy
inactive (29)	inactivo, inactiva
incisor (CC)	incisivo
incomplete (29)	incompleto, incompleta
incorrect (29)	incorrecto, incorrecta
independent (29)	independiente
inner ear (CC)	oído interno
insulation (CC)	insulación
interesting (25)	interesante
intersecting (CC)	cruzando
interview (CC)	entrevista
into (10)	en, por
Inuit (CC)	inuita
invention (27)	invento
invisible (29)	invisible
invite (11)	invitar
iris (CC)	iris
iron (31)	planchar; plancha
island (25)	isla
it's (17)	es

J

January (10)	enero
jaywalking (CC)	cruzar la calle imprudentemente
jewels (CC)	joyas
juice (22)	jugo
July (21)	julio
jump shot (CC)	lanzamiento con salto
June (33)	junio

K

Kansas (3)	Kansas
kayak (CC)	kayac
key sequence (CC)	secuencia de teclas
kicks (CC)	patear
kitchen (7)	cocina
kneel (2)	arrodillarse
knit (2)	tejer
knob (2)	tirador
knot (2)	nudo
know (2)	saber
known (25)	conocido, conocida
Kwanza (33)	Kwanza

L

ladies' (34)	de las damas
lady's (34)	de la dama
Lake Erie (CC)	lago Erie
Lake Huron (CC)	lago Huron
Lake Michigan (CC)	lago Michigan
Lake Ontario (CC)	lago Ontario
Lake Superior (CC)	lago Superior
lamb (2)	cordero
landforms (CC)	accidentes geográficos
larger (5)	más grande
largest (5)	el más grande, la más grande
lately (27)	últimamente
latitude (CC)	latitud
laughed (3)	reír (pasado)
lay-up (CC)	(en baloncesto) lanzamiento desde abajo del aro
lazy (16)	perezoso, perezosa
lead (CC)	párrafo introductor
leaders (CC)	líderes
least (9)	el menos, lo menos
length (CC)	largo
lens (CC)	cristalino; lente
let's (17)	vamos a
lettuce (8)	lechuga
librarian (CC)	bibliotecario, bibliotecaria
library (CC)	biblioteca
limb (2)	rama
line (CC)	recta
lion (11)	león
liquid (14)	líquido
local (CC)	local
location (27, CC)	localidad
lock (CC)	esclusa
longitude (CC)	longitud
loose (35)	suelto, suelta
lose (35)	perder
loud (21)	fuerte
love (CC)	amar

M

machine (31)	máquina
magnet (CC)	imán
magnetic field (CC)	campo magnético
magnetism (CC)	magnetismo
marble (CC)	mármol
March (7)	marzo
matter (8)	importar
May (33)	mayo
mean (13)	tener la intención; malo, mala; querer decir
meant (13)	tener la intención (pasado)
Memorial Day (33)	Día de conmemoración de los caídos
memories (15, CC)	recuerdos
memory minus (CC)	tecla de memoria para el signo menos
memory plus (CC)	tecla de memoria para el signo más
memory recall (CC)	tecla de llamada de la memoria
menu (22)	menú
meridians (CC)	meridianos
meteorologist (CC)	meteorólogo, meteoróloga
meter (13)	metro
metric (13)	métrico, métrica
middle ear (CC)	oído medio
might (25)	poder
misbehave (29)	portarse mal
misled (29)	engañar (pasado)
misplace (29)	extraviar
missed (16)	perder; echar de menos (pasado)
misspell (29)	deletrear mal
mistreat (29)	maltratar
model (32)	ejemplo; modelo
moisture (CC)	humedad
molar (CC)	muela
moment (31)	momento
money (9)	dinero
monkey (9)	mono, mona
monkeys (15)	monos, monas
mood (22)	humor
morning (20)	mañana
motor (32)	motor
motorcycle (26)	motocicleta
mountain (21)	montaña
mountains (CC)	montañas
movement (28)	movimiento
Mr. (33)	Sr.
Mrs. (33)	Sra.
Ms. (33)	Srta., Sra.
muffin (3)	panecillo
myself (26)	yo mismo, yo misma
mysteries (15)	misterios

natural gas | punishment

N

natural gas (CC)	gas natural
Navajo (CC)	návajo
needleleaf (CC)	hoja de aguja
negative (CC)	negativo
neighbor (19)	vecino, vecina
nephew (22)	sobrino
nerve (20)	nervio
newspaper (26)	periódico
nighttime (26)	noche
November (33)	noviembre
number (32)	número
number keys (CC)	teclas de números
number sentence (CC)	expresión numérica

O

oak (CC)	roble
October (32)	octubre
odd (8)	raro, rara
of (35)	de
off (35)	apagado, apagada; de
offer (8)	ofrecer
office (CC)	oficina
often (25)	a menudo
oil (CC)	petróleo
oil gland (CC)	glándula sebácea
omnivore (CC)	omnívoro
only (19)	sólo
opened (4)	abrir (pasado)
opening (4)	abriendo
operation key (CC)	tecla de operación
optic nerve (CC)	nervio óptico
orchestra (CC)	orquesta
other (32)	otro, otra
our (35)	nuestro, nuestra
outer ear (CC)	oído externo
outside (21)	afuera
oven (32)	horno

P

paddle (8)	remar; canalete
painful (27)	doloroso, dolorosa
panic (CC)	dejarse llevar por el pánico
parallel (CC)	paralelo, paralela
parallel circuit (CC)	circuito paralelo
parallels (CC)	paralelos
parents (CC)	padres
Parthenon (CC)	Partenón

participate (CC)	participar
pavement (28)	pavimento
payment (28)	pago
peace (23)	paz
peaceful (27)	pacífico
pedestrians (CC)	peatones
people (32)	gente; personas
perfect (20)	perfecto, perfecta
perimeter (CC)	perímetro
perpendicular (CC)	perpendicular
photo (3)	foto
pickle (19)	pepino
piece (19, 23)	trozo; pedazo
pint (11)	pinta
pistil (CC)	pistilo
pitcher (7)	lanzador, lanzadora
plains (CC)	praderas
plateau (CC)	meseta
plates (CC)	placas
pocket (3)	bolsillo
point (CC)	punto
polar bear (CC)	oso polar
poles (CC)	polos
pollen (CC)	polen
pollution (27)	contaminación
pond (10)	charco
pore (CC)	poro
portrait (CC)	retrato
pottery (CC)	loza
pour (20)	verter
power (21)	poder; fuerza
powerful (27)	poderoso, poderosa
predator (CC)	depredador, depredadora
pressure (CC)	presión
prey (CC)	presa
prime meridian (CC)	línea de Greenwich
print (CC)	impresión
probably (31)	probablemente
producers (CC)	productores, productoras
products (CC)	productos
proud (21)	orgulloso, orgullosa
psychologist (CC)	sicólogo, sicóloga
pudding (21)	pudín, budín
pueblo (CC)	pueblo
punish (7)	castigar
punishment (28)	castigo

pupil (22, CC)   alumno, alumna; pupilo, pupila

Q

quart (14)   cuarto

queen (14)   reina

quick (14)   rápido, rápida

quiet (35)   silencio; quieto, quieta

quilt (14)   colcha de retazos

quit (35)   abandonar

quite (35)   muy

quotient (CC)   cociente

R

rain gauge (CC)   pluviómetro

rattle (19)   sonaja

ray (CC)   rayo

Rd. (33)   ruta

react (29)   reaccionar

really (25)   verdaderamente

reason (9)   razón

rebound (CC)   rebote

rebuild (29)   reconstruir

recall (29)   recordar

record (3)   disco

recover (CC)   recobrar

reflector (CC)   reflector

relate (13)   relacionarse; contar

relative (13)   pariente

relatives (31)   parientes

relax (14)   relajar

remainder (CC)   residuo

remember (25)   recordar

remote (11)   remoto, remota

replace (29)   reemplazar

represent (CC)   representar

reproduce (CC)   reproducir

republic (CC)   república

rescue (CC)   rescatar

research (CC)   investigar

reservation (CC)   reservación

result (CC)   resultado

retina (CC)   retina

reuse (29)   reusar

Richter scale (CC)   Escala Richter

ridden (8)   montado

rim (CC)   aro

river (10)   río

robbed (4)   robar *(pasado)*

robbing (4)   robando

rough (3)   desigual; difícil; áspero, áspera

S

sadder (5)   más triste

saddest (5)   el más triste, la más triste

safely (27)   con toda seguridad

sagebrush (CC)   artemisa

said (19)   decir *(pasado)*

scarier (5)   más espantoso, más espantosa

scariest (5)   el más espantoso, la más espantosa

school (22)   escuela

scrapbook (CC)   libro de recuerdos

scratch (1)   rascar; arañazo

scream (1)   grito; gritar

screen (1)   biombo

scrub (1)   fregar

seal (CC)   foca

season (9)   estación

seed (CC)   semilla

segment (CC)   segmento

seismograph (CC)   sismógrafo

September (33)   septiembre

series circuit (CC)   circuito de series

serve (20)   servir

set (35)   poner

several (25)   varios, varias

shampoo (22)   champú

shared (CC)   compartir

she'll (17)   ella + *(futuro)*

shelter (7)   refugio

shoot (22)   tirar; sacar una foto

short (7)   corto, corta

shouldn't (17)   no deber

shower (21)   ducha

shown (7)   mostrado

shudder (8)   estremecerse

shutter (CC)   obturador

sign (2, 13)   señal; letrero; seña

signal (13)   señalar; señal

silver (CC)   plata

simple (32)   simple; sencillo

siren (CC)   sirena

sit (35)   sentarse

skateboarding (CC)   patinaje

skirt (20)   falda

skyscraper (1)   rascacielos

slam-dunk (CC)	(en baloncesto) lanzamiento desde arriba del aro
slipped (4)	resbalarse *(pasado)*
slippers (8)	zapatillas
slipping (4)	resbalándose
slowly (27)	despacio
smaller (5)	más pequeño, más pequeña
smallest (5)	el más pequeño, la más pequeña
smoke (11)	humo
snack (3)	bocadillo
snapshot (CC)	fotografía instantánea
soft (13)	suave; blando, blanda
softball (26)	sóftbol
soften (13)	suavizar; ablandar
softness (28)	suavidad
something (26)	algo
sometimes (26)	a veces
somewhere (7)	en alguna parte
sources (CC)	fuentes
speak (9)	hablar
special (CC)	especial
spider web (CC)	telaraña
spores (CC)	esporas
spotless (28)	inmaculado, inmaculada
square (1)	cuadrado
squeal (1)	chillido; chillar
squeeze (1)	exprimir
squirm (1)	retorcerse
squirt (1)	dejar salir a chorros
stamen (CC)	estambre
state (CC)	estado
statement (28)	declaración
station (11)	estación
steal (9)	robar; marcharse furtivamente *(pasado)*
steel (CC)	acero
stiff (3)	tieso, tiesa
St. Lawrence Seaway (CC)	Ruta marítima de San Laurencio
stole (11)	robar
stomach (31)	estómago
stood (21)	parar
stopped (4)	cesar; parar; detenerse *(pasado)*
stopping (4)	deteniéndose; parando
storm (20)	tormenta

strange (1)	raro, rara
strategy (CC)	estrategia
strawberry (1)	fresa
street (1)	calle
strength (1)	fuerza
strengths (CC)	fuerzas
strike (1)	golpe; golpear; prender un cerillo
stroke (CC)	brazada
studied (4)	estudiar *(pasado)*
studying (4)	estudiando
successful (CC)	exitoso, exitosa
sudden (32)	imprevisto, imprevista
suddenly (27)	de repente
suffer (8)	sufrir
suffixes (15)	sufijos
suit (22)	traje
Sun. (33)	dom.
supper (8)	cena
supplies (15)	provisiones; materiales para escuela
support (31)	apoyo
suppose (31)	suponer
surprised (25)	sorprendido, sorprendida
sweat gland (CC)	glándula sudorífera
swimming (25)	nadando

T

Taj Mahal (CC)	Taj Mahal
taxes (15)	impuestos
teacher's (34)	del maestro, de la maestra
teachers' (34)	de los maestros, de las maestras
tears (CC)	lágrimas
temperature (CC)	temperatura
temple (CC)	templo
Texas (14)	Texas, Tejas
than (35)	que
that's (17)	eso es
their (23)	su (de ellos, de ellas), sus (de ellos, de ellas)
them (9)	ellos, ellas, los, las, les
then (35)	entonces; luego
there (23)	ahí, allí
they (25)	ellos, ellas
they'd (17)	ellos + *(condicional)*, ellas + *(condicional)*
they'll (17)	ellos + *(futuro)*, ellas + *(futuro)*

they're (23)	ellos (ellas) son, ellos (ellas) están
thirsty (20)	tener sed
thoughtful (27)	considerado, considerada
threat (1)	amenaza
thrill (1)	emoción
throat (1)	garganta
throne (23)	trono
through (1)	por, a través de
thrown (1, 23)	tirado, tirada
thumb (2)	pulgar
tigers (15)	tigres
title (32)	título
to (23)	a, hacia
toes (19)	dedos de los pies
tomb (CC)	tumba
tomorrow (8)	mañana; demasiado, demasiada
too (23)	también;
took (21)	tomar; llevar (pasado)
tough (10)	duro, dura
track (3)	vía; pista
trash (7)	basura
treads (CC)	pedalea en agua
treat (9)	convidar; tratar; gusto
treatment (28)	tratamiento
tremendous (CC)	tremendo
trouble (10)	preocupar; dificutad
truthfully (27)	verdaderamente
tundra (CC)	tundra
two (23)	dos

U

ugly (16)	feo, fea
unknown (2)	desconocido, desconocida
until (16)	hasta
upon (16)	sobre
upstairs (26)	arriba
useless (28)	inútil
usual (22)	usual
usually (31)	usualmente

V

vacation (11)	vacación
Valentine's Day (33)	día de San Valentín
valley (9)	valle
verify (CC)	verificar
vertex (CC)	vértice

village (14)	pueblo
volcano (CC)	volcán
volume (CC)	volumen

W

walrus (CC)	morsa
want (16)	querer
washed (16)	lavar (pasado)
wasn't (16)	no era, no ser, no estar (pasado)
waste (23)	desperdiciar
watch (7)	observar; reloj
water fountain (CC)	fuente de agua
waterway (CC)	vía fluvial
weaknesses (CC)	debilidades
weaving (CC)	tejido
Wed. (33)	miér.
weekend (26)	fin de semana
weekly (27)	semanal
weight (19, CC)	peso
weird (19)	raro, rara
welcome (31)	bienvenido, bienvenida
we'll (17)	nosotros + (futuro), nosotras + (futuro)
went (9)	ir (pasado)
were (35)	ser; estar (pasado subjunctivo)
we're (35)	somos, estamos
we've (17)	hemos
whale (CC)	ballena
what's (17)	qué es
whatever (7)	todo lo que
wheat (7)	trigo
when (35)	cuando, cuándo
whenever (7)	cuando sea
where (35)	donde, dónde
wherever (7)	donde sea
who's (35)	quien es, quien está
whole (11)	entero, entera
whose (35)	de quien
width (CC)	anchura
wild (11)	salvaje
win (35)	ganar
wind vane (CC)	veleta
window (10)	ventana
with (10)	con
wood (21, 23)	madera
worried (4)	preocupado, preocupada; preocuparse (pasado)

worry | your

worry (8)	preocuparse
worrying (4)	preocupándose
worthless (28)	sin valor
would (23)	*(condicional)*
would've (17)	*(condicional)* + haber
wouldn't (17)	no + *(condicional)*
wreath (2)	guirnalda
wreck (2)	restos (de un auto); accidente
wren (2)	reyezuelo
wrench (2)	llave inglesa
wrist (2)	muñeca
writing (2)	escribiendo
written (8)	escrito, escrita

Y

yesterday (31)	ayer
you'd (17)	tú + *(condicional)*, usted + *(condicional)*
you're (23)	eres, estás
young (10)	joven
your (23)	tu, tus, su, sus